Entrepreneurship and Business Culture

10

100

Entrepreneurship and Business Culture

Studies in the Economics of Trust
Volume One

Mark Casson

Professor of Economics, University of Reading, UK

Edward Elgar

Aldershot, UK • Brookfield, US

Published by
Edward Elgar Publishing Limited
Gower House
Croft Road
Aldershot
Hants GU11 3HR
UK

Edward Elgar Publishing Company
Old Post Road
Brookfield
Vermont 05036
US

British Library Cataloguing in Publication Data
Casson, Mark
　　Entrepreneurship and Business Culture:
　　Studies in the Economics of Trust
　　I. Title
　　338.04

Library of Congress Cataloguing in Publication Data
Casson, Mark, 1945–
　　Entrepreneurship and business culture: studies in the
economics of trust / Mark Casson.
　　　　p.　cm.
　　1. Entrepreneurship. 2. Corporate culture. 3. Business ethics.
I. Title.
HB615.C372　1995
302.3'5—dc20
　　　　　　　　　　　　　　　　　　　　　　　　　　　94–48413
　　　　　　　　　　　　　　　　　　　　　　　　　　　CIP

ISBN 1 85898 229 4

Printed and bound in Great Britain by
Hartnolls Limited, Bodmin, Cornwall

Contents

Figures

Tables

Preface

This book is a collection of papers written over the period 1984–94. Some of the papers have previously been published and others have not. All have been thoroughly revised over the summer of 1994. Although a collection of papers can only be an imperfect substitute for a specially written book, I have done my best to eliminate duplication of material and to link up the arguments of the different chapters as closely as possible.

The aim of the book is to synthesize the analysis presented in two of my previous books, *The Entrepreneur: An Economic Theory* (1982) and *The Economics of Business Culture* (1991). A variety of special topics are addressed in which insights from these two earlier books are combined. In this way an extended theoretical framework is developed through a series of distinct, though related, applications.

The original papers (with the exception of Chapter 3) were all typed by Jill Turner, and she typed up the revisions too. It is quite amazing how she can combine this work with her other duties as departmental secretary – I am very grateful to her for doing such a thorough job. My staunchest critic has always been my wife, Janet, and I must thank her for all the suggestions which she has made to improve the text, suggestions which were not always gratefully received at the outset, I might add.

A number of publishers to whom copyright has been assigned have kindly agreed to the republication of journal articles and chapters in edited books. I am grateful to Basil Blackwell for permission to reprint Chapter 1 from J. Creedy (ed.), *Foundations of Economic Thought* (1988), to Plenum for permission to reprint Chapter 2 from *Human Relations*, volume 46, to Manchester University Press for permission to reprint Chapter 4 from J. Brown and M.B. Rose (eds), *Entrepreneurship, Networks and Modern Business* (1993) and to the University of Michigan Press for permission to reprint Chapter 6 from Y. Shionoya and M. Perlman (eds), *Innovation in Technology, Industries and Institutions*, 1994. Chapter 7 is reprinted from the *Journal of Comparative Economics*, volume 17, by courtesy of Academic Press, San Diego, Chapter 9 is reprinted from G. Jones and N.J. Morgan (eds), *Adding Value: Brands and Marketing in Food and Drink* (1994), by courtesy of Routledge, and Chapter 11 is reprinted from P.J. Buckley and P.N. Ghauri (eds), *Economics of Change in East and Central Europe* (1994), by courtesy of Academic Press, London. Chapter 10 is based on a consultancy commissioned by Menter a Busnes, Aberystwyth and, of course, reflects only my own personal views on the subject and not those of Menter a Busnes itself. I am also grateful to Peter Buckley, the co-author of Chapter 2, for agreeing to the inclusion of this paper in the book.

Finally, I should like to thank the publisher Edward Elgar and his enthusiastic team for the interest that they have taken in this work, and in previous work of mine that they have published as well.

Mark Casson

PART I

Cultural Issues in Economic Perspective

1. From 'economic man' to 'ethical man'

1.1 INTRODUCTION

Economists fall into two main groups: those who believe that there is a crisis in their subject, and those who believe that there is not. The crisis school typically alleges that conventional economic theory is irrelevant to major real-world problems (Wiles and Routh, 1984). Such problems do not occur neatly packaged as 'economic', they claim, but rather their economic aspects are intertwined with social and political aspects too. Looking at the intellectual division of labour within the social sciences, economics seems to be isolated from other disciplines. Economists fail to collaborate effectively with sociologists and political scientists: the different disciplines seem to produce conflicting analyses of similar aspects of a problem, rather than complementary analyses of different aspects, as they should.

One reason for its isolation, the critics allege, is that conventional economic theory does not do full justice to the cultural and historical dimensions of its subject. The accusing finger is pointed at the way that economics substitutes for a realistic account of human nature the artificial construct of economic man (Hollis and Nell, 1975; Leibenstein, 1976). Economic man – or 'economic person', as some prefer to call him – is the representative individual who appears in many economic models, particularly the so-called 'neoclassical' ones. He is usually assumed to be optimizing, selfish and materialistic (these terms are defined later). Because of these assumptions, explanations of behaviour couched in terms of economic man often conflict with the evidence of introspection and appear repugnant in terms of conventional moral values (Sen, 1985). (It is worth noting that most economists do not describe their own motivations in terms of economic man; they speak instead of the fearless pursuit of truth and of dedication to the advancement of learning. If economists *really* believe in economic man then their professional rhetoric is essentially hypocritical.)

Defenders of orthodoxy (for example, Friedman, 1953) claim that criticism of economic man in terms of the realism of the assumptions is misplaced. The relevant comparison is not between theory and reality, but between one theory and another. Economics should focus on explaining the behaviour of the system as a whole. It cannot expect to explain every act of every single individual within it. Individuals exist only as typical elements which can be aggregated to form a profile of the population as a whole. The system is so complex that there is room for only a very simple account of individual behaviour within it. Economic man merely personifies a parsimonious set of assumptions about human motivation that generate a mutually consistent set of testable hypotheses about system behaviour. The onus is on the critics, it is suggested, to propose an alternative set of assumptions which can perform better in terms of this criterion. It is by no means obvious, however, what this alternative should be.

1.2   OPTIMIZATION AND COMPARATIVE STATICS

An appraisal of economic man must inevitably range widely, because the concept of economic man is inseparable from the nature of economic theory as a whole. Conventional economics is committed to methodological individualism (Boland, 1982, ch. 2): the economist accepts an obligation to explain social processes as a result of the interplay of separate individual decisions. Economic theorizing cannot therefore begin until the fundamentals of human motivation have been established.

Economic man is essentially man the decision maker. Decisions imply choice, and choice implies the existence of alternatives. Conventional economics is an applied theory of choice. To explain why someone acted in the way they did is to explain why they chose not to act in some other way.

Three main presuppositions underpin the theory of choice. The first is that in identical situations a given person will make the same choice. Since the same person does not make different choices in the same situation, this suggests that behaviour is systematic rather than erratic. This rules out schizophrenic personality, for example. The second is that a given person may, in different situations, make different choices. Since the person does not resolutely adhere to the same action, this suggests that he is adaptable. Behaviour is not governed by a simple rule which ignores the characteristics of the environment. The third is that there is a discernible pattern in the response to the environment which is compatible with purposeful and intelligent behaviour.

A purposeful agent distinguishes between ends and means. An intelligent agent pursues his ends by selecting appropriate means. He selects the means by constructing a mental model of the environment which is consistent with the information at his disposal.

The most powerful forms of explanation address themselves to comparative evidence obtained under controlled conditions. Because economic conditions are difficult to control, explanation is usually conducted on *ceteris paribus* assumptions. Much of the comparative evidence used in conventional economics relates to how people's behaviour varies across different market or fiscal environments (see below). Given this emphasis on cross-section variation, the theory of choice highlights the margin at which one course of action is substituted for another.

Emphasis on the margin has implications both for the nature of the individual's preferences and for his perception of constraints. An individual who has a very strong preference for acting in one particular way may never act otherwise. To rule out such cases, it is useful to distinguish between a high-order objective such as utility, to which the individual is invariably committed, and lower-order objectives which are instrumental in generating utility, such as the consumption of particular goods. It is assumed that no single lower-order objective dominates. There are instead several conflicting lower-order objectives which must be traded off against each other.

Failure to perceive alternatives could also lead to invariant behaviour. To rule this out, it is assumed that the individual can perceive all available alternatives, because his mental model of the environment accurately reflects the options available.

The handling of the trade-off is considerably simplified if only marginal alternatives need to be considered. A sufficient condition for this involves quasi-concavity of the utility function and convexity of the feasible set. If an option can be identified for which no marginal variation yields a utility improvement then, under these conditions, no extramarginal alternative will yield an improvement either.

When the utility function and the relevant boundary of the feasible set can be represented in simple mathematical terms (using, for example, continuous and differentiable functional forms) then the condition relating to marginal variations can be expressed in equation form (or some variant, such as a system of inequalities). Decision making then reduces to calculation, and intelligence implies optimization. This view of decision making based on the calculation of an optimum reflects the standard conception of economic man.

Using this approach, variations in behaviour are induced by implementing an exogenous parameter shift in the model of environmental constraints. Comparative static analysis examines the change in behaviour in terms of the substitution of a new best response to the environment. Under suitable assumptions (of the kind indicated above) continuity of response is guaranteed. An arbitrarily small change in the parameter generates an arbitrarily small change in behaviour. The direction of response can often be identified as well without any knowledge of the preference function other than its quasi-concavity. The classic example is the proof, using revealed preference theory, that a non-zero substitution effect is always negative. According to the Samuelson–Le Chatelier correspondence principle, such qualitative results are also associated with important dynamic properties of the system.

All conventional comparative static analysis, whether qualitative or quantitative, is predicated on the assumption that preferences are fixed. Changes in individual behaviour are explained by changes in the alternatives available to the decision maker, and not by changes in his preferences. The autonomy of individual preferences is widely regarded as crucial (Becker, 1976; Becker and Stigler, 1977). This is presumably because changes in alternatives are related to changes in the environment which are easily measurable, whereas changes in preferences might be related to psychological characteristics which cannot be objectively measured. Allowing for the presence of such changes, it is suggested, would undermine the ability to identify the impact of measurable environmental change on individual choice.

This argument is, however, spurious. While the psychological characteristics themselves may not be measurable, there are measurable factors which govern psychological characteristics in a determinate way. It is therefore possible to develop a predictive theory showing how changes in these factors combine with other changes in the environment to affect choice.

1.3　THE CONCEPTUALIZATION OF ALTERNATIVES

Critics of economic man typically take a different view of economic explanation. Their emphasis is on explaining the initial position rather than the response to change. Although conventional economics restricts preferences to a quasi-concave function, it does not provide a unique specification of preferences. (Whilst applied econometricians often select specific functional forms, their criteria concern the identification of parameters and the computability of estimators, and often result in choices that appear ad hoc from a strictly economic point of view.) The non-uniqueness of the postulated preference structure leaves conventional economics powerless to account for the initial position.

Explanations of the initial position attempt to circumvent the difficulty in three main ways. The first is to postulate a single dominant objective which encourages people to act persistently in a particular way. This view is characteristic of those who explain behaviour in terms of what people want to do rather than in terms of the constraints upon them.

The second is to argue that in practice people have few alternatives. This approach is typical of those who see individuals as victims of some kind of class conspiracy. All of the alternatives to the chosen course may be so unpleasant that they are not worth detailed consideration. This suggests that the constraints do not afford the decision maker a continuum of choices, but present a small discrete set in which one is much more preferable than the others.

The third approach is to deny that people can perceive alternatives even when they exist. It may be claimed, for example, that individuals cannot visualize hypothetical alternatives that they have never tried (or seen others try) before. Another possibility is that people are so busy that they have no time to investigate alternatives and so continue, through inertia or habit, to repeat the choices they have made before. A more extreme approach argues that people can be conditioned to ignore alternatives. The Stalinist view of human nature, for example, suggests that people's minds are like blank sheets of paper on which preferences can be stamped through propaganda or brainwashing. A leader can therefore persuade his followers that there is no alternative to the choice he wants them to make.

It is worth noting that all of these approaches provide a simple account of the initial position by implicitly denying the possibility of adjustment to incremental change. These accounts work by denying that there is a margin around which minor modifications of behaviour will occur. The more extreme accounts deny that any kind of adaptation will occur, whilst the more moderate ones suggest that adaptation will occur only through discrete jumps triggered by very major changes in the environment.

Scholars who adopt this alternative perspective on choice frequently talk about 'power'. Power has little significance for an economic man preoccupied with marginal choices between many correctly perceived alternatives, but it does have considerable significance where perceived alternatives are few and the margin is remote. The power of the leader of an organization, for example, stems from his capacity to punish those who do not conform by obeying the rules – either by exacting penalties or by withholding rewards. The near certainty of unavoidable punishment removes disobedience from marginal consideration. The power of a leader also stems from his ability to mould followers' preferences so that they dedicate themselves to a single course of action (see below). The leader may also control their knowledge of alternatives by encouraging the conservative inward-looking attitude that there is no feasible alternative to doing things the way they are already done within the group.

1.4   GENERAL EQUILIBRIUM THEORY

The single most important factor explaining the influence of economic man on the thinking of professional economists is his role in the neoclassical general equilibrium (GE) model. Economic man provides a remarkably parsimonious micro-foundation for this model. Many of the assumptions about economic man are, in fact, finely tuned to the specific needs of the GE model.

The high profile of the GE model stems partly from the fact that it tackles an important issue relating to the resolution of human conflict which goes back to antiquity. The issue is whether paternalism and hierarchical organization are necessary to maintain social order (Goldsmith, 1985; Myers, 1983). The movement towards individualism at the end of the Middle Ages revived intellectual interest in this issue, while the trend towards individuals holding property absolutely and in their own right, rather than as members of a family, made it of practical political concern (Macfarlane, 1978).

The Newtonian revolution in physics drew yet more attention to this issue. Newton showed how harmony in the heavens was maintained by an equilibrium of gravitational forces. If there is harmony in the heavens, it may be asked, why is there so much conflict on earth? This question directs attention to the search for social and economic forces which have similar equilibrating tendencies. Adam Smith (1776) identified these forces with the invisible hand. He showed how the balance between supply and demand sustained a harmonious division of labour which evolved naturally in a progressive fashion. This revealed market forces as the providentially ordained forces of a self-adjusting social system. A precise correspondence with Newtonian mechanics could not be achieved, however, until the theory of the market had been placed upon secure mathematical foundations.

The development of Benthamite utilitarianism provided a philosophical framework within which individual preferences could be given a simple mathematical form (Steintrager, 1977). It seems doubtful whether the economists who developed applications of utilitarianism appreciated the full impact of modelling human behaviour in these terms, though there is no doubt that the philosophical standpoint appealed to the Whiggish rationalism of many nineteenth century intellectuals. The harnessing of utilitarianism was a crucial element in the marginalist revolution of the 1870s (Barrientos, 1988; Stigler, 1982) which narrowed the focus of economics to the study of decentralized decision making within a market system. The broader concerns of the classical economists were largely abandoned. Not surprisingly, the tightly focused research agenda attracted many able mathematicians to the study of economics and, following important work by Walras, Marshall, Cassel, Hicks and Samuelson, the application of topological fixed-point theorems led to the classic formulation of GE theory by Arrow and Debreu (1954).

In the GE model individual preferences are specified in a very particular way. The low-level objectives which appear as arguments of the utility function are confined exclusively to the individual's own consumption of tangible goods and services, whilst the quasi-concavity assumption implies, amongst other things, that the individual is never satiated by the consumption of any of these goods. The individual is also assumed to have perfect information about market prices.

These assumptions impose crucial restrictions on the individual's supplies and demands in each market. These restrictions ensure that, when supplies and demands are aggregated, the excess demand schedules in the various markets have the properties needed to guarantee the efficiency of the market system. It can therefore be seen that both the preference structure and the information set associated with economic man are finely tuned to supporting the efficiency results obtained in GE theory.

To appreciate the logical steps involved in this argument, it is useful to begin by noting that, for a general equilibrium to prevail, the total values of supplies must equal the total value of demands. Otherwise, it would be impossible to have simultaneous equilibrium in all markets. Whilst this requirement is always satisfied *ex post*, in the sense of accounting for realized outcomes, equilibrium requires that it applies *ex ante* too. A simple way of meeting this requirement is to postulate that each individual's demands and supplies exactly satisfy his budget constraint. Since profit is defined as a residual, the firm's budget constraint is the profit identity and so is always satisfied. In a GE system the burden of maintaining budgetary discipline therefore falls upon the household. The householder must correctly perceive all prices and also correctly anticipate the profit of each firm in which he holds shares. He therefore requires perfect information on prices and on the profit implications of firm's production plans. To determine firms' production plans, he must know factor prices and their technological parameters too. He must also have sufficient calculating ability to ensure that his demands and supplies are consistent with budgetary balance. Under these conditions, the aggregation of demands and supplies across all firms and households leads to Walras's Law. There is overall budgetary balance, so that equilibrium in all markets except one ensures that there is equilibrium in the last market too.

To guide the system to equilibrium it is sufficient that market excess demands are uniquely defined as continuous functions of prices. Optimization provides a convenient framework within which to derive this result. Since the budget constraint determines a bounded and weakly convex feasible set, quasi-concave household preferences of the usual type guarantee a unique optimum which exactly satisfies the constraint. This optimum responds smoothly to changes in prices.

For GE to be efficient it is necessary that all the coordination that needs to be done is done through markets. This imposes exceptionally strong conditions, namely that no-one interacts with others except through markets, and that the markets that handle these interactions work perfectly. If these conditions are not satisfied then externalities arise. One individual's actions affect another's welfare and there is no way the victim of an action can influence its perpetrator. In the absence of such influences, a Pareto-inefficient decision may be made.

The need to avoid externalities helps to explain the focus of GE theory on private rather than public goods. For a given level of production of a private good, an additional unit of consumption by one person denies a unit of consumption to someone else. This does not apply to public goods. Any individual procuring the production of a public good indirectly benefits other people. This encourages selfish people to wait for others to provide the good, and so generates a 'free-rider' problem.

Most pure public goods are intangible – tangible goods usually have some capacity limit which, once reached, means that each user precludes another, as with a private good. Information is a good example of an intangible public good. The fact that the acquisition and dissemination of information is not usually treated explicitly in GE theory has much to do with the fact that the procurement of information is an indivisible activity which confers significant external benefits, so that the optimal provision of costly information cannot be guaranteed in a conventional GE framework.

Another source of externality is found where one individual is concerned about the consumption pattern of another individual. This individual can then influence the welfare of the first by the way he acts. To rule this out, GE theory requires that each individual is concerned only with his own consumption pattern. He is purely selfish, in other words. A selfish individual who demands only tangible rather than intangible goods may be said to be materialistic. In this sense, selfish and materialistic preferences are hallmarks of conventional economic man as he appears in the GE model.

1.5   UNCERTAINTY

The assumption about perfect information made in the GE model can be relaxed without causing too much damage to the efficiency results. Lack of information implies uncertainty and it was thought at one time that the presence of uncertainty would render optimization so fuzzy that the approach would become practically useless. But this is not, in fact, the case. The crucial requirement for optimization is that both objectives and constraints should be precisely specified. Perfect specification, rather than perfect knowledge, is what is required. Uncertainty can be handled very easily when it is assumed that the decision maker is able to identify a set of mutually exclusive and collectively exhaustive possible states of the environment, and to associate a subjective probability with each of them. His preferences can then be defined, not over the set of all outcomes in a given state, but over the set of all possible combinations of different outcomes in different states. Moreover, preferences over the contingent outcomes may well satisfy the quasi-concavity condition, so that the decision problem remains sufficiently well-defined for optimization to yield a unique choice.

When modified in this way, the GE model shows that, while the presence of uncertainty leads to sub-optimization compared to full information, the allocation of resources will still be efficient conditional on the availability of information and its distribution between individuals. This qualification is nonetheless significant, because it means that some trade may occur which appears efficient *ex ante* but is not so *ex post*. In the context of speculative behaviour, for example, two people who attach different subjective probabilities to the outcome of some event can both gain *ex ante* from betting with each other, but one individual is bound to lose *ex post*. This individual is the one who attaches the lowest subjective probability to the outcome that actually occurs. The *ex ante* mutual welfare gain translates into an *ex post* redistribution of income between the winner and the loser. For the loser, optimization with imperfect foresight makes him worse off than he would have been had he adopted the sub-optimizing strategy of not placing a bet at all.

The treatment of uncertainty in GE theory illustrates why conventional theory is criticized for being inherently static. In simple GE models no new information is ever generated in the course of the decision-making process. In a typical multi-period model, for example, the individual makes a single integrated lifetime plan at the outset which he has no reason to revise later because no new information emerges before the plan has expired. If such information does become available, it is assumed that the possible forms this information might take have been anticipated in advance, and a contingent plan drawn up as to how it would lead to subsequent behaviour being modified. This means that only information of a type that can be anticipated will appear. It also means that all learning activity is telescoped back into the present, in the sense that before taking the initial decision, the issue of what one would infer from certain information, were it to emerge, has already been considered.

A full analysis of uncertainty requires a notion of information cost, however. The reason many people act in ignorance is simply that the information they require is just too expensive for them to collect. The calculus of information gathering lies beyond the scope of GE theory because, as noted above, information is a public good and GE theory has difficulty accommodating public good effects. It is not that it cannot cope at all, but that when several public goods are introduced the model quickly becomes too cumbersome to be of very much use.

The decision on whether information is worth collecting itself requires information, and the decision on whether, in turn, to collect this information could prove to be the start of an infinite regress. To break into this regress it is necessary to have a simple rule for gathering information, a rule that can be applied when little information is available (Simon, 1983). The rule is needed to structure the sequence in which information is required, indicating at what point enough information has been obtained to allow a commitment of resources to be made.

An obvious way of developing such a simple rule is to formulate a procedure linked to a performance norm. A performance norm identifies a degree of success in decision making which is considered satisfactory. A shortfall with respect to a performance norm indicates a problem, whose solution competes attention away from other matters. Another kind of norm is an expectation of what an observation, or similar item of information, will turn out to be. Discrepancy between expectation and realization causes surprise (Shackle, 1979). Surprising information points to the existence of a situation which previously seemed unlikely and suggests that plans may need to be revised.

An individual who takes a realistic view of his own state of ignorance is well equipped to choose the best of the available procedures. The available procedures are those which begin by using only the information that the individual is endowed with and subsequently use only this together with any other information which has been acquired in earlier steps of the procedure. The selection process reflects the individual's subjective beliefs about all the other factors on which no information is to hand. Individual behaviour therefore appears to be governed by a simple procedure, but it is, nevertheless, a procedure which in the light of the initial endowment of information, and the costs of adding to it, has been selected by the individual as the optimal one.

1.6   AN ALTERNATIVE RESEARCH AGENDA

Preoccupation with the specific issue of the efficiency of the market system has led to a concept of economic man which has little relevance to wider issues. It is the inability of conventional theory to tackle pressing practical problems outside the market arena that reveals the most serious limitations of economic man.

Recent concern over faltering productivity growth, for example, has focused attention on the discretionary nature of effort within teams and organizations. It is often difficult for supervisors to monitor effort and for owners of firms to monitor managers. Agency theory demonstrates that this gives selfish people an incentive to slack (see, for example, Arrow, 1985). Conventional economic man cannot be trusted: he is sure to take advantage of the situation. He must be given pecuniary rewards which, in the absence of direct measurements of effort, must be related through contingent contracts to a performance measure based upon output. Pecuniary incentives do not provide a complete solution to the problem, however, since when individual effort cannot be observed it is the output of the team or organization as a whole, and not the output of the specific individual, to which the payment is related.

Many of the most successful firms, it appears, tackle this problem not with pecuniary incentives but through moral suasion. They encourage individuals to supply effort unselfishly, by developing their commitment to various causes promoted – directly or indirectly – by corporate activity. In one version of efficiency wage theory (Yellen, 1984) such commitments are reinforced by paying wages which workers perceive as being fair and equitable. Individual preferences which are broad enough to encompass aspects of social welfare replace the narrowly self-centred interests of economic man (Akerlof, 1983).

The persistence of collusion between individuals is also difficult to explain in conventional terms. Trade union power relies heavily on the unwillingness of workers to compete for jobs by undercutting the wages of those already in employment (Akerlof, 1980) and on solidarity amongst strikers (Naylor, 1987). Informal collusion between producers through price leadership requires the leader to trust the followers not to undercut prices covertly. There are many other examples where collusion is sustained despite a short-term incentive for each individual party to cheat on the understanding or agreement. The Prisoner's Dilemma model shows that cheating may be individually rational independently of whether or not other individuals are expected to cheat (Schelling, 1960). While in some cases cheating can be punished by collective action against the culprit, such collective action is itself subject to cheating, whereby not everyone participates in the punishment process. This is a special case of the more general 'free-rider' problem, which inhibits economic man from successfully providing public goods to members of a group (Ng, 1979). The cohesiveness of social groups, whether collusive or not, is thus difficult to explain in terms of the behaviour of economic man.

In unemployment theory, the microfoundations of wage and price stickiness are also difficult to explain in conventional terms. While nominal rigidities can be attributed to money illusion, it is difficult to explain why such illusion should persist if individuals are fully rational and basically well informed. Rigidities in real wages are difficult to account for, too, except in terms of employee preferences which include the persistence of a customary minimum standard of living and the maintenance of traditional differentials between occupations. Stickiness of retail prices is often explained in terms of goodwill, established through implicit contracts – or 'invisible handshakes' (Okun, 1981) – and sustained through reciprocity. Since the obligation to reciprocate cannot be legally enforced, however, it is once again difficult to rationalize such behaviour in terms of purely selfish motives.

There are certain areas of economics where conventional theory is notoriously weak. Scholarship in these areas is often dominated by economists who have defected from the mainstream of the profession and see the study of their field as providing an inductive basis for the creation of an alternative theory (Coleman, 1987; Hill, 1986; Meier and Seers, 1984). In the fields of economic history and economic development, for example, there is a long-standing difficulty in explaining international and interregional disparities in the standard of living and the rate of growth. Observed differences cannot be fully accounted for by differences in resource endowments and technological capabilities. Cultural factors, such as the Protestant work ethic, and the prevalence of entre-preneurial attitudes are said to be important, but proof is difficult because these factors are hard to quantify.

The preceding remarks suggest that economists should switch their attention to an alternative research agenda centred on the historical evolution of economic institutions and the impact of such institutions on economic performance (Foster, 1987; Hodgson, 1988). This agenda embraces the establishment and growth of both formal institutions, such as governments and firms, and informal institu-tions, such as work groups, friendship circles and so on. The focus is on the comparison of institutional arrangements rather than on the more conventional comparison of market equilibria under different fiscal regimes.

A suitable theme for the new agenda is that individuals take a much wider view of their environment than does conventional economic man, and care about things which may not directly affect them in a purely materialistic sense (Elster, 1989; Etzioni, 1988; Frank, 1987). This wider interest may seem, from a con-ventional standpoint, to lead to unwarranted interference in other people's affairs. From another standpoint, however, it highlights the ability of individ-uals to encompass their own immediate problems within a much wider view and to resolve conflict with others, not merely through market forces, but also through institutions which engineer the convergence of their preferences to reduce the scale of conflict between them.

1.7   INSTITUTIONAL INFLEXIBILITY

It is a feature of many of the problematic phenomena noted above that they involve the persistence of a particular pattern of behaviour, when conventional theory suggests that repeated short-term adaptations might be expected instead. When adjustment does occur, it is normally discrete, as when a new institutional form supplants an old one. The lumpiness of adjustment is most readily explained by fixed costs of evaluating and implementing adjustment.

When fixed costs of adjustment are large it is simply uneconomic continu-ally to re-evaluate policy in the light of every minor change in the environment. Costless adjustment may well be a reasonable assumption when individuals are simply making buying and selling decisions in Walrasian markets. It may even be a reasonable approximation to the situation in real markets where there is intense competition and the costs of switching between alternative trading partners are negligible. But it does not apply in the context of organizational behaviour because organizations are created to deal with complex problems which conventional markets cannot easily solve. Short-term efficiency within an organization normally requires individuals to conform in their commitments to decision rules and working habits. The rules and habits to which members conform can normally be changed only by the leader, who may take some time to recognize the need for change. Such institutional inertia can significantly reduce the frequency, and increase the lumpiness, of adjustment.

Because of the time that must be invested in appraising change there is a tendency for leaders of different organizations to 'free-ride' on one another's efforts (Conlisk, 1980). Each leader adopts a no-change strategy until he observes someone else make a change. He uses this as a cue to begin his own evaluation and then take the experience of the innovator as an input to his own calculations. This can lead to a delay in making the initial change and cause bunching as each leader subsequently makes up for lost time.

Another reason for the persistence of behaviour patterns is that it helps to build up both personal and corporate reputations, which enhance the efficiency of organizations and also facilitate trade by reducing transaction costs. To appreciate the significance of reputations it is necessary to present a critique of Walrasian market assumptions.

1.8 THE NON-WALRASIAN ENVIRONMENT

Real markets operate in a manner that is substantially different from the Walrasian model. The main reason stems from the spatial dimension of trans-actions. This spatial dimension means that most transactions stem from bilateral encounters between individuals. These encounters are typically face to face. Sometimes the encounters are deliberately planned for purposes of trade, as when people go shopping, and sometimes they are a by-product of other activities – leisure and recreation, for example.

Another consequence of the spatial dimension is that encounters themselves are spatially dispersed. This means that when negotiating a price in any encounter neither individual can be really sure of what price he would be able to obtain in an alternative trade.

Negotiation may be seen as a process in which each party attempts to influence the other party's perceptions of opportunity costs. A successful negotiation terminates when each party believes that the gain from further manipulating the other party's perceptions by protracting the negotiations is just outweighed by the advantages of concluding an agreement immediately. As a result, price setting is much more time consuming than in a Walrasian system. There will, moreover, be a spatial dispersion of prices across simultaneous transactions which will be greater, the greater are the geographical distances involved and the poorer the quality of communications.

The execution of the resulting contract may also pose problems, for when exchanging bulky goods in a spatial economy it is often difficult to synchronize payment and receipt. The existence of leads and lags exacerbates the risk of default. Spatial dispersion also creates information asymmetry, where the seller knows the quality of the product better than the buyer, a factor which is difficult to correct for where quality is not reflected in the appearance of the good.

Transactions, it can be seen, involve a number of stages. Each stage typically involves an element of reciprocal externality: each party can take a decision which affects the other's welfare. At stages such as search and negotiation, which come before the contract has been concluded, there is no way of eliminating these externalities by incorporating incentives into the structure of the contract itself.

Transaction costs are typically fixed costs, independent of the volume and value of trade (Casson, 1982). This means that many markets in highly specialized rights cannot function because the potential gains from trade are insufficient to cover the fixed transaction costs. Trading in such goods will be diverted into markets for more versatile goods and services which can then be allocated to a specific use once the owner has gained possession of them.

Versatile goods are often traded between institutions (households, firms, government bodies) and within these institutions the markets that are too specialized to operate externally operate internally between the members of the institutions. Institutions are therefore a mechanism for internalizing the externalities that arise from the fact that conventional trade is costly to arrange. To economize on internal transaction costs the institution uses principles of trading very different from the external market. It places considerable emphasis on spontaneous cooperation underpinned by the trust that members of a stable group learn to place in one another.

Individual members may develop a strong commitment to their institution. They form a social group whose organic structure becomes a vital concern of the members. This organic structure is the product of a division of labour within the group. Individuals may identify closely with their role within the groups, particularly if they are assigned to them on a long-term basis. Other social sciences – notably sociology – take the existence of the social group as in some ways more fundamental than that of the individual. Their analysis begins with the group as an organic entity, rather than with the individual as an isolated social atom. This organic view has much to recommend it, as it emphasizes the strength of the long-term non-market relations that exist between individuals in both their consumption and production activities. Conventional economics, with its emphasis on the individual isolated from others except through market transactions, is potentially misleading in this respect. Its valid commitment to methodological individualism should not obscure the importance of social groups in economic coordination, and the consequent restraint that this places on the speed with which the system adjusts to small environmental changes.

1.9 REPUTATION AND COMMITMENT WITHIN A TRANSACTION GAME

In the absence of Walrasian markets, almost any attempt at coordination must address a situation in which there are reciprocal externalities. The previous section showed that the typical transaction in fact involves a sequence of such reciprocal externalities.

Reciprocal externalities are the basis of non-cooperative games. When each stage of a transaction is considered separately, the pay-offs associated with the resultant games commonly share certain properties. The games belong to a small number of types, such as 'chicken' and 'Prisoner's Dilemma' (Schelling, 1960). When these games are considered in the context of the entire sequence, however, the later games become sub-games within an encompassing sequential game pertaining to the transaction as a whole (for biological analogies, see Smith, 1982). At any one stage, the nature of the game that is entered at a subsequent stage depends upon the outcome at the current stage. The most obvious manifestation of this is that certain combinations of strategies at any stage can cause the transaction as a whole to fail and the rest of the sequence to abort.

Given that individuals move on, within a spatial economy, from one encounter to another, each transaction has a potential successor. The outcome of one transaction can influence the nature of subsequent transactions through reputation effects. These occur when someone observes how a party behaves in a given transaction and uses it to infer how they are likely to behave in future transactions. Reputation mechanisms are most effective when bilateral transactions are readily observed by third parties; third parties constitute a reasonably impartial source of information on the transaction and act as a conduit for the dissemination of this information to people who are likely to deal in future with the partner concerned. Third party observation is most likely to occur amongst a relatively small number of transactors who are members of a stable group engaged in regular face-to-face contact within a compact territory.

Reputation effects mean that each transaction must itself be considered as an element within a sequence, with decisions made at any stage having the capacity to affect all future stages of the sequence. Given that each transaction is itself a sequence, the problem of deciding the optimal strategy at any given stage then becomes incredibly complex (on complexity, see Loasby, 1977).

One way of coping with such complexity is to exploit the repetitive nature of the transaction experience and derive simple rules for transacting which can be applied without further analysis in each subsequent transaction (Axelrod, 1984). The fixed cost of developing the rule is then spread over a number of transactions. With sufficient repetition, these rules may be applied almost subconsciously because the individual has become habituated to them. The most widely studied rules involve trigger mechanisms that punish opponents who refuse to reciprocate cooperative behaviour.

A major cause of the complexity in sequential games is that each party is playing against an intelligent opponent. When the parties are equally intelligent, an attempt to find a winning solution that outwits the opponent may well be self-defeating. For every strategy one party investigates, the other will investigate the counter-strategies. As each attempts to uncover possible strategies that the other has overlooked, the dimensions of the game increase and the complexity accelerates further.

It is worth noting that conventional economic analysis typically handles such problems by restricting the vision of one or more of the players. In the Cournot model of oligopoly, for example, both players have restricted vision, in the sense that each takes the other's output as given when he could, in fact, influence it. The Cournot equilibrium is inherently myopic, which is confirmed by the fact that both parties could do better through collusion. In the Stackelberg model, the leader's vision of the game encompasses the follower's Cournot response, and so the follower's behaviour is endogenized in the leader's calculation of his optimal strategy. When both players have an encompassing vision, however, problems arise if they both persist in pursuing strategic self-interest. Neither can outwit the other through quantity adjustment, and any recourse to other instruments, such as advertising and R & D strategies, can also be matched by the other party. They are therefore driven towards collusion, but the organization of collusion becomes itself just another game. Each is trying to outwit the other in extracting concessions over the distribution of profit.

Each party would find the game much easier to play if the other party were committed to a simple rule. But the other party would not make such a commitment because he would fear that he could be exploited. If one party could make a commitment to non-exploitation, however, then the other party might well find it worthwhile, because of decision-making economies, to adopt a simple rule. Thus commitment by one party to a rule, and by the other to non-exploitation, may confer mutual benefit. Other forms of commitment, such as mutual commitment to complementary rules, might afford similar economies; but non-exploitation, being a principle, is potentially more flexible. There are two main problems with non-exploitation. The first is to define exactly what it means and the second is to explain why a commitment to non-exploitation could ever be credible.

Non-exploitation is essentially a state of mind. It involves forbearing from pursuing one's own interests by exploiting a knowledge of other people's patterns of behaviour. It is impossible for observers to test for it directly, but there are certain symptoms by which it can be identified. One of these is a symmetric distribution of the benefits of a transaction. Benefit, of course, must be measured relative to opportunity cost, and is therefore a subjective concept itself. A group of independent observers may nonetheless be able to reach consensus over the degree of symmetry in the transaction, even if this consensus differs according to the cultural values of the group. A culturally specific concept of non-exploitation can then be defined.

Assume, therefore, that exploitation is detected through the distribution of benefits. Commitment to non-exploitation could, in principle, be encouraged through a system of rewards and penalties, but this leaves open the question of who is to have the power to enforce them. One solution is for people who are likely to transact with each other to enter into a preliminary contract in which they determine a mechanism for identifying exploitation according to agreed criteria, and surrender to an enforcing power whatever instruments they have for evading or countering punishment. This, however, only pushes the problem back one stage further, because whoever is given such power is clearly in a strong position to exploit those who have surrendered it to them. How could the party concerned be trusted to exercise restraint?

Ultimately, it seems, the commitment to non-exploitation must be based on a credible personal commitment to exercise restraint in pursuit of self-interest. Such a commitment must have the property that the individual would punish himself were he to break it. He must be emotionally committed, in the sense that default will cause feelings of guilt. To enter into such a commitment there must be some compensating advantages, however. Commitment to non-exploitation must have certain rewards of its own, which are anticipated at the time the commitment is made, and are sufficiently real for the individual to remain fearful of default. These rewards, it may be suggested, stem from the more intense psychic benefits obtained from outcomes which acquire special significance because they promote the objective to which the individual is committed.

Individuals may differ in their capacity for commitment of this kind. An individual with an established reputation for commitment to non-exploitation is likely to attract people to trade with him. He will benefit from this, provided he is not himself the victim of exploitation. Since non-exploitation is a principle rather than a rule, an intelligent individual is not too vulnerable in this respect. He may also emerge into a leadership role in which people trust him and rely upon him as an independent third party to monitor their transactions. Part of the payment offered by the transactors may be their active support in punishing those who do attempt to exploit the leader.

This leadership role is, in fact, rather akin to the role of the auctioneer in the GE system. The auctioneer is trusted by all transactors with the crucial role of setting price, acting as a clearing house for orders and consignments, and ensuring that contracts are enforced. Not only is he perfectly efficient, in the sense of operating costlessly, but he exercises remarkable self-restraint in not using his position as intermediator to set a monopolistic margin between buying price and selling price in each market. In practice, only an individual with impeccable credentials for non-exploitation would ever be entrusted with the responsibilities of the Walrasian auctioneer.

1.10   THE SOCIAL GROUP

Commitment, it has been suggested, provides both direct emotional benefits and indirect benefits through the reduction of transaction costs. The benefits from commitment are often most easily generated within the framework of a social group. A social group contains individuals who share the same commitment. Thus individuals who join the same group benefit both directly from the emotional support of the others and indirectly from the fact that transaction costs are lower when they trade with other members of the same group (Granovetter, 1985).

From an economic point of view, a particularly interesting type of group is the workgroup. Workgroups are found in firms both in shop-floor production and among managers making collective decisions. Within a workgroup individuals typically operate as a team, which means that failure by any one individual can seriously damage overall group performance. Within a team, the leader typically assigns each individual member to a role, and sets a performance norm. In a well-run group the member will receive practical and emotional support in attaining these norms. If he is successful, he will experience satisfaction, and receive the approval of the leader. If he fails, he will normally quit the group, finding another group – possibly committed to some other objective – within which he can perform better. The benefits of group membership can usually be assessed accurately only through experience. Individuals who are still seeking a worthwhile commitment and a workgroup to support it will tend to circulate between groups, whilst those who have found what they are looking for will stay with their group.

The fact that breaking a commitment generates feelings of guilt discourages individuals from 'shopping around' once they have made their decision. When membership of a group is voluntary, leaders can be regarded as effectively competing for the most able members in order to further their objectives. They may also compete on other fronts too, because their objectives conflict. While competition between groups can often be useful in setting external norms against which each group can judge its performance, it can also degenerate into warfare unless all groups respect the rules of the competitive game. In this respect the morality of leaders themselves is crucially important. Integrity requires that they should be personally committed to the official objectives of their group, but not so committed that they abandon self-restraint by punishing weaker members severely for underperformance or attacking rivals on the basis that victory is to be obtained at all costs. The requisite combination of dedication and restraint seems to be difficult to find in practice.

1.11   ETHICAL MAN

This chapter began by inquiring whether there was a more relevant alternative to economic man. The preceding discussion suggests that an alternative may indeed exist. There may well, in fact, be several alternatives, but it is convenient to focus on just one. This alternative may be termed 'ethical man'. It articulates a broader concept of human nature than the conventional economic man who is finely tuned to the requirements of GE theory. As indicated in Chapter 3, ethical man has, in fact, a number of distinguished antecedents in the literature of economic philosophy (see, in particular, Hoyt, 1926; Knight, 1935; Macfie, 1936,1943).

Ethical man, like economic man, is purposeful and intelligent (in this respect, but only in this respect, he is also similar to 'Austrian' man (Kirzner, 1986)). These restrictions mean that the concept is certainly not a vacuous one. Unlike economic man, however, his purposes are fixed only in the very general sense that he is seeking peace of mind. In any given situation this general purpose is translated into more proximate objectives. These proximate objectives are more precise, and resemble more closely the preferences of conventional economic man. These proximate objectives are not autonomous, however. They can be influenced by the social group (or groups) to which the individual belongs. The individual searches across groups in pursuit of commitments that will give peace of mind. Within any group he conforms to the pursuit of the collective goal, willingly when membership is voluntary, but possibly as a result of coercion if it is not. Because the mechanism of preference change is well specified, the criticisms of endogenous preferences that are usually advanced do not apply.

Unlike economic man, ethical man is sufficiently intelligent to recognize the limitations of the 'human situation'. He realizes that there are significant costs in collecting sufficient information to be fully informed about each and every issue. He may therefore choose to remain ignorant of some aspect of his circumstances because the expected value of the outcome of his decision would increase by less than the cost of collecting the relevant information. Ethical man does not therefore extol the rationality of what he does, but frankly admits that he often chooses to act on the basis of his personal judgement.

In one sense, therefore, ethical man may appear irrational. But in another sense he is actually more rational than economic man. This is because he is analysing and responding rationally to the problem of what information to collect when information is a scarce resource. This is not an issue that troubles conventional economic man at all.

It is, in fact, a complex issue, for a given item of information may have implications for several different fields of action. Moreover, the decision whether to collect a given item of information is itself conditioned on, or framed by, information that was collected before. One of the simplest ways of deciding what information to collect is to adopt a performance norm in each area of activity and to use shortfalls with respect to this norm to trigger investigations of whether an unexpected change of circumstances has occurred. Because he works with norms, ethical man regards 'standards' as very important in identifying problems that actively require investigation.

There is another sense in which ethical man is more rational than conventional man. Ethical man often takes a broader view of a problem than does economic man, encompassing aspects of the environment that economic man ignores. This is particularly true of the behaviour of other major players in the environment. Economic man often fails to endogenize the responses of others to his own decisions. Ethical man endogenizes such responses, but does so in a simple way because he recognizes the strategic complexities that are involved. Ethical man, for example, has sufficient vision to realize that, when playing against an equally intelligent opponent, cooperative strategies must be developed which involve reciprocal commitments. In some cases reputation effects may be sufficient to make commitments credible, whereas in other cases emotional commitment, secured by peace of mind, on the one hand, and guilt-feelings, on the other, are necessary. Shared membership of a social group is instrumental in enhancing both reputation effects and emotional attachments, and so joining a group, even though it involves tampering with proximate preferences, can still be perceived as a reasonable step to undertake. Ethical man has sufficient intelligence to perceive this, but regrettably economic man, because of the narrow vision engendered by the Walrasian environment in which he operates, cannot. Ethical man is social, and indeed gregarious, whereas economic man is not (Hirschman, 1982; McIntosh, 1969; Roberts and Holdren, 1972).

Ethical man's capacity for commitment appears indirectly in game-theoretic analysis of reputation. Some models (for example, Rosenthal, 1981) postulate a small probability of 'irrational' behaviour by potentially reputable people. The capacity for commitment may be interpreted as a 'rationalization' of such 'irrational' behaviour, as it is commitment to a particular pattern of behaviour that is crucial in such analysis.

The concept of ethical man demonstrates that people differ in many respects, and not just in their preferences for material goods and services. People differ in the objectives to which they are committed, in their personal norms, in their capacity to handle complex decisions, in the knowledge and in the biases they have inherited from previous experience, and so on. The concept of ethical man therefore makes it possible to recognize genuine personality differences between people, and to address the crucial economic issue of how people with different personalities are to be matched to different roles within a social group. It is possible, in principle, to examine the requirements of each role in terms of the responsibilities that go with it, and the qualities that are consequently needed to perform it effectively. This provides a much richer analytical structure than conventional economic theory with which to investigate the performance of groups, both large and small, from shop-floor workgroups to large firms and even to nation states.

An important aspect of the division of labour within a group is the relation between leader and follower. Leaders have a valuable role in intermediating between followers and most particularly in building up trust between them. In one sense a leader resembles economic man more closely than does his followers, for his preferences tend to exhibit a higher degree of autonomy and his decision making is often more calculating too.

A crucial issue is how far leaders also resemble economic man in being potentially devious and untrustworthy. It is important for the functioning of groups that leaders are committed both to the official objectives of the group and, in particular, to the non-exploitation of other people's commitments. The performance of the group hinges on the leader being trusted, and indeed it is often the most trusted individual who emerges as the leader of a group. Because the concept of ethical man is so much broader than that of economic man, it provides plenty of opportunity to analyse the role of personality factors in leadership and to relate group performance to leadership style.

Ethical man is also better suited than economic man to dynamic analysis. Ethical man does not attempt to telescope the whole of the future into his present decisions, because he appreciates the complexity of decision making that would result. Neither does he expect other individuals to enter into sophisticated contingent forward contracts for his benefit. The transactions costs involved are prohibitive. He recognizes that moral commitments to simple principles or rules are in many cases an adequate substitute. He copes with problems as and when they arise, relying for support upon the goodwill of other members of his social group. He recognizes, in other words, that economic success is not just an individual, but also a group phenomenon.

1.12 CONCLUSION

It is a hopeful sign that in the last 25 years or so the narrow concept of economic man has been steadily weakened – if not undermined – in the course of a number of imaginative applications of economic analysis to subjects of wider import (in addition to earlier references, see Margolis, 1982, Sugden, 1986). This success has allowed economics to function, to some extent, as an imperialist science, bringing the standpoint of methodological individualism to bear on social issues previously analysed chiefly from an organic standpoint (Hamlin, 1986). It has allowed economics to regain some of the ground that was lost to sociology and political science in the aftermath of the marginalist revolution (Hirshleifer, 1985), a point developed further in Chapter 2.

It has been argued in this chapter that the concept of ethical man provides a more appropriate basis on which to continue this imperialistic movement. Ethical man harnesses the power of methodological individualism to analyse behaviour in a manner complementary to, rather than in conflict with, the insights that emerge from the organic perspective. Methodological individualism, through ethical man, can provide the 'bottom up' perspective on the same sort of issues for which the organic perspective provides the 'top down' view. This should permit a more sensible intellectual division of labour within the social sciences. The methods of economics can be used to develop the individualistic perspective across the whole range of sciences analysing the social system. Other social sciences can concentrate on the elaboration of the organic perspective. Because of the role of markets in decentralizing decisions, the individualistic perspective will tend to be of greatest relevance in analysing market behaviour. Conversely, within strictly hierarchical organizations, the organic view will reveal its greatest relative strength. Thus there will continue to be some association between market analysis and individualism, on the one hand, and hierarchical analysis and the organic approach, on the other, but where they interface a better intellectual 'fit' should, in future, be obtained.

ACKNOWLEDGEMENTS

I am grateful to Peter Buckley, John Creedy, Jim Pemberton and Alan Roberts for their comments on an earlier draft.

REFERENCES

Akerlof, G.A. (1980) A theory of social custom, of which unemployment may be one consequence, *Quarterly Journal of Economics*, **94**, 719–75.
Akerlof, G.A. (1983) Loyalty Filters, *American Economic Review*, **73**, 54–63.
Arrow, K.J. (1985) The Economics of Agency, in J.W. Pratt and R.J. Zeckhauser (eds) *Principals and Agents: The Structure of Business*, Boston, Mass.: Harvard Business School Press, 37–51.

Arrow, K.J. and G. Debreu (1954) Existence of equilibrium for a competitive economy, *Econometrica*, **22**, 265–90.

Axelrod, R. (1984) *The Evolution of Cooperation*, New York: Basic Books.

Barrientos, A. (1988) Economic Man, Mathematics and the Rise of Neoclassical Economics, *Ealing Working Papers in Economics*, No. 5.

Becker, G.S. (1976) *The Economic Approach to Human Behavior*, Chicago: University of Chicago Press.

Becker, G.S. and G.J. Stigler (1977) De gustibus non est disputandum, *American Economic Review*, **67**, 76–90.

Boland, L.A, (1982) *The Foundations of Economic Method*, London: Allen and Unwin.

Casson, M.C. (1982) *The Entrepreneur: An Economic Theory*, Oxford: Martin Robertson.

Coleman, D.C. (1987) *History and the Economic Past: An Account of the Rise and Decline of Economic History in Britain*, Oxford: Clarendon Press.

Conlisk, J. (1980) Costly Optimisers versus Cheap Imitators, *Journal of Economic Behaviour and Organisation*, **1**, 275–93.

Elster, J. (1989) Social Norms and Economic Theory, *Journal of Economic Perspectives*, **3**, 99–117.

Etzioni, A. (1988) *The Moral Dimension: Towards a New Economics*, New York: Free Press.

Foster, J. (1987) *Evolutionary Macroeconomics*, London: Allen and Unwin.

Frank, R.H. (1987) If *Homo Economicus* could choose his own Utility Function, would he want one with a Conscience?, *American Economic Review*, **77**, 593–604.

Friedman, M. (1953) The methodology of positive economics, in M. Friedman, *Essays in Positive Economics*, Chicago: University of Chicago Press, 3–43.

Goldsmith, M.M. (1985) *Private Vices, Public Benefits: Bernard Mandeville's Social and Political Thought*, Cambridge: Cambridge University Press.

Granovetter, M. (1985) Economic Action and Social Structure: The Problem of Embeddedness, *American Journal of Sociology*, **91**, 481–510.

Hamlin, A.P. (1986) *Ethics, Economics and the State*, Brighton: Wheatsheaf.

Hill, P. (1986) *Development Economics on Trial: the Anthropological Case for a Prosecution*, Cambridge: Cambridge University Press.

Hirschman, A. (1982) *Shifting Involvements: Private Interest and Public Action*, Oxford: Martin Robertson.

Hirshleifer, J. (1985) The Expanding Domain of Economics, *American Economic Review*, **85**(supplement), 53–68.

Hodgson, G. (1988) *Economics and Institutions*, Oxford: Blackwell.

Hollis, M. and E. Nell (1975) *Rational Economic Man: A Philosophical Critique of Neo-Classical Economics*, Cambridge: Cambridge University Press.

Hoyt, E.E. (1926) *Primitive Trade: Its Psychology and Economics*, London: Kegan Paul, Trench, Trubner.

Kirzner, I.M.(ed.) (1986) *Subjectivism, Intelligibility and Economic Understanding: Essays in Honour of Ludwig M. Lachmann on His Eightieth Birthday*, London: Macmillan.

Knight, F.H. (1935) *The Ethics of Competition: And Other Essays*, London: Allen and Unwin.

Leibenstein, H. (1976) *Beyond Economic Man: A New Foundation for Microeconomics*, Cambridge, Mass.: Harvard University Press.

Loasby, B.J. (1977) *Choice, Complexity and Ignorance*, Cambridge: Cambridge University Press.

Macfarlane, A. (1978) *The Origins of English Individualism: The Family, Property and Social Transition*, Oxford: Blackwell.

Macfie, A.L. (1936) *An Essay on Economy and Value: Being an Inquiry into the Real Nature of Economy*, London: Macmillan.

Macfie, A.L. (1943) *Economic Efficiency and Social Welfare*, London: Oxford University Press.

Margolis, H. (1982) *Selfishness, Altruism and Rationality: A Theory of Social Choice*, Cambridge: Cambridge University Press.

McIntosh, D. (1969) *The Foundations of Human Society*, Chicago: University of Chicago Press.

Meier, G.M. and D. Seers (eds)(1984) *Pioneers in Development*, New York: Oxford University Press.

Myers, M.L. (1983) *The Soul of Economic Man: Ideas of Self-Interest, Thomas Hobbes to Adam Smith*, Chicago: University of Chicago Press.

Naylor, R. (1987) Strikes, Free Riders and Social Customs, *Warwick Economic Research Papers* No. 275.

Ng, Y-K. (1979) *Welfare Economics: Introduction and Development of Basic Concepts*, London: Macmillan.

Okun, A.M. (1981) *Prices and Quantities*, Oxford: Blackwell.

Roberts, B. and R.R. Holdren (1972) *Theory of Social Process: An Economic Analysis*, Ames, Iowa: The Iowa State University Press.

Rosenthal, R.W. (1981) Games of Perfect Information, Predatory Pricing and the Chain-Store Paradox, *Journal of Economic Theory*, **25**, 92–100.

Schelling, T.C. (1960) *The Strategy of Conflict*, Cambridge, Mass.: Harvard University Press.

Sen, A. (1985) The moral standing of the market, in E.F. Paul, F.D. Miller, Jr. and J. Paul (eds) *Ethics and Economics*, Oxford: Blackwell, 1–19.

Shackle, G.L.S. (1979) *Imagination and the Nature of Choice*, Edinburgh: Edinburgh University Press.

Simon, H.A. (1983) *Reason in Human Affairs*, Oxford: Blackwell.

Smith, A. (1776) *An Inquiry into the Nature and Causes of the Wealth of Nations* (ed. R.H. Campbell, A.S. Skinner and W.B. Todd, Oxford: Clarendon Press, 1976).

Smith, J.M. (1982) *Evolution and the Theory of Games*, Cambridge: Cambridge University Press.

Steintrager, J. (1977) *Bentham*, London: Allen and Unwin.

Stigler, G.J. (1982) *The Economist as Preacher*, Oxford: Blackwell.

Sugden, R. (1986) *The Economics of Rights, Co-operation and Welfare*, Oxford: Blackwell.

Wiles, P. and G. Routh (eds)(1984) *Economics in Disarray*, Oxford: Blackwell.

Yellen, J.L. (1984) Efficiency wage models of unemployment, *American Economic Review (Papers and Proceedings)*, **94**, 200–205.

2. Economics as an imperialistic social science

2.1 INTRODUCTION

Economic theorists are by nature system builders. Successful system building in the social sciences requires fearless simplification. Any theoretical system that corresponds too closely to complex social reality will be too complicated to be of any use. But simplification invites criticism, for there is always something of potential importance that gets left out of a theoretical system. The system builders need their critics, both to remind them of their system's limitations and to suggest ideas for improvement. For system builders are proud of their constructions and tend to place too much confidence in them.

Equally, the critics need the system builders. Because of its formality and rigour, a good system has a logical transparency which the verbal expressions of the typical critic usually lack. Without a transparent system to criticize, the critics will soon be out of business. While the critics can, of course, criticize each other, no-one else is likely to take much notice of this. For, while a system is typically founded on fixed ground, critics frequently shift their position and so are difficult for other critics to pin down successfully.

Critics of economic theory often find it difficult to understand how economics manages to survive what they perceive to be their devastating criticisms. One reason is that they do not offer a better system – just the prospect of a more complicated system, or even no system at all. Sometimes they rather peevishly claim that the mathematical formalism of economic theory gives it pseudoscientific legitimacy, because people who do not understand mathematics often stand in awe of those who do. Certainly the use of mathematics is a powerful symbol of the internal logical consistency to which economics aspires, and it may indeed convey mystique to the uninitiated. But it can equally well be argued that it is not the difficulty of the mathematics, but the elegance and simplicity of the underlying logic, that is the real attraction of economic theory.

Because the legitimation of one's beliefs is as difficult as it is important, people like to have a theoretical system to which they can refer for intellectual support. And because abstract thinking is difficult, people like the assumptions of the theory to be simple and straightforward. The assumption of rational behaviour, which is central to economics, satisfies this criterion very well. Moreover, the fact that people are assumed to be rational gives a kind of intrinsic necessity to the theory's results. Things cannot really turn out differently from what the theory says, it would seem, because this would imply a waste of resources which rational people would seek to correct. This points to a paradox: that it is because people are, in fact, of limited rationality that it is useful for them to assume that other people are perfectly rational when interpreting their behaviour. Only a perfectly rational person could possibly analyse the behaviour of a society by explaining the mental processes of each individual using a fully-fledged model of the human brain – assuming that a satisfactory model of this kind were actually available. The economist's assumption of rationality is not, therefore, a piece of misguided psychology, but an effective response to a practical need to explain social behaviour in simple terms.

Another reason why economic theory withstands criticism so successfully is that it is much more versatile than its critics realize. The critics are always 'firing at a moving target', because the theory is continually being adapted to meet previous criticisms. When the theory was criticized by the early American institutionalists for assuming perfect competition, the theory of monopoly was developed, and an early theory of oligopoly due to Cournot was rediscovered and refined. When business economists criticized the theory for assuming perfect certainty, the theory of uncertainty was developed and triumphantly applied to explain the pricing of insurance and other financial claims. When the theory was criticized by later institutionalists for modelling the firm as a 'black box', the theory of transaction costs was developed to explain how the boundaries of the firm are set. Finally, the growing emphasis on business strategy has stimulated game-theoretic analysis of the competitive process. By adding game theory to its repertoire of techniques, economics has finally evolved to the stage where it is able to take on other social sciences on their own terms.

This record of adaptation is inconsistent with the view that economic theory is rigid and dogmatic. The core assumptions of economics are compatible with a wide range of human behaviour – not just in the economic field, but in social and political fields as well. The predictions of economics come from combining the core assumptions with a wide variety of specific assumptions. The sheer diversity of the specific assumptions that can be accommodated gives the theory enormous 'survival value'.

All the predictions of economics derive from a combination of general core assumptions and specific applications-centred assumptions. The core assumptions are always the same, but the specific assumptions may vary from case to case. The two main core assumptions are optimization and equilibrium. The first describes how individual plans are formulated and the second how conflicting plans are reconciled. The standardization of core assumptions guarantees the internal coherence of different economic models at a reasonable level of generality. Problems can arise, however, if a specific model is utilized outside its intended field of application, where it may conflict with another specific model developed using different assumptions chosen with that field particularly in mind.

The combination of assumptions involved in any one prediction means that the falsification of any one prediction does not strike directly at the core assumptions. It simply invites refinement of the specific assumptions with which the core assumptions are combined. This distinction between the general core and the specific applications is not, of course, unique to economics: it is widely used in the natural sciences, and elsewhere, to immunize general principles against specific criticisms. It serves to emphasize the point made earlier, though, that the core assumptions themselves are never directly tested. People who state, for example, that 'Experience shows that many economic decisions are irrational' simply demonstrate their ignorance of economic methodology, for rationality is a core assumption whose implications for behaviour are always conditioned on the decision maker's preferences and their perception of constraints. The specification of these preferences and constraints involves specific assumptions, and any instance of predictive failure can always be imputed to errors in these specifications rather than to a flaw in the core assumptions themselves.

Since core assumptions, by themselves, imply little or nothing, their usefulness resides mainly in extracting meaning from other sets of assumptions. As noted above, it is by combining two different kinds of assumption that predictions are derived. The ease of derivation, and the breadth and depth of the topics to which the predictions relate, are the principal criteria by which the core assumptions must be appraised. Good core assumptions will afford a wide range of predictions which are interesting because they are not immediately obvious. The predictions may run counter to untutored common sense: it is only on reflection that the inner necessity mentioned above will be revealed. Weak core assumptions, on the other hand, will provide a small number of predictions which follow fairly obviously from the specific assumptions to which they have been applied. The weakness in the core of many other social sciences is revealed by the fact that it is often difficult to distinguish between a prediction and the assumption from which it is supposed to have been derived.

2.2   EXPANDING THE DOMAIN OF ECONOMICS

This chapter is not a straightforward defence of conventional economics, however. Following the theme of Chapter 1, the thrust of the argument is that economists have been too cautious and unimaginative in the way that they have applied their ideas. They have presumed that their core assumptions are useful mainly in the domain of economic behaviour, whereas in fact they are of much wider validity within the social sciences.

Moreover, within the field of economics, too much emphasis has been placed on the explanation of market rather than non-market behaviour (Tullock, 1972; Udéhn, 1992). As a result, a division of labour has evolved in the social sciences whereby economists apply their principles mainly to market behaviour whilst other social scientists apply a rather different set of principles to non-market behaviour. This arrangement fails to exploit the economies of scope available from utilizing the same general principles in several different subject areas. It also fudges the issue of whether one of these sets of principles is superior to the other, or whether the two sets of principles should coexist indefinitely side by side.

Attempts to apply non-economic principles to economic behaviour are exemplified by the literature of political economy, which seeks to place economic issues within a broader social and political context. The fact that economic activity is embedded within a framework of social and political institutions is indisputable and, in so far as conventional economics has ignored this, the literature of political economy provides a valuable corrective.

But the principles on which political economy is based are extremely diffuse and eclectic, and the analysis often relies heavily on ill-defined concepts such as power and hegemony. This raises the question of whether the social and political context of economic activity might not be better understood in terms of more conventional economic concepts such as optimization and equilibrium. This means that, in the context of Table 2. 1, the appropriate movement is not from left to right along the bottom row of the table – extending non-economic principles to market behaviour – but from right to left along the top row of the table – applying economic principles to non-market behaviour. The thrust of this chapter is therefore to show how economic principles can elucidate not only the market process itself, but the institutional framework within which that process takes place. It is claimed that extending the domain of conventional economics, and not promoting an eclectic form of political economy, is the most appropriate way to standardize the conceptual framework of the social sciences.

Table 2.1   The relation of theoretical framework to field of study

	Field of study	
Framework	Market	Non-market
Economic	Conventional economics	Imperialist economics
Non-economic	Political economy	Other social sciences

If extending the domain of economics is so fruitful, it might be asked, why have economists not been more active in this respect? The explanation seems to be that economics is a conservative profession, so that economists have exploited the versatility of their core assumptions only when under threat. When left to their own devices, much of their research effort has gone into greater refinement of a few simple models, notably the general equilibrium model of competitive markets. For many economists, general equilibrium (GE) theory is the crowning glory of the economics profession, because of its Newtonian quality of reconciling counteracting forces of demand and supply in a harmonious way. In fact the GE model is only one of the many kinds of model that the core assumptions of economics will support. If economics is to respond to contemporary threats, moreover, it will have to develop these other kinds of model, and this chapter indicates some of the ways in which this is being done.

A major contemporary threat comes from the accumulating evidence that cultural factors are key determinants of economic performance. Economists can no longer afford to regard culture simply as an exogenous factor impeding the modernization of primitive societies. Nor can they continue to treat it just as a residual factor in their empirical research. For culture appears to be a significant positive factor promoting the growth of advanced economies. If culture is, in fact, a valuable intangible resource then it is important not only to measure the benefits of it but also to compare these benefits with the cost of acquiring and sustaining it. Culture can be thought of as an important component of human capital, for example. As such it can influence national productivity and comparative advantage. Thus workers with similar technical skills may be more productive in one country than another because the moral content of the local culture makes them better motivated.

Another manifestation of cultural difference is the way that some regions successfully exploit inter-firm networks to coordinate product flow and infrastructure development, whilst coordination in other regions is impaired by conflicts between different factions. Similar contrasts can be observed in industrial relations and, at the national level, in areas such as industrial policy.

Finally, at the firm level, there is growing evidence for the influence of corporate culture on growth and profitability. While managers of some firms appear to demoralise their workers with intrusive supervision and overcentralized administration, others successfully empower their subordinates to contribute to corporate objectives in a satisfying way. This suggests that managers who trust their employees obtain better results than those who do not – a result which is confirmed by anecdotal evidence from high-growth innovative industries.

If economists are to analyse the cultural determinants of economic performance then the question naturally arises as to whether they should analyse culture *per se*. Should they tackle head on some of the core issues of social anthropology, for example, or carefully circumvent them in order to preserve traditional subject boundaries as far as possible? It is suggested in this chapter that economists should tackle such issues head on. It is in the best traditions of economics to focus on the key issues – to abstract from detail, to discard the peripheral and to provide a simple account of the essential elements. If this can be done successfully, moreover, then enormous benefits will be obtained. For, if economics can indeed tackle issues of this kind, then it has the potential to supply a unifying framework of analysis for social science as a whole.

Many readers may be taken aback by this conclusion. It is often suggested that economic theory stands apart from social science theory as a whole and therefore has no place within a unified social science. The unification of social science, on this view, will finally expose economic theory as a rationalist impostor. But the present line of argument suggests that economic theory stands apart only because it is more advanced than other subjects in its theoretical development. It does, after all, have a long and distinguished intellectual tradition, and has assimilated many useful mathematical and statistical techniques from other disciplines. It is only lack of imagination that has prevented economists from applying their methods in other fields. A more imaginative research agenda will allow other social sciences to benefit from these techniques. They in turn can assimilate the techniques that have so much enhanced the reputation of the economics profession.

There are already important examples of 'economic imperialism' in the social sciences from which lessons can be drawn. It is useful to compare two cases, one very successful and the other less so. The success is public choice theory. By examining the logic of the democratic process (Downs, 1957; Buchanan and Tullock, 1962) and its relationship to collective action (Olson, 1965) economists clarified issues which political scientists had earlier failed to resolve. The economists' emphasis on the rationality of individual choices illuminated issues which the more organic approach of the traditional political scientist had obscured.

The less successful case is the economics of the family (Becker, 1976). While this theory has had notable achievements in demography, through its analysis of the demand for children, it has not fulfilled its claim to explain the key features of family behaviour in purely economic terms. Part of the problem seems to be that altruistic behaviour is more important at the level of the family than at the level of the nation state. The common tendency of economists to identify rationality with selfishness (see below) is less damaging in the political context than it is in the family one. It is necessary, it seems, for economists to be even more inventive in their theory when discussing the family than when discussing political choices, and so far they do not seem to have been inventive enough.

Thus it is evident that successful imperialism involves more than just the extension of conventional models to new fields: it involves innovating new models, or at least significantly modifying existing ones. A lazy approach, which merely adapts a model to a new situation by relabelling the variables, reflects unwarranted arrogance, and brings economics into disrepute. Successful imperialism requires that only the core assumptions remain unchanged; the more specific assumptions must be altered to accommodate the special features of the new situation.

2.3 OPTIMIZATION AS A CORE ASSUMPTION

The difficulty with this research programme is to distinguish properly between what is core and what is not. One reason why economists have been so unimaginative in their application of theory seems to be confusion over this very issue of where the boundaries of the core are to be set. Historically, there has been a tendency to include too much in the core. Assumptions useful in just one particular field have acquired the status of core assumptions and have subsequently been applied to other fields where they are much less suitable. This has meant that the extension of economic theory in certain directions has produced poor results, and discouraged further attempts of this kind.

In this chapter only one assumption is taken as unconditionally core, and that is that people optimize. A second assumption – the existence of an equilibrium – is also employed, but with reservations that will be discussed later on. Since people cannot meaningfully optimize unless they can rank alternatives in order of preference, it is assumed that optimization is with respect to a well-behaved objective function. What enters into this objective function is left fairly open. It may be consumption goods, as in conventional specifications of a consumer utility function. Alternatively, it may be strategies, as in the specification of game-theoretic pay-off functions. Although the consumption of a good does not naturally suggest itself as a strategy, and strategies such as cheating are not naturally interpreted as the consumption of particular goods, it is important to realize that the logic of the theory does not discriminate in any essential way between these two cases. This is illustrated, for example, by the role of effort, which is crucial in any discussion of cultural influences on economic performance. Effort can be thought of either as a strategy – hard work rather than shirking, for example – or as a negative good – an undesirable sacrifice of leisure. What matters for the theory is only the valuation of effort, and not how it is described. Thus in general both strategies and goods can enter simultaneously into an individual's objective function.

Similarly with the objective function itself, the use of the expression 'utility function' in connection with individual objectives has misleading connotations. It tends to be assumed that a utility function must specify selfish materialistic wants. The hedonistic tradition of utility theory, commencing with the Benthamite calculus of pleasure and pain, continues to influence the way that utility functions are perceived even though, as a logical construct, the modern utility function can just as easily represent altruistic feelings and emotional needs. Thus many economists continue to believe that an assumption of selfishness is core, even though altruists are just as capable of optimizing as anyone else.

Some critics of economics also mistakenly believe that selfishness is core: they dub altruism irrational, and then criticize economists for focusing exclusively on rational behaviour. In fact they should emphasize that altruism is perfectly rational (if preferences are altruistic to begin with) and criticize economists for retaining an assumption of selfishness, as if it were core, in situations (such as family life) where such an assumption reduces rather than enhances the theory's predictive power.

Another feature of the utility function, as commonly specified, is that everything which appears in it is controlled by the individual concerned. There is no interdependence, such that one person cares about something which another person decides. Thus utility has no vicarious components. Interdependencies of this kind are rejected in conventional theory because it is widely believed that the additional complications inevitably undermine the theory's predictive power. This is another reason why selfishness is assumed in conventional theory, for altruistic preferences exhibit interdependence whereas selfish preferences do not. But the loss of predictive power caused by interdependence affects some models more seriously than others. The GE model is very seriously affected and, because of the prestige that this model has enjoyed in the past, this has been sufficient reason for many economists to reject preference interdependence altogether. Outside the GE context, though, preference interdependence can in fact be a source of enhanced predictive power.

Preference interdependence means that one person can manipulate another person's behaviour. Suppose, for example, that individual A's preferences relate to a variable under individual B's control. Suppose, furthermore, that this variable is a complement or a substitute for another variable entirely under A's control. For example, A may like to work just as hard as B does, so that the harder B works, the lower is the disutility of effort experienced by A. If B knows about A's preferences, then B can exploit this knowledge to manipulate A's behaviour. By working hard himself, B lowers A's disutility of effort and encourages A to substitute hard work for leisure. Thus, because A's effort and B's effort are complements within A's preferences, A will tend to match the level of effort expended by B. It could be said that hard work by B is a 'stimulus' to which A responds; in this case preference interdependence is indistinguishable from a 'behavioural' explanation of A's behaviour. Alternatively, it could be said that A tries to conform with B, in which case the explanation is indistinguishable from a purely sociological account of the group dynamics involving A and B. Finally, it could be said that A desires to reciprocate B's effort. This would be appropriate if both A and B are members of a team and supposedly working towards a common cause; B's commitment of effort to this cause is then reciprocated by a similar commitment from A. This account expresses the result in terms of morale and motivation, rather than in terms of behaviourism or conformity as before. It is all the same phenomenon, however, and preference interdependence is arguably the most straightforward way in which it can be explained.

2.4   LEADERSHIP IN SOCIAL GROUPS: AN ECONOMIC APPROACH

The use of utility functions with preference interdependence is thus a powerful method of integrating social influences into the analysis of economic behaviour. Almost any kind of behaviour can be rationalized by the specification of an appropriate interdependent utility function. However, it is only by imposing restrictions on the forms of interdependence allowed that predictions can be obtained about the kinds of behaviour that will be observed in particular circumstances.

The success of the theory depends, of course, on the choice of appropriate restrictions. There are many possible sets of restrictions which could be imposed. Each set of restrictions represents a particular view of how the economy and society interact. To illustrate the economic approach to social issues it is sufficient to make just one selection from the extensive menu of possible restrictions. The restriction made here is designed to illustrate how a leader can improve economic performance by engineering the culture of a social group (Casson, 1991).

First, it is assumed that every individual belongs to a social group and that each social group has a leader. The leader is autonomous, in the sense of having independent preferences, whilst the other members of the group (the followers) have interdependent preferences. While a follower's interdependence may relate to other followers' behaviour, it is generally focused on the leader.

Secondly, some of the follower's own strategies are complementary to some of the leader's strategies. Thus an action performed by the leader increases the value of some particular action by the follower, and so increases the likelihood that an optimizing follower will act in this particular way.

Thirdly, it is assumed that the leader knows the interdependencies within the follower's preferences and can exploit them for his own particular ends. These are not necessarily selfish ends: besides being concerned with his own material interests, the leader is assumed to attach some weight to the overall performance of the group. The leader then optimizes his own actions by calculating the responses of followers to various actions of his own and assessing their impact on his overall ends.

Because the leader knows the way that the follower's preferences relate to his own actions, the follower's preferences are essentially endogenous from the leader's point of view. In other words, if the follower's utility function is redefined to include only the variables which the follower controls, then the form of this new utility function is conditional on the leader's actions. This rather surprising result shows that debating whether preferences are exogenous or endogenous, as economists have tended to do in the past, is liable to miss the basic point, which is not whether they are endogenous, but *to whom* they are endogenous. Whoever perceives another person's preferences as endogenous has the power to manipulate them, provided they can find the appropriate variable to control. Power and influence therefore depend not only on monopolistic control of resources, as in conventional economics, but on the ability to manipulate other people's preferences too.

When a leader stands in one-to-one relation with each of his followers then the principle of optimization is quite sufficient to explain their joint behaviour. The leader calculates how each follower will rationally respond to each manipulative act and then rationally chooses his manipulation strategy. Assuming that the leader has all available information on the follower's preferences and constraints, and the follower is content to act passively in taking the leader's behaviour as a datum, then both will be satisfied with the outcome.

An important implication of optimization is that trade-offs can be made. If the environment changes, then strategy can adapt to conserve resources that have become more scarce. This applies to individual followers who, with given group incentives, will modify their plans as circumstances change, and to the leader too. Since the leader's strategy is concerned with cultural engineering, this means that culture too will change in response to environmental change.

The principle of optimization therefore provides a useful antidote to the popular view of culture as a rigid, historically inertial system of beliefs which causes decisions to be made on emotional instead of rational grounds. In fact, culture simply provides a framework within which followers behave quite rationally and is itself a framework which is purposefully adapted to the changing environment of the group.

The engineering of culture becomes a more complex issue, however, when the followers interact directly with each other as well as with the leader of the group. For example, when the followers trade amongst themselves it is important for the leader to influence not only the followers' behaviour towards himself, but their behaviour towards each other too. To do this effectively, he needs to understand the nature of the interaction between the followers and the results to which this leads.

To predict the outcome of such interactions it is natural to suppose that the process of interaction between the followers will continue until none of them perceives any advantage from initiating further change. Loosely speaking, this means that the process of interaction will adjust to an equilibrium.

2.5   THE CONCEPT OF EQUILIBRIUM

One of the weaknesses of modern economics is that it has little to say about how an equilibrium is achieved. Indeed, critics of economics would be well advised to focus their attacks on equilibrium, where the theory is particularly vulnerable, and leave rationality alone. Out of equilibrium, individuals face difficult issues which disappear once equilibrium has been achieved. The most important of these is learning. Each step in the process of adjustment to equilibrium generates new information which must be fed back to guide the next step. Successful adjustment requires efficient use of this information. If information processing were costless then individuals could guide their steps using a perfectly logical learning procedure such as Bayesian inference. But if information processing is costly it may be optimal to switch to a simpler non-Bayesian method. A rational choice must therefore be made between different learning procedures. While the chosen procedure may not be 'rational' in the Bayesian sense, the choice will be made on 'rational' criteria. There are, therefore, two concepts of rationality which need to be distinguished: rationality in the sense of optimizing choice, which is core, and rationality in the sense of perfectly logical inference, which is not.

This chapter follows conventional economics in invoking the equilibrium principle, but differs from conventional theory in providing a very simple account of how the adjustment process works. It is assumed that the leader of the group provides all the information people need by producing an accurate forecast of what the equilibrium will be. The leader is regarded by the followers as an authoritative source whose pronouncements are interpreted as prophecies. The authority of the leader is reinforced by the fact that in many situations forecasts of an equilibrium have a self-fulfilling quality. This quality, where relevant, is present in the three examples given below.

Motivation and Productivity

The leader wishes to stimulate productivity through greater effort by members of a group. In this context the leader could be the owner–manager of a firm and the followers his employees. Followers have a choice of working fast or slow, and the owner finds it difficult to monitor what they do. He wishes to exploit preference interdependence in order to encourage them to work fast. He realizes that, under certain conditions, this may be cheaper than a bonus system based on measured output, because of the costs of metering involved.

He knows that the followers regard their effort and his own effort as complementary goods. Followers can observe his effort even though he cannot observe theirs. More precisely, followers can observe a token of his effort in the care and consideration he gives to providing them with a good working environment. The leader can turn this to his advantage by investing in the work environment in order to induce reciprocity by the employees in the form of harder work. On the other hand, if the cost of such gestures is great, and the cost of metering very low, he may prefer the bonus system. In other cases it may even pay to tolerate a slow pace of work to avoid the costs of both metering and manipulation. Theory can predict how the chosen strategy will reflect the underlying costs and benefits, and thereby relate management style to the characteristics of the social and technical environment.

Transaction Costs in a Trading Economy

Consider now the political leader of a nation who wishes to encourage greater participation in market activity. He observes that the process of economic development is being held up by the large number of people who produce only at subsistence level. They prefer to remain self-sufficient rather than participate in a division of labour because they do not trust the market process. In particular they believe that those with whom they trade will cheat them, taking their goods but reneging on payment. When the legal system is weak (as it is in many emergent societies) this can be a serious problem, for, in a one-off trade, cheating is usually the best strategy in purely material terms. If the other party is actually honest, you can 'take them for a sucker', whereas if they also plan to cheat then you minimize your losses by cheating them at the same time. In game theory terms, the trading game is a Prisoner's Dilemma and has a single equilibrium – mutual cheating. Given that everyone expects that they are going to be cheated, there is no point in attempting to trade in the first place.

A progressive leader who seeks to promote development must make mutual honesty an equilibrium too. If he can make honesty the best response to honesty, successful trading can take place, and this will encourage everyone to join in. A leader who undertakes a conspicuous act of reciprocity – for example, by sacrificially serving those who elected him to power – encourages them to imitate his gesture by making reciprocation a rule of life. In particular they will reciprocate honest behaviour by their partners in trade. Formally, the followers' strategy of reciprocity is (by assumption) complementary to the leader's strategy of reciprocity within the followers' preferences. A leader who is aware of this complementarity can engineer reciprocity in his followers through conspicuous reciprocity of his own.

To engineer trade through reciprocity, however, it is also necessary for people to believe that their partners will be honest, for if the partner cheats the best response is still to cheat. Beliefs about the integrity of other people are therefore crucial: optimism encourages honesty, and pessimism encourages cheating. In the aggregate, therefore, beliefs tend to be self-fulfilling. Optimism about one's partner encourages honesty, validating the partner's belief that one will be honest too. Conversely, pessimism about one's partner encourages cheating, validating the partner's belief that one will cheat.

Because beliefs of this kind tend to be self-fulfilling, a leader who makes prophetic announcements can achieve a good track record. Provided all the followers believe the prophecy, the prophecy will come true. Hence the role of leader as prophet can complement the role of leader as exemplary reciprocator in engineering mutually honest trades.

Networks and Hierarchies

The nature of the firm is one of the key issues in modern microeconomics. It is now recognized that, if all markets worked perfectly, as assumed in conventional general equilibrium theory, there would be no need for the firm. It is unnecessary to create a managerial hierarchy to coordinate flows of resources that arm's-length contracts can coordinate just as well. Thus firms exist because markets are imperfect: that is, because they incur transactions costs of the kind alluded to above. When transaction costs between firms are high, firms will tend to trade with themselves. The boundaries of the firm will expand to internalize key markets for intermediate products such as proprietary knowledge. The higher are arm's-length transaction costs, the greater are the economies of internalization and the wider are the boundaries of the firm.

It is frequently observed, however, that firms in some countries and districts are on average much smaller than those elsewhere because they do not internalize their operations to the same extent. Inter-firm trade amongst small firms replaces intra-firm trade within a single large firm. Textiles which in one country are produced by a single vertically integrated firm may in another country be produced just as successfully by a network of small firms who trade part-finished goods between themselves. Assuming that both managements respond rationally to local conditions, and have similar access to management techniques, it seems likely that inter-firm transaction costs are much lower in one area than in another.

These lower transaction costs may be imputed to effective leadership of the social group to which the owner–managers of the small firms belong. Maybe they share a common educational background (the 'old school tie' effect in the

City of London, for example) or political or religious affiliation (the Communist Party and the Roman Catholic church in the Italian textile districts of the 1960s, Quakerism in nineteenth-century Lancashire textile towns, and so on). In each case, theory predicts, preference interdependence exhibited by the owner–managers bonds them to each other because, for them, loyalty to their group is complementary to some token act of moral significance made by the leader of this group. This token act may have occurred some time ago. Thus bonding effected by schools and churches often takes place during people's youth and only pays substantial dividends when the members achieve positions of business responsibility in middle age.

Conversely, theory predicts that internalization will emerge as a rational organizational response to the higher transaction costs encountered where social bonds of this kind are weak. The United States, with its relatively high levels of immigration and internal geographical mobility, exemplifies this weakly socialized environment, and it is entirely consistent with the theoretical approach that it is in the United States that the use of hierarchy rather than networks is particularly noticeable.

2.6 CONCLUSIONS AND IMPLICATIONS FOR FUTURE RESEARCH

While the preceding examples illustrate a variety of contexts in which an economic theory of interdependent preferences can be applied, they certainly do not do full justice to the generality of the approach. To begin with, it should be recognized that there are typically several different kinds of interdependence linking leader and follower, so that the leader has a choice of which kind of interdependence to operate on. Thus, in the second example above, it was assumed that the leader would reduce transaction costs by exploiting the ethic of reciprocity, whereas he could, in fact, have used a stronger kind of moral imperative instead. Had the leader performed a token act to emphasize that the intention to cheat is morally wrong, whether the trading partner cheats or not, he could not only have created an equilibrium of mutual honesty but at the same time have eliminated the equilibrium of mutual cheating too. By his emphasizing the intrinsic guilt of the cheater, honest trading could have been established without the use of prophecies as described above.

For an optimizing leader it is essentially a question of cost-effectiveness whether to play on the guiltiness of the cheat or rely on a combination of reciprocity and optimism instead. By examining this choice in detail it is possible to obtain an additional set of predictions describing which particular ethic – and hence which particular form of interdependence – the leader will exploit under each set of circumstances.

It is also likely that in many situations a follower's preference interdependence is focused not only on the leader but on other followers too. Complementarity between one's own actions and other followers' actions is the basis of conformity in social behaviour. Certain actions performed by followers raise the marginal utility of similar actions performed by oneself, leading to imitation and hence to conformity across the group (Jones, 1984).

This idea can be extended even further by allowing the leader to manipulate the pattern of conformity within a social group. This involves postulating a three-way complementarity between the leader's actions, the follower's own actions and the actions of the other followers within the group. The leader acts first by performing some token gesture which highlights the importance of organic unity within the group. This activates the follower's desire to match other followers' acts of a certain kind, so that, if any other follower performs this act for any reason, the first follower will perform it too. The use of communal assemblies in Japanese factories may be interpreted as an example of a leader activating conformist preferences amongst his followers using symbolic collective acts. (The social rituals of many other institutions, such as the sharing of meals within a family, may be interpreted in these terms as well.)

Not only are there many options for developing the present approach, but there are already other analytical approaches to social issues which complement the one set out here. The theory of repeated games, for example (Axelrod, 1984) shows how cooperation can evolve without the intermediation of a leader, provided that encounters between the same individuals are replicated an indefinite number of times. Again, the theory of clubs (Buchanan, 1965; Olson, 1965) shows how groups can help organize the supply of goods which the insiders can share whilst outsiders are excluded from their use. Frank (1988) has shown how valuable reputation effects can emerge when people are known to signal their moral commitments in various involuntary ways. Integrating these approaches with the present one helps to explain, for example, what kinds of groups need leaders and what kinds can do without, and also what kinds of group charge membership fees and what kinds do not.

Although it is claimed that the present approach, and others like it, can tackle almost any aspect of social behaviour, there is still an important role for the critic to play. First, it is still the case that the theory oversimplifies reality and ignores many important features of social life. For example, leadership has been portrayed above as a unitary role, and as a paramount influence on the behaviour of the group. In practice individuals are exposed to different kinds of leadership in different contexts. They belong not only to workgroups, but to families, local communities, trades unions, clubs and, of course, to churches, political parties and alumni groups, as noted above. Any leader's influence is therefore constrained by that of other leaders, who head other groups to which the individual belongs.

Even within a given group there may be competition for leadership. Furthermore, if the leader is elected, each leader may have too short a term of office to have much influence on the membership as a whole. More work is required to address such issues within the framework set out in this chapter, and critics can provide valuable advice on where change is most required.

The extension of the scope of economic method proposed in this chapter does require the critics to modify the tenor of their criticisms, though. To put it bluntly, the theory shows that economics can do many things that self-styled method-ologists of social science have claimed it cannot do. It is wrong to claim that its postulate of rationality disables economics from explaining common patterns of behaviour, for all economics does is to infer from observed behaviour the nature of the preferences and beliefs that underlie it. Economics can actually help to derive hypotheses about how such preferences and beliefs are formed, and thereby contribute to social science research as a whole.

The long-run ideal of a unified social science may therefore be closer than most people think. For it is usually assumed that the unification of social science will be effected using some set of general principles that have not yet been discovered. It is possible, however, that some of the relevant principles are already available, and are simply waiting to be used in a more imaginative way. These are the core principles of rationality and equilibrium found in conventional economics. By extending the field over which these principles are applied, economic imperialism may serve to unify social science within the foreseeable future: it may be misguided to wait for a still undisclosed set of principles to materialize for this purpose.

Because core principles can be combined with many different assumptions, accepting the core of economics does not mean accepting all the policy impli-cations and historical interpretations of conventional economics as well. For the use of interdependent preferences effects a major change in the way that these core assumptions are applied and requires economists, as well as other social scientists, to reconsider some of their most cherished beliefs. Economic imperialism therefore has important implications for economics too. In particular, the emphasis on markets in contemporary economics is likely to be further weakened once non-market mechanisms such as cultural manipulation are expressed in economic terms. Economists will discover that in many cases the market is not the best coordinating mechanism. One of the effects of economic imperialism may be that economists are forced to admit that on many policy issues the non-economists were right after all.

ACKNOWLEDGEMENTS

I am grateful to my co-author Peter Buckley for allowing me to reprint our paper. I should also like to thank Ray Loveridge and the anonymous referees of *Human Relations* for their helpful comments.

REFERENCES

Axelrod, R. (1984) *The Evolution of Cooperation*, New York: Basic Books.

Becker, G.S. (1976) *The Economic Approach to Human Behavior*, Chicago: University of Chicago Press.

Buchanan, J.M. (1965) An Economic Theory of Clubs, *Economica* (New Series), **32**, 1–14.

Buchanan, J.M. and G. Tullock (1962) *The Calculus of Consent*, Ann Arbor: University of Michigan Press.

Casson, M.C. (1991) *Economics of Business Culture*, Oxford: Clarendon Press.

Downs, A. (1957) *Economic Theory of Democracy*, New York: Harper and Row.

Frank, R.H. (1988) *Passions within Reason*, New York: W.W. Norton.

Jones, S.R.G. (1984) *The Economics of Conformism*, Oxford: Blackwell.

Olson, M. (1965) *The Logic of Collective Action*, Cambridge, Mass.: Harvard University Press.

Tullock, G. (1972) Economic Imperialism, in J.M. Buchanan and R.D. Tollison (eds) *Theory of Public Choice: Political Applications of Economics*, Ann Arbor: University of Michigan Press.

Udéhn, L. (1992) The Limits of Economic Imperialism, in U. Himmelfarb (ed.) *Interfaces in Economic and Social Analysis*, London: Routledge.

3. Economic analysis of society: the contribution of Frank Knight

3.1 INTRODUCTION

This chapter examines a relatively neglected aspect of Frank Knight's work. Knight spent many years puzzling over the social problem of how individuals (and nations too) can coexist peacefully when they have different views about the most desirable direction in which society should progress. The chapter seeks to demonstrate that, once the difficulties created by Knight's manner of exposition are removed, it is possible to discern an underlying unity in his social thought. It is claimed that Knight's social thought has important implications for current debates in economic theory and policy.

Frank Knight's economic methodology has received an increasing amount of attention lately, including a centenary symposium and a major doctoral study by Emmett (1990). Aspects of his thought dealing with social issues remain relatively neglected, however. Since one of the main aims of this book is to develop the interface between economics and sociology, it is appropriate to examine Knight's work in social theory. Those who are already familiar with the incisiveness of Knight's logic in other fields will not be surprised to learn that he has much of importance to say on this subject. His analysis, which first appeared in the politically troubled 1930s, has obvious relevance for social issues of today.

Frank Hyneman Knight (1885–1972) was born just over one hundred years ago in White Oak Township, McLean County, Illinois. The eldest of 11 children, he was raised on a farm as a God-fearing Protestant. The farm and the religion were soon abandoned. An erratic early career included working as a stenographer at the Jamestown Exposition in Norfolk, Virginia, from 1906 to 1908, acting as an assistant in chemistry at the University of Tennessee, and writing a Master's essay on 'Gerhard Hauptmann as an Idealist' (American Economic Association, 1973). In 1913, he enrolled at Cornell University to major in philosophy, taking a minor in economics under Alvin Johnson. Endowed 'with dyspepsia and a graven expression of pessimism', he was told by his tutor in philosophy that he was totally unfit to teach anything. 'It isn't that he is devoid of ability,' the tutor complained to Johnson, 'but with his ingrained skepticism he repudiates all the values of philosophy. As a teacher or writer he will not be just the blind leading the blind into pitfalls. He will destroy the true philosophic spirit wherever he touches it' (Johnson, 1952). Knight switched to economics instead.

Within three years of commencing economic studies, he had completed a PhD which won second prize in the Hart, Schaffner, Marx essay competition for 1917. Herbert Davenport, who was visiting Cornell, was a major influence on Knight, and so too was J.M. Clark of Chicago, under whom he revised his dissertation for publication during the period 1917–19. Following eight years at the University of Iowa, he was appointed Professor of Economics at Chicago in 1927, where he became Distinguished Service Professor of Social Sciences and Philosophy in 1945 and Professor Emeritus in 1952 (Patinkin, 1973).

The philosophy that Knight practised in his later years as Professor of Philosophy was not professional academic philosophy; he did not, for example, discuss technical issues of semantics. He belonged to what might be called, somewhat uncharitably, the Mark Twain school of social philosophy. He was 'imbued with the robustness of the open plains and with the strong independence of the yeoman' (Schultz, 1973, p. 517; see also Wick, 1973, p. 513). His philosophy was based on 'obstreperous facts' about human nature and was expounded with a sardonic wit. The anxiety generated by the continual questioning of fundamental issues can often be alleviated by a strong dose of humour. This was particularly important in Knight's case because of the unpalatable nature of many of the conclusions. He liked 'to take the bull by the tail and look the situation square in the face' (Knight, 1956, p. 255).

As a teacher and lecturer, therefore, Knight talked good old-fashioned horse sense. The role of a sceptic, he perceived, was not to create a climate of nihilism, but rather to debunk exaggerated intellectual claims which ignored the fact of human fallibility. Claims to produce an exact science of human behaviour based on laws akin to those of the natural sciences, and rationalistic schemes for planning and social reform, were, in his opinion, legitimate targets for the sceptic. Knight's scepticism permitted common sense postulates to be used as the basis for a deductive economic theory, provided the limitations of the resulting theory were appreciated. Like many other great economists, he believed that economic theory was founded upon a few basic truths, which were obvious when you knew them, but which were often ignored by non-economists in discussions of practical issues.

Knight is best known amongst economists for his dissertation, published as *Risk, Uncertainty and Profit* in 1921. This classic work is in two main parts. The first examines the scope and limitations of the static theory of competition, while the second develops a dynamic theory of profit in which entrepreneurs are rewarded for the specialized bearing of uncertainty. Knight's ideas on entrepreneurship are considered further in Chapter 5.

For present purposes, it is important to recognize that his work on entrepreneurship represents only a preliminary exercise, clearing the ground for a much

broader project which absorbed him for the rest of his life. He was preoccupied with the 'social problem', the difficulty of getting people to live together
harmoniously without relying on coercive measures that stifle human progress.
In discussing the social problem, he ranged widely over ethics (the problem of
defining and criticizing 'values'), methodology (the differences in the status of
knowledge in the natural and social sciences), politics (the nature of nationalism and the character of international relations), anthropology (the comparison
of institutional arrangements in different cultures) and social history (the
evolution of group ideologies and methods of social control).

This broader project is hinted at in the preface to the first edition of *Risk,
Uncertainty and Profit*, even though it was not fully developed until later. He
indicates that his principal motive for writing the book is that he 'cherishes, in
the face of the pragmatic philistine tendencies of the present age...the hope that
careful rigorous thinking in the field of social problems does after all have some
significance for human weal and woe'. He is concerned with the role of the free
enterprise system in 'securing and directing cooperative effort in a social group'.
His study begins by 'refinement not reconstruction' of the theory of competition. Analysis of the entrepreneur is the 'particular technical contribution' of
the book, although in relation to the wider problem 'there is little that is fundamentally new'.

Knight's subsequent speculations on the social problem led him to develop,
in outline, an economist's theory of society. It is, however, necessary to know
beforehand what one is looking for in order to synthesize this theory from his
writings. The principal source for this theory is a collection of his essays, *The
Ethics of Competition and Other Essays* (1935). Knight consented to, but did
not actually participate in, the production of this volume. It was compiled by
some of his most distinguished students – Milton Friedman, Homer Jones,
George Stigler and Allen Wallis – who complained, incidentally, that they
were hampered in their compilation by the fact that Knight kept no record of
his publications. His theory is elaborated further in *Freedom and Reform:
Essays in Economics and Social Philosophy* (1947), *On the History and Method
of Economics* (1956) and *Intelligence and Democratic Action* (1960). He col-
laborated with a liberal theologian, Thornton W. Merriam, on *The Economic
Order and Religion* (1948) and published his Chicago lecture notes as *The
Economic Organisation* (1951). *Freedom and Reform* and *History and Method*
were also compilations undertaken by Knight's students, the former by Hubert
Bonner, William Grampp, Milton Singer and Bernard Weinberg, and the latter
by William Letwin and Alexander Morin. *Intelligence and Democratic Action*
was prepared for publication by James Buchanan and Warren Nutter from tape
recordings of a series of lectures delivered at the University of Virginia.

It is evident that more than half of Knight's published work concerns the social
problem in the large rather than specifically economic issues. It is perhaps not

surprising that most economists have simply ignored this aspect of Knight's work, concentrating instead on his reformulation of the theory of capital and interest, his criticisms of Marshallian dynamics, his controversy with Pigou over social cost, and his criticisms of Hutchison's empiricist methodology (see, for example, Blaug, 1978, 1980). Buchanan (1968), Gonce (1971) and Vining (1984) have examined the social aspects of Knight's thought, though Gonce concentrates mainly on its methodological foundations and Buchanan on its constitutional implications. Knight's social thought has had some influence on sociologists such as Edward Shils (Bulmer, 1984, p. 193).

Many readers of Knight fail to find any systematic body of theory expounded in his work. What they do find, however, are insights which help to crystallize their own thoughts. Knight's work, therefore, is to some extent a mirror, reflecting back to the reader a sharper image of his own ideas. It is perhaps for this reason that some of Knight's own students, notably Buchanan, Patinkin and Stigler, have subsequently chosen to emphasize very different aspects of his thought.

Nevertheless, it is quite clear that there are certain themes which recur regularly in Knight's work. The object of this chapter is to explore possible connections between these themes and to suggest how they can be placed in a logical sequence. Sections 3.2–3.6 below develop the themes, relying heavily upon direct quotation. The quotations that have been selected are never merely passing remarks: almost every one of them could be matched by a similar quotation taken from another of his works. The result of this exercise is something like the unified body of theory that many people would hope to find in Knight. It is not claimed, however, that the interpretation of Knight offered here is definitive: there is no intention to rule out alternative interpretations, nor to claim that, 'if Knight were alive today', he would necessarily endorse it.

A full account of Knight's thought would trace the influences on him back through Max Weber, Thorstein Veblen and Alfred Marshall to the Scottish Enlightenment, whose thinkers took a similarly pragmatic view of 'what people are really like'. But this is a difficult course to chart because of the sheer diversity of the influences involved, and because Knight did not bother to cite his authorities in most of his work. This chapter confines itself to setting out in a systematic way what Knight actually said, as an essential preliminary to this more ambitious exercise. Fortunately, by the time Knight began his major writing on the social problem he seems to have evolved a mature position from which he did not depart significantly later on. It is therefore feasible in his case to present an account of his work as if all his writings were a part of the same overall piece.

Conventional interpretations of Knight emphasize his view that economic theory is a purely abstract system (see, for example, Seligman, 1962), but what they do not explain is *why* he was at such pains to emphasize the point. It is argued below that Knight believed that economics achieved practical relevance only in conjunction with ethics. The connection arises because economics is the rational study of *means* whilst ethics is the rational study of *ends*. Economic theory provides a basis for the criticism of means – for evaluating alternative methods of achieving a *given* end. Ethics provides a basis for the criticism of ends. Ethical criticism is a continuous, indeed never-ending, *process*, carried on by individuals within a social group. This intellectual process causes the ends of group activity to change, and these changing ends in turn imply the adjustment of means. The historical record of changing means forms the past data on economic decision making. Changes in the choice of means are to be interpreted primarily in terms of changes in the underlying ends, as recorded in the cultural history of the group. Changes in technology and in the relative scarcities of factors of production also influence the choice of means, but they play only a secondary role in Knight's interpretation of history.

If this account is correct, then Knight has successfully developed an economic theory incorporating endogenous changes in preferences. Individual preferences are subject to social influence, and these influences are generated by a continual process of ethical criticism. This affects both the form of economic organization adopted by the society and the pattern of market outcomes. In short, Knight's approach affords a possible explanation of how changing cultural values can influence the economic performance of a society. Thus an abstract economic theory, when placed within the wider context of social dynamics, acquires relevance to important issues in economic growth and development.

It is strange that work of such importance should have received so little recognition. The explanation seems partly to lie with Knight himself, and partly with the positivist neoclassical hegemony in post-war US economic theory, which has led many historians of thought to distort the nature of Knight's intellectual contribution. Knight's personality is considered in section 3.7, conventional interpretations of Knight are examined in section 3.8; his intellectual contribution as a whole is appraised in section 3.9.

3.2   UTILITY AND ETHICS

The foundation of any satisfactory analysis of social groups has to be a theory of human motivation. Knight (1947, p. 287) believes that human activity can be analysed on six main levels. Man can be regarded as

1. physical mechanism (for example, the use of muscle for moving jointed bones);

2. a biological organism, with characteristics extending 'from those of the lowest plant to the highest animal in the biological scale';
3. a social animal (a gregarious animal living in small communities governed by custom);
4. an instrumental problem solver, choosing the most appropriate means to achieve given ends;
5. an ethical problem- solver, judging between alternative ends; and
6. a social being, deliberately participating in instrumental cooperation, ethical debate and so on.

It is widely recognized that there is an implicit bias towards 'reductionism' in the social sciences, where the researcher attempts to explain as much behaviour as possible in terms of the simplest possible mechanisms. Knight is particularly sensitive to this aspect of modern thought, and sees it as part of a spurious 'scientism' that permeates the social sciences:

the real beginning of modern natural science was the discovery that the inert objects of nature are not like men, i.e. subject to persuasion, exhortation, coercion, deception, etc., but are inexorable. The position which we have to combat today seems to rest upon an inference, characteristically drawn by the 'best minds' of our race, that since natural objects are not like men, men must be like natural objects. (Knight, 1947, p. 270)

Aspects 1–3 of human behaviour are of little relevance to advanced societies, except in so far as the acquisition of habits – so characteristic of lower animals – may help people to coordinate their routine activities with those of others. Habits, when they acquire the universality of custom and are reinforced by the authority of tradition and religion, are powerful conservative forces that help to maintain the unity of social groups. Economic theory is principally concerned with behaviour of type (4). 'Economic man' is simply a personification of *economizing behaviour*, which involves choosing the most suitable means of achieving given ends.

To integrate economic man within a wider study of human motivation it is necessary to abandon the crude utilitarian or hedonistic interpretation of the utility function. In taking this view, Knight follows the same line of thought as Mises (1933) and Robbins (1932). Utility theory can be preserved only if it is regarded as a highly abstract framework; it merely commits the economist to the view that people behave as if they were trying to maximize something, without specifying exactly what that something is.

A science of conduct...is possible only if its subject-matter is made abstract to the point of telling us little or nothing about actual behaviour. Economics deals with the form of conduct rather than its substance or content. We can say that a man will in general prefer a larger quantity of wealth to a smaller (the principal trait of economic man) because in the statement the term 'wealth' has no definite concrete meaning; it is merely an abstract term covering everything which men do actually (provisionally) want. The only other important economic law of conduct, the law of diminishing utility, is almost as abstract; its objective content is covered by the statement that men strive to distribute income in some way most satisfactory to the person at the time among an indefinite number of wants and means of satisfaction rather than to concentrate upon one or a few. Such laws are unimportant because they deal with form only and say virtually nothing about content, but it is imperative to understand what they do and what they do not mean. (Knight, 1935, p. 36)

Utility theory has been uncritically applied in the past, Knight argues, particularly by those who have taken a purely hedonistic view of utility. Typical targets of Knight's criticism, it seems, would be Jevons and Edgeworth, and particularly the latter's 'Conception of Man as a Pleasure Machine' (Edgeworth, 1881, p. 15). One reason for the popularity of hedonism is that people have an emotional need to think of a 'driving force' underlying human behaviour, analogous to the physical force used to explain mechanical behaviour. Hedonism meets this need because it postulates a kind of psychic gravitational force that attracts people to sources of pleasure and repels them from sources of pain. However, just as the validity of mechanics is independent of our subjective feeling of force, so the validity of utility theory does not depend upon any psychic force. Our intuition may tell us that our actions are governed by the force with which objects attract us, countered in some cases by the opposing force of our will, but the true scientist does not make the validity of his theory depend upon introspection of this kind.

A related point is that the hedonistic interpretation of utility theory

comes near to being the fulfilment of the eighteenth-century craving for a principle which would do for human conduct and society what Newton's mechanics had done for the solar system. It introduces simplicity and order, even to the extent of making it possible to state the problems in the form of mathematical functions dealt with by the methods of infinitesimal calculus. Moreover, in harmony with eighteenth-century cravings, it claims to furnish a guide for social policy...The utility theorists were contemporaries of Herbert Spencer, and were philosophically his comrades in arms. (Knight, 1935, pp. 158–9)

The principal error of hedonism is that it reduces human wants to a stable requirement for material consumption of one kind or another. As a result, the ends of human activity are incorrectly specified. The chief error lies in a failure to recognize that the ends are in a constant state of flux.

Wants...not only *are* unstable, changeable in response to all sorts of influences, but it is their essential nature to change and grow; it is an inherent inner necessity in them. The chief thing which the common-sense individual wants is not satisfactions for the wants that he has, but more, and better wants. The things that he strives to get in the most immediate sense are far more what he thinks he ought to want than what his untutored preferences prompt. The feeling for what one *should* want, in contrast with actual desire, is stronger in the unthinking than in those sophisticated by education. It is the latter who argues himself into the 'tolerant' (economic) attitude of *de gustibus non disputandum.* (Knight, 1935, p. 22)

Thus 'the real ends of action are not mainly of the concrete quantitative sort represented by utility functions.... Every end is more or less redefined in the process of achieving it, and this redefinition is one reason for desiring the activity' (Knight, 1935, p. 281).

The ends of action are modified chiefly through three channels. First, an individual may be disappointed once he has attained an end – the emotional satisfaction may be less than anticipated – and so he may decide to pursue another end instead (Knight, 1956, p. 175).

Second, a person may become so committed to the means he has adopted to achieve his end that the means becomes an end in itself, and in the process the original end is lost sight of: 'Men seem to have an inherent disposition to erect instrumental interest in absolutes, and a positive yearning for absolutes' (Knight, 1947, p. 253). This tendency to erect means into ends may itself be a response to the fact that ends often seem to recede in the process of our trying to attain them. Knight, nearly always a pessimist, suggests that 'man is committed...to strive towards goals which recede more rapidly than he as an individual, or even society, advances toward them' (Knight and Merriam, 1948, p. 56). It is only natural, therefore, that nearer goals should be substituted for further goals in the process.

Third, the most important channel for modifying ends is a social one. In line with the modern sociological view of man, Knight argues that, to a significant extent, man is a product of his environment. Many of the influences occur during childhood:

in a world in which individuals grow old and die and are replaced by new units who are born as infants and are necessarily reared and educated in the society in which they are to live and function as members, it is merely absurd to treat the individual as a datum for purposes of decisions regarding social policy. (Knight, 1956, p. 170)

Conventional economics omits all three of these channels, but the omission of the third is the most serious. It must be emphasized that

'economic man' is not a 'social animal' and economic individualism excludes society in the proper human sense. Economic relations are *impersonal*. The social organisation dealt with in economic theory is best pictured as a number of Crusoes interacting through the markets exclusively... Economic theory takes all economic individuals in an organisation as *data*, not subject to 'influence', and assumes that they view each other in the same way. (Knight, 1935, pp. 282–3)

Knight argues that the reductionist bias in scientific thinking has led to a serious underestimation of the influence of ethical principles on human behaviour. A good deal of the influence exerted on individuals in a civilized society involves the transmission of ethical values. It is tempting for the economist to dismiss commonsense ethical systems on grounds of their naivety, but this is wrong. The feelings and emotions out of which ethical attitudes are formed are the same feelings out of which our entire picture of the external world is constructed.

> For those to whom ethics is only a more or less 'glorified' economics, virtue is correspondingly reduced to an enlarged prudence. But the essential element in the moral common sense of mankind seems to be the conviction that there is a difference between virtue and prudence, between what one 'really wants' to do and what one 'ought' to do; even if some religious or other 'sanction' makes it ultimately prudent to do right, at least it remains true that it is prudent because right and not right because prudent or because there is no difference between the two....
>
> The disillusioned advocate of hard-headedness and clear thinking would usually admit that the 'moral illusion' has stood the pragmatic test and concede its utility while contending that scientifically it is a hoax. But it is pertinent to observe that the brick-and-mortar world cannot be constructed for thought out of purely objective data. There is always a feeling element in any belief. Force and energy are notoriously feelings of ours which we read into things, yet we cannot think of anything as real without force as real. Apparently we are incapable of picturing anything as existing without putting a spark of our own consciousness into it. Behind every fact is a theory and behind that an interest. There is no purely objective reason for believing anything any more than there is for doing anything, and if our feelings tell us nothing about reality then we know and can know nothing about it. (Knight, 1935, pp. 37–9)

Knight argues that our feeling of repugnance towards those who dismiss our cherished ethical precepts only serves to confirm the potential strength of ethical considerations in social and economic behaviour.

3.3   THE ROLE OF PLAY

In his discussion of human behaviour, Knight continually emphasizes the same small set of motives. Briefly, it is Knight's thesis that people, above all, enjoy play – both real and make-believe. The practical side of play is manifest in physical absorption in workmanship and in mental absorption in instrumental problem solving. This aspect of play falls directly within the province of the economist. The make-believe side of play is manifest in romance, in the ritual enactment of magic and the supernatural, and so on. The two facets of play are, however, closely linked. Comparison of the real world with the make-believe one makes man continually dissatisfied with his situation: at the same time, the hope of narrowing the gulf between fantasy and reality supplies him with the motive to continue attempting to realize his dreams.

Play can be both a solitary activity and a social one. In the social sphere, play is normally competitive, except where religious influences are dominant. For a society to achieve progress, while maintaining social harmony, it is necessary to achieve a delicate balance between the competitive and non-competitive aspects of play. This balance is extremely difficult to maintain, and the major purpose of economic study is to advise, from the limited standpoint of instrumental behaviour, about the form of economic and social organization best adapted to this purpose.

To provide a 'realistic study of human nature, it would appear that we should give at least equal consideration to the spontaneous activities of recreation, as compared with those of work' (Knight, 1935, p. 301). Thus 'it is an old and ever fascinating dream that all work might be converted into play under the right conditions. We know that almost any kind of work may become infused with the play spirit, as is more or less true of the creative arts, the higher professions to some extent, and notably business itself'. (Knight, 1935, p. 62)

We do things to prove that we can, and to find out whether we like to; the problem is largely to understand the problem itself, and as with smaller problems, understanding it largely carries the actual solution with it as a matter of course. The consumer and producer of wealth commonly does not realise it, but it is true that much of his activity is in response to the poetic injunction, 'Know thyself'. Curiosity is very largely synonymous with the supposedly broader term, 'interest'. Knowledge of self cannot be separated from knowledge of the world, nor either knowledge from that which is known. As we know more, both the self and the world are enlarged, and this growth is life. (Knight, 1935, pp. 101–2)

...in the ordinary day's work, men constantly risk life, or knowingly shorten it, and in the last resort throw away a life by no means intolerable, for the chance of a 'better' life, for themselves or for others. That human beings are by nature idealists and sentimentalists seems to be as incorrigibly and obstreperously a 'fact', for practical purposes, as any verifiable scientific observation. (Knight, 1935, p.100)

A lot of play is structured around the exploration of possible solutions to a problem – both practical ones and purely intellectual ones. True freedom is not, therefore, freedom from problems, but freedom to solve problems in one's own way, the freedom to make one's own mistakes: '*Activity is problem-solving*, which is the primary ultimate or indefinable reality of thinking in general; the terms "activity", "problem-solving" and "freedom" refer to the same fact in different aspects or connection' (Knight, 1947, p. 246).

Intellectual problems are never really solved until they have been simplified to the point where they can be answered in terms of a single principle: 'Man as intellectual inquirer is characterised by a craving for simplification and unification, for "*monism*" as against pluralism' (Knight, 1947, p. 275).

The play of the imagination generates romantic cravings which can never really be satisfied. Amongst the young, it may be suggested, there is always hope of betterment, but amongst the old disillusionment may set in. Knight's reflections on this subject seem to be partly autobiographical:

> man is a dissatisfied animal, a critic of other men, of society, of the world, and even of himself. He has intelligence, in varying amount and kind, but is more conspicuous for egotism, boundless imagination, and manifold romanticism. Roughly in proportion to his human development, he finds nearly everything to be wrong, and for this he is disposed to blame other people and social institutions; and especially he lays the blame for the institutions on particular individuals who seem to be beneficiaries of their wrongness, those who are, or whom he imagines to be, in power. (Knight, 1947, p. 196)

Knight is sympathetic to people who crave for progress and improvement – for the continuation of the struggle for a better life – but cannot sympathize with those who seek communal reconciliation with their lot through religion: 'there are two possible ways for securing harmony between man's restless spirit and his world. One way is to change the world. This way is emphasised by the liberal philosophy of life....The other way of reconciliation is for man to find the wrong in himself and to change his own nature, to suppress and extirpate his restless cravings and "accept the universe". This is the religious way' (Knight, 1947, p. 197).

> The urge to dominate, or craving for power, without regard to any use to be made of it, is more commonly a subject for comment, but a mystical craving for fellowship, in which individuality is lost, is comparable in frequency of occurrence and is perhaps equally inimical to sane living. (Knight, 1947, p. 253)

Play is to a large extent a social activity, and much of it is competitive in spirit. But it takes place within a framework of rules which are designed to curb the urge to achieve complete dominance.

> ... it is a sobering reflection that the competitiveness of play is a phenomenon indefinitely older and more general than the competitive organisation of economic life. There is a strong case for the view that the whole development of economic and political individualism represents essentially a release of general, if not universal, human tendencies which were formerly held in leash by institutions. (Knight, 1947, p. 51)

> When we are freest to do what we want to do, the first thing we generally do is start a competition of some sort, either to engage in directly, or as a spectacle which we enjoy by vicarious participation; and the interest of the direct participants is largely dependent on the size and character of a spectator group. (Knight, 1935, p. 301)

It is this aspect of play – indulgence in competitive games – that is of most relevance to economic study. It received considerable attention from Knight, as explained below. But Knight never achieved his ambition of developing a full theory of human motivation. He took the view that human nature had so many facets that it could never be grasped as a whole. He was, indeed, rather prone to overstate this view in somewhat nihilistic terms: 'human nature as we know it...is a tissue of paradox. It would be difficult to make any general statement about "man" which would not contain substantial truth; and this means that the antithesis of every statement, or, indeed, several antitheses, would also be partly true and, on the average, equally so' (Knight, 1947, p. 359).

3.4   THE COMPETITIVE GAME AND ITS DISORDERS

The 'competitive game' has a central role in Knight's analysis of the free-enterprise system. It should not be confused with the game theory of von Neumann and Morgenstern (1944). A game is defined essentially by its rules, which are usually framed through custom or law. 'Playing the game' generates its own satisfactions in addition to those of 'winning'. The more interesting a game, the more satisfaction it generates for all the players. The free-enterprise system may be thought of as a gigantic game in which practically everyone is involved.

A good game is not only interesting but also fair; that is, it is *perceived* as fair by all the contestants. Games are rendered unfair when one player's over-weaning desire to win spoils the game for others, for example by his cheating. A still more serious problem arises when the winner abuses his position to redefine the rules so that he keeps on winning and other players have no chance of dislodging him.

Some games, such as board games, are played for purely notional stakes, but the free-enterprise game is played 'for real'. Also it is difficult for a loser to withdraw voluntarily from the free-enterprise game. The free-enterprise game, moreover, has an inherent tendency to become unfair because competition is unstable relative to monopoly. Once a competitive game has been won, and a monopoly has been established, the monopolist becomes a powerful vested interest, capable of changing the rules in his own favour. If this tendency goes unchecked, the capitalist system sows the seeds of its own destruction. Growing sentiment that the game is unfair leads to social protest by the losers and, if this protest goes unheeded, political revolution may ensue.

There is a 'special psychology of competitive games' which differentiates these games from solitary games and from non-competitive social ceremonial (Knight, 1935, pp. 63–4). An enjoyable game is one in which the outcome is determined by the appropriate combination of ability, effort and luck. The abilities of the players should be reasonably well matched. Knight hints that the able players might consent to be handicapped in the interests of the game:

'the hunter who considers himself a sportsman always gives his quarry a chance'. It should not, however, be too easy to measure ability before the game, for part of the fun of the game is to discover one's ability through play. A good game always compels the players to effort: 'Effort is called forth by interest, and intelligent interest is dependent on the fact that effort makes some difference in the result.'

'The result must be unpredictable: if there is no element of luck in it there is no game. There is no game in lifting weights, after one once knows how much can be lifted, even though the result measures capacity. Where "records" are made, the interest centres in the unpredictable fluctuations in the powers of men (or horses, etc.) from one trial to another.' Pure chance exerts a special fascination, although on reflection most people would concede that games of skill are 'superior' to games of pure chance.

Knight suggests that free enterprise has two main shortcomings as a game, although in practice these shortcomings tend to offset one another. First, 'its outcome is a very inaccurate test of real ability, for the terms on which individuals enter the contest are too unequal'. It is not clear what is meant here by 'real ability'. It may refer to innate ability, as opposed to education 'acquired from the previous expenditure of effort in play or practice, or perhaps in some closely related activity of either a recreative or serious character'. But it seems more likely that it refers to unequal possession of financial wealth at the start of the game. In his later work, however, Knight treated everything except innate ability as capital, and so the distinction between education and financial wealth becomes blurred.

> The sharp distinction made in popular and reformist thinking between labour-power and property in external means of production is for the most part spurious. All forms of productive activity are ultimately capital and are to be traced back to the same complex of factors – inheritance, the activity of the individual owner and other persons (primarily his parents), social processes and accident. Property is practically as much, or as little, as personal capacity, an attribute of personality. (Knight and Merriam, 1948, p. 91)

On this view, Knight's criticism reduces to the claim that the inequality of the outcome of the free-enterprise game reflects inequalities in the capital of those who participate in it. In view of the very general concept of capital adopted by Knight, this proposition is almost a tautology.

The second shortcoming is that luck plays too large a part in the free-enterprise game. The pure economic profit earned in free enterprise is on average zero, or even negative, according to Knight, because people tend to be overconfident. Large gains are offset by equally large losses in the long run. The gains and losses are far more a matter of luck than the successful participants in the game will ever admit.

And this luck element works cumulatively, as in gambling games generally. The effects of luck in the first hand or round, instead of tending to be evened up in accord with the law of large numbers in the further progress of the game, confer on the player who makes an initial success a differential advantage in succeeding hands or rounds, and so on indefinitely. Any particular individual may be eliminated by the results of his first venture, or placed in a position where it is extraordinarily difficult to get back into the game. (Knight, 1935, pp. 63–4)

The 'natural' tendency is for a game to deteriorate, if the participants follow their primitive impulses without conscious exercise of moral restraint. No game is possible unless the players have the attitudes and interests to which the term 'sportsmanship' is understood to refer. The modern conception of society, economic and political, is that of an organization of people pursuing individual interests; and the problem of morale is probably harder in an individualistic organization than in a group united under some mystical common purpose.

The minimum problem in a group or society is that of preventing 'cheating' and unsportsmanlike practice. 'The operation of the tendency to cheat is insidious; if one player cheats a "little", or even creates a suspicion that he is cheating, the thing tends to become contagious and progressive' (Knight, 1935, pp. 302–3).

Cheating is not the only problem. The most serious problem is instability in the game itself. Knight argues:

(a) that *any* form of power may be used to get more power in the same or other forms,
(b) that in a culture in which men's chief interests and psychological drives centre in power, it will be so used, and
(c) that the consequent, inevitable concentration of power will destroy freedom, or reduce it to an empty form. (Knight, 1935, pp. 297–8)

The problems are compounded by the difficulty of the loser in withdrawing from the game. Their choice between 'exit' and 'voice' (Hirschman, 1970) is heavily weighted in favour of 'voice':

the individual who wants to maintain the game in its integrity confronts two alternatives: he may either organize group pressure to correct the evil, or withdraw from the game. But in the larger, political game, peaceful withdrawal is impossible, and those persons who care for ordered society must face the problem of organized compulsion, i.e., of law. (Knight, 1935, p. 303).

The political option of exercising voice is no solution to the problem, however, for the political game is played by politicians, and the way they play it is simply as a variant of the competitive game! When the losers in the economic game turn to their political leaders, they turn to people who are simply playing the 'democratic game' of competing for their votes.

When the 'economic game' of free enterprise becomes intolerable through the growth of individual inequality and of monopoly, the next recourse of the masses who get the worst of it – or of their more or less self-appointed saviours from the ranks of the labour movement and the social-reform minded intelligentsia – is to politics. This has meant, in the first instance, to *democratic* politics. (Knight, 1935, p. 293)

But 'as it has worked out in the modern world, *democracy is competitive politics*, somewhat as free enterprise is competitive economics (though inherently a competition for a monopolistic position), and shows the same weaknesses as the latter' (Knight, 1935, p. 295).

In the economic game there are just a few winners and many losers; in other words, its tendency is inherently non-egalitarian. The many losers, who dominate the electorate, are naturally disposed to collective stupidity; whether this is due to some kind of irrational crowd psychology in the democratic process or to the same individual stupidity that caused the losers to fail in the economic game in the first place is not made clear. The losers vote into power men whose main ability lies in exploiting the political process to gain power. They may, in some cases, even be the same people who have already succeeded in the economic game – the very people whom the political process is supposed to hold to account!

Democratic politics works out in practice as campaigning, electioneering, and 'organiz-ation', featuring the type of human capacity suggested by such terms as 'spell-binder', 'boss', and 'machine'. Such abilities are more unequally distributed among men by nature than is economic ability or power of any other kind, and also tend more strongly to cumulative increase through their own exercise. This growth through exercise does not come about solely or chiefly because a technique improves with practice. A far more important reason is that the largest element in the ability to influence people is prestige, reputation, or prominence. Only persons of some degree of prominence find it easy to get a hearing at all, and one who is prominent enough, for whatever reason, is readily accepted as an authority and guide on almost any subject – regardless, in both cases, of real knowledge or competence, or even moral trustworthiness.

Thus liberal economics and liberal politics are at bottom the same kind of 'game'. The fundamental fact in both is the moral fact of rivalry, competitiveness, and the interest in power. (Knight, 1935, pp. 296–7)

The evils of democratic politics stem from a failure of leadership: 'It is surely self-evident that organized social action on any large scale, unless conditions are purely traditional and stationary (except for such unconscious "drift" as characterizes linguistic change), must depend on *leadership* and the general willingness to accept and follow leadership' (Knight, 1935, pp. 304–5).

True social leadership is based on the single-minded pursuit of certain ethical values. What passes for leadership in the typical democracy is actually 'fol-lowership', in which the crowd of dissatisfied losers determines the values and the would-be leaders adapt their own opinions to suit. An appropriate metaphor is of a church with the pulpit at the back.

Under these conditions, a democratic assembly ceases to function as a forum for honest discussion of social values and becomes instead a market-place where elected representatives promote the vested interests of their constituents. Such a system cannot, in the long run, meet the legitimate social aspirations of the majority of the electorate, and will be superseded eventually through revolutionary change. Thus Knight claims to follow Plato and Aristotle in predicting 'a cyclical oscillation, from freedom to autocracy and back to freedom by way of revolution' (Knight, 1935, p. 299).

3.5   SOCIAL GROUPS AND THEIR LEADERS

To analyse fully the mechanics of leadership it is necessary to understand the principles underlying the organization of social groups. A social group is much more than a 'team' or 'club' formed to accomplish some limited well-defined objective. This narrowly economic rationale of the group ignores the enormous emotional satisfactions that people derive from merely 'belonging' to the group and sharing in its values and experiences. If, for example, the group is to be explained in terms of interpersonal complementarities in production then it is the production of values and common experiences that is crucial; or if the explanation involves the consumption of the services of an indivisible public good then it is values and experiences that are 'consumed'. Although Knight did not express himself in these terms, the meaning of his remarks on the subject is fairly clear. Even if one cannot approve of such group-inspired emotions, it is still necessary to appreciate their importance in group behaviour.

Social–moral motivation must rest on more than pure, abstract ethical idealism. It has a quality properly called religious. As there is really no human life apart from group life, so there is probably no group life without real 'devotion', in a religious sense, of the members to the group as a more or less 'mystical' entity, and beyond it to some set of values for which the group is supposed in an especial way to stand. I offer this as a simple fact, a fact of 'observation' in the only sense in which really human data ever are observed. The degree to which this element in motivation is present is of course variable. Some individuals, such as great world conquerors and great 'crooks', may be nearly free from it, looking upon society not in terms of participation, but as something entirely outside themselves, to be treated as a toy or an instrument for purely private ends. But such cases are hardly pure types and are exceptional.

Complete indifference to the interests of one's group is hardly conceivable. The concept of devotion as a motive applies conspicuously to men at both ends of the scale of thoughtfulness. For those who are distinctly thoughtful, and attempt to rationalize their existence as individuals, the craving for such a super-individual end or object of devotion is an outstanding fact, and if it is not more or less satisfactorily gratified, symptoms of morbidity are likely to appear. On the other hand, it is apparent that the great mass of men have always lived in some society characterized by a religion which each accepts and organizes into his own system of values. They seem to require for normal living the feeling of a 'destiny' and mission pertaining to a group to whose life they contribute. This motif is conspicuous in Medieval ideals; the individual lived to save his own soul, but salvation consisted in 'belonging' to the Blessed Community, the City of God. (Knight, 1935, pp. 321–2)

It would be wrong, however, to assume that Knight adopted an 'organic view' of social groups. Human beings are not preprogrammed into spontaneous cooperation in the manner of insects and lower animals. Human society is not like the society of termites, or of Mandeville's bees. Social ties between humans are not purely instinctive, but are regulated by intelligence.

The familiar adage that [man] is 'naturally' a social (or political) animal is misleading. In sharp contrast with insect society, in which there is relatively perfect 'law and order', but neither courts nor legislature, human society must in large part both enforce and make its 'law'. And it does both very imperfectly indeed! It is permeated with immorality, criminality, conflict and disorder, and would surely seem intolerably anarchic to a termite with intelligence enough to judge. (Knight, 1947, p. 223)

The forces moulding human society 'belong to an intermediate category, between instinct and intelligence. They are a matter of custom, tradition, or institutions. Such laws are transmitted in society, and acquired by the individual, through relatively effortless and even unconscious imitation, and conformity with them by any mature individual at any time is a matter of "habit" (Knight, 1947, p. 224). Habit is an important aspect of coordination in unsophisticated social groups.

One individual can choose or plan intelligently in a group of any size only if all others act 'predictably' and if he predicts correctly. This means, *prima facie*, that the others do not choose rationally but mechanically follow an established and known pattern, or else that the first party has coercive power, through force or deception. (...) Without some procedure for coordination, any real activity on the part of an individual, any departure from past routine, must disappoint the expectations and upset the plans of others who count on him to act in a way predicted from his past behaviour. (Knight and Merriam, 1948, p. 60)

Formal coordination of group activity depends crucially upon language. Language, however, is not used exclusively for instrumental activities such as coordination, but is also used for ethical discourse. It has a strong emotional content and its vocabulary is heavily laden with the values of the group: 'The primary use of speech amongst civilised men today is doubtless the expression and communication of emotion, including playful and esthetic matter, and including also the formulation of inexpressed mental content' (Knight, 1947, p. 345); 'The learning and use of language is inseparable from the acquisition of the content, also cultural, whether intellectual and emotional or merely trivial...' (Knight, 1947, p. 346).

Sophisticated groups rely for coordination, not upon habit or custom, but upon law. Law is the product of intelligent communication, and its primary function is to fix the terms and conditions of membership of the group. The freedom of the individual within the group is determined by three main factors: the nature of the law to which he must conform, his right to leave, and his right to participate in changing the law (Knight and Merriam, 1948, p. 64). Ideally, law should be made only on the basis of unanimous support, but in practice majority rule is often a necessary compromise, in which case the minority may feel that conscience dictates rebellion.

> Even in connection with the most legitimate law, the individual may confront the duty as well as the right of quiet disobedience, ranging to open defiance, resistance, and organised insurrection. There is no formula which will solve these problems. The individual can only use his best judgement and strive to make his judgement as good as possible. (Knight and Merriam, 1948, p. 66)

Given the conservative nature of custom and tradition in most groups, major steps in progress very often come about through open defiance of them.

Knight distinguishes two main types of group – the family and the nation – although he recognizes others, such as the business firm and the local community. He also recognizes that each individual can be a member of several different groups, and will be influenced by each of them: 'Man belongs to infinitely many societies extending from his family and accidental conjunctions with his friends and acquaintances, to his national status, usually to some group of allied nations, and finally the world' (Knight, 1960, p. 53).

Knight seems to analyse group membership on the implicit assumption that each individual has a limited stock of altruism, or goodwill, so that the more goodwill he lavishes on fellow-members of his own group(s), the more hostility he will show towards the members of other groups. Thus, while Marshall and other economists have praised the family for strengthening the feelings of altruism and of social responsibility, Knight regards the family as a socially divisive force. It strengthens bonds with the family at the expense of weakening bonds between members of different families. He even suggests that love for one's own children makes it practically impossible to love other people's children as well!

> the selfishness or self-interest of the family, as against other families, is far greater than that of the individual against other individuals. Or, the selfishness of parents for their children is greater than that for themselves. The ethical injunction to 'love one's neighbour as one's self' does not get to the heart of the problem at all... The crux is rather for loving one's neighbour's children as one's own. (Knight, 1947, p. 191)

Nationalism, particularly the sort fuelled by patriotic feeling, has even less to recommend it than the family. Small groups, such as the family, at least have the advantage to the individual of affording 'fellowship', and some measure of enhanced productivity through teamwork. The nation, on the other hand, tends to promote unity purely by fostering enmity towards foreigners, and thereby promotes social divisiveness on a global scale. Knight sees this as part of a general tendency for people 'to gravitate into groups in which one of the main effective bases of internal unity is a sentiment of opposition to or competition with other groups' (Knight, 1935, p. 320).

Combining this analysis with the discussion of section 3.4 suggests that many competitive games are played out, not between individuals, but between social groups. The appropriate metaphor for competition, therefore, is not necessarily an individualistic game, such as tennis, but a team game, such as football. Individuals join teams and then the teams compete against each other. The individual thus enjoys both the fellowship within the team and the thrill of participating in the game between the teams. This is an important idea. In the context of the labour market, for example, it means that the individual, in choosing between different teams, is choosing between alternative leaders under whom he will serve. 'Freedom of exchange works out into the somewhat paradoxical situation that the chief freedom you can have is a freedom to choose your boss' (Knight, 1960, pp. 113–14).

Inter-firm rivalry may be interpreted, in similar fashion, as competition between social groups. It is organized initially within the framework of a game but, as the game degenerates, it develops into a fight to the death. Strong groups develop an imperative for continuing growth which leads, in the long run, to the elimination of their weaker rivals. This applies particularly to rivalry between nations.

> Groups could not exchange their culture if they would; and in fact, each thinks its own is best and wishes to preserve and propagate it, and in this wish, this loyalty, most human moral values are bound up. There is always cooperation between groups, as well as competition, but the combination of the two relationships only complicates the moral problem... Any group, from a family to an international alliance, must finally choose, consciously or unconsciously, between increase and decline, and ultimately between survival and extinction, along with all distinctive features of its culture – and/or its race. (Knight and Merriam, 1948, p. 71)

Most social groups exhibit some division of labour, and one of the most important aspects is the division between those who specialize in taking key decisions about group activity, and those who specialize in implementing them.

> The most important differentiation in function, or division of labour, between individuals is the separation between direction and execution, or the specialisation of

leadership. It may well be true that able leaders are in general also more competent workers or operatives, but the gain from superior direction is so much more important than that from superior concrete performance that undoubtedly the largest single source of the increased efficiency through organisation results from having work planned and directed by the exceptionally capable individuals, while the mass of the people follow instructions. (Knight, 1951, p. 17)

A crucial aspect of group organization is the way that the leader is selected. Leadership may be hereditary within a ruling family or high caste. The leader may select himself by forming the group *ab initio*; this is the case with the entrepreneur who founds a firm. Very often, however, the leader is selected by the members of the group themselves. This method, in Knight's view, encounters insuperable problems of adverse selection and is responsible for an almost universal failure of leadership in democratic societies.

A little reflection about the simplest type of problem in the field of leadership, say, that of the relation between a technical counsellor and his client, or more specifically, a physician and his patient will show four things: First, it is impossible for a leader to be selected intelligently, in the scientific sense. In order to select his doctor scientifically, the patient would have to know all the medical science known by all the candidates under consideration, and in addition know how much of this knowledge was possessed by each separate candidate. Secondly, the relation between leader and follower must be a moral relation, one of confidence and trust on the part of the client and of moral integrity and of candour tempered by judgment on the part of the counsellor. Thirdly, where the leader is chosen by the follower or client on the basis of active competition for the position, the follower becomes the real leader; for the methods of competition by those seeking appointment will run largely to competition in promising to do what the client wants done, and by debating technical details will make him the judge of these, and to promising results of whose probability of realization the counsel-seeker must judge. And all this is the more certainly true where the follower is a group, amenable to manipulation through crowd psychology. Fourthly, active competition for positions of leadership, especially leadership of groups of considerable size, means the progressive degradation of the entire system through the use of salesmanship or 'influence' – flattery, cajolery, outright deception, and sheer pressure of suggestion and assertion. (Knight, 1935, pp. 304–5)

In the case of a large group such as a nation state, the process of leadership selection can have pathological results. Knight may have had one eye on Nazi Germany when he wrote of the leader whose

chief attribute is an absolute and fervid faith in his own 'call' to the position of representing and speaking and acting for the group, and a belief that all opposition reflects immoral motives, or hopeless stupidity. His own conviction on this point is contagious by its intensity. At bottom this is because he is peculiarly endowed with the sense of unity which others crave, and with an especial sensitiveness to popular ideas and sentiments. (Knight, 1935, p. 323)

Knight's view of society is thus an extremely pessimistic one. He is, at heart, a liberal who believes that intelligent free discussion should govern social policy. But society has a natural tendency to fragment into groups, or cliques, who seek to differentiate themselves from others, and in the process become rivals or even enemies. The unifying force within these groups is a mystical feeling of fellowship which unscrupulous individuals can exploit. If only the groups could select a better type of leader, the leaders could agree to contain their rivalry within the framework of an enjoyable and worthwhile competitive game. This is, in essence, the solution offered by ethical liberalism. But the solution is unstable because the unscrupulous leaders merely seek domination for their particular group. They are unwilling to engage in the kind of constructive criticism of ethical values which, in Knight's view, offers the best prospect of progress for society as a whole.

This pessimistic outlook is confirmed by the experience of the nineteenth century, which is a test-case for all who believe in the practical possibility of sustained social progress. For a time conditions were particularly favourable for the development of society along ethical liberal lines, but ineradicable human failings caused the liberal experiment to fail. When writing from the standpoint of the 1930s, Knight perceived nationalism as the natural reaction to liberal failure. Liberalism may have its chance again, he believed, when society has in turn become disillusioned with nationalism, but conditions are unlikely to be as favourable in the future as they have been in the past.

3.6 KNIGHT'S POLITICAL PHILOSOPHY

It was noted in Section 3.1 that different people find in Knight support for, and clarification of, different views of their own, and nowhere is this more so than in Knight's discussion of political issues. Patinkin (1973), for example, finds in Knight's writings of the early 1930s a sympathetic attitude to the managed economy. He draws attention to Knight's support for discretionary monetary management, and suggests that Knight's hostility to Keynes's *General Theory* arose from his opposition to Keynes's analysis of the interest rate as a monetary phenomenon rather than from hostility to the social and political implications of the theory. Buchanan (1968, 1982), on the other hand, by emphasizing Knight's later writings, places him in the tradition of Edmund Burke, Adam Smith and the American Founders, as someone looking for the reform of existing institutions in line with the ground rules of a progressive liberal society. Some other scholars detect in Knight a strain of anarchism or even nihilism, arising from his philosophical scepticism and his unwillingness to prescribe general rules of conduct, whether for individuals or for society as a whole.

The structure imposed on Knight's thought in the preceding sections of this chapter draws attention to another dimension of his political thought. Knight recognized that some form of social control was necessary to preserve individual freedom – there must be some power of custom or law. He stressed that not everyone can have unlimited freedom, and that the question of who is to be most free cannot be separated from the question of who is to have the most power. Freedom and power are two sides of the same coin. Knight did not consider that human beings were sufficiently responsible to use their power in the public interest, however, and those who deliberately sought power were likely to be the worst offenders in this respect. All true liberals must therefore face up to the dilemma that, while individuals desire freedom, freedom depends upon power, and power is liable to be abused.

Knight was critical of those who sought to circumvent this dilemma by over-simplifying the case for liberalism. He suggests, in some places, that the main enemy of liberalism is not socialism or nationalism, but the perversion of liberalism into a creed concerned almost exclusively with the defence of private property. This was the creed elaborated by many nineteenth-century intellectuals. They advocated what would now be called a property-owning democracy. It is popular rejection of this false liberalism that leads to nationalism and socialism, and their associated evils, Knight claims.

In the nineteenth century the economic frontier was still open, most particularly in North America. Intellectuals had the material comforts and the leisure time required to support ethical speculation, and economic conditions gave them every encouragement to develop a true philosophy of freedom. But, according to Knight, all they did was to elaborate a negative concept of freedom based on the sanctity of property, using the ideas of the French economists and Adam Smith: 'This unexamined, emotional–religious absolute which, objectively viewed, is Property, was generally called by the more appealing name of Liberty. It is a purely negative idea, meaning freedom to use power, and without power, completely empty' (Knight, 1947, p. 32).

The confusion of property and freedom arises from the 'fundamental error' of thinking of the individual as a 'social atom', someone totally non-social, and concerned only with excluding other people from the material things that he enjoys. Instead of emphasizing freedom as an end in itself, the intellectuals concentrated on property rights, which are simply a means to this end. In the manner described in section 3.2, through their fixation on the means they lost sight of the end. They emphasized the defence of property, rather than the positive virtues of freedom and the moral development of the individual.

'Thus an age with unprecedented opportunities for worthwhile philosophical speculation became, instead, an age of "scientificism", and of "management"; in philosophy it was the age of utilitarianism, which evolved, in America, around the turn of the century, into pragmatism, the negation of philosophy, philistinism transformed into a cult' (Knight, 1947, p. 31). The greatest historical opportunity to pursue 'the ideal of free society' that 'social problems should be settled in their large outlines by discussion' was wasted.

'The specialized, professional intellectuals have shown pathetically little capacity to maintain the spirit of discussion, even in small groups and under what should be extremely favourable conditions; and of their ability to settle issues and solve serious problems by discussion among themselves, it is more pleasant not to speak' (Knight, 1935, p. 353). Intellectual leaders, it would appear, are no better than political leaders at resolving the social problem.

3.7   'A PUZZLER IF THERE EVER WAS ONE'

It is instructive to consider why so few of Knight's insights into the relation of economics to society have been developed further. Knight himself must bear much of the responsibility. He never formalized his social theory in the same way that he formalized his economic ones. Of course, formalizing a social theory is a formidable problem, but he could have made a start by putting his ideas into some sort of sequence, as has been attempted in this chapter. He was a poor writer: his punctuation is sparse, he 'jumbled together' his major points, and some of his arguments are so condensed as to be practically unintelligible.

The key to these shortcomings seems to be Knight's personality. Hayek (1978) distinguishes two types of mind: the 'master of his subject' and the 'puzzler'. The master 'has at his ready command the whole theory and all the important facts of his discipline and is prepared to answer at a moment's notice all important questions relating to his field' (p. 50). He is, we may say, the conventional type – up to date with the state of the art, thoroughly imbued with conventional wisdom, an authority dictating tidy scientific results to students and ready-made advice to laymen, tolerant of proselytizing doctoral students, and so on. Hayek cites Böhm-Bawerk, Schumpeter and Viner as masters of their subject, though the validity of these examples might be challenged; Friedman and Stigler might be better examples.

Knight certainly does not conform to this type: 'He did not seek the trappings of the modern academic elite. He did not succumb to conferences and consulting. He was not dependent upon foundation grants and on a retinue of graduate students. His wants were few and simple, as he, by himself and alone, sought the key to ... the lack of social unity' (Schultz, 1973, p. 516). Similarly, Stigler (1973, p. 519) notes that, unlike the master of his subject, Knight 'had an unfailing suspicion of authority'. Thus 'Knight's immense influence did not generate imitative discipleships, partly because he applied to himself the suspicion of authority. Indeed, none of us believed that we were capable of dealing with his range of problems at his level, and we were surely right.'

Knight is much more the 'puzzler' type. The puzzler has very few firm doctrines. He is constantly at work on problems and has little interest, or confidence, in other people's solutions of them until he has solved them for himself. He finds that the solution merely clarifies the nature of the question, and therefore suggests a sequel of many further questions which immediately demand attention. The original solution, once obtained, loses all interest, and the puzzler cannot pause in order to communicate his solution to other people because of the fascination exercised by the new questions that have arisen. The main way that other people learn of the puzzler's solution is by inviting him to give a public lecture or to review a book. The spell upon him is temporarily broken by this distraction and his solution of the problem appears *en passant* in the course of a discussion of other people's views on the subject. Hayek admits to being a puzzler himself, but indicates that he is far surpassed in this respect by Knight, who was 'a puzzler if there ever was one'(Hayek, 1978, p. 51). Wick (1973, p. 513) emphasizes the same trait when he describes Knight's 'first intellectual love' as 'philosophy in its ancient character as an activity which has no end, and produces no authoritative doctrines, just because it reflects critically on the aims, interrelations, limitations and distortions of all doctrines'.

Wick continues (p. 514) that no man of his acquaintance has been more concerned with moving, not from principles to inferences by means of deduction, but in the opposite direction by 'questioning such relatively established principles, noting in turn their presuppositions and their limitations, in the attempt to discern more clearly how they might fit together in some order according to principles more comprehensive and, of course, more elusive'.

The puzzler, it may be suggested, spends too much time in general reading and reflection, and too little time writing down and summarizing his thoughts. Unless he is fortunate enough to have the discipline of writing imposed upon him at an early age, his thinking may develop into an almost anarchic process. When responding to invitations, he cannot adjust to the time limit imposed, and he finds it impossible to structure his thoughts and to condense them to a few fundamental points. This is very characteristic of much of Knight's later writing. His papers often ramble, approaching the central point through ever-decreasing circles, without ever quite arriving there.

The puzzler typically ponders over fundamental questions and in the course of this he may discover that other people's answers must be qualified in some way. (Since most fundamental questions do not permit of simple yes/no answers, it is only in exceptional cases that the puzzler achieves fame by demonstrating that the received position is completely wrong.) The puzzler, therefore, becomes a critic of the received position: his criticisms cannot easily be answered, but it may be possible just to ignore them. He challenges the 'core' of his subject, and a conspiracy of silence ensures that the issues he raises will not be discussed (Lakatos, 1978). As Buchanan (1982) notes, Knight was a critic *par excellence*. Not only did he criticize what he saw as a widespread abuse of economic theory (see above), but he also became a critic of moral values – the very things, as he observed himself, that most social conventions exist to protect from criticism.

Hayek argues that the puzzler has a short memory. His mastery is of the process of thought rather than of its results. He keeps very few formulae in his head. He reads so widely that he needs to forget the detail in order to make room in his memory for the most important points. He has actually forgotten more than most people will ever know. As a result, he is unsure where to begin when expounding his ideas to others. He has forgotten what it was like to be ignorant, and he therefore overestimates how much his audience already knows.

Patinkin (1973, p. 806) remarks that he attended Knight's lectures on price and distribution theory twice, and although the course remained practically the same, he took down two completely different sets of notes. On his first contact with Knight he was confused by the rambling presentation and eventually gave up and re-enrolled the following year. Towards the end of his graduate studies he sat through the course again and, whereas the first set of notes 'is filled primarily with economic matters proper, the second contains less of these, and more of long digressions on the nature of man and society – and God'. It appears that those who know economics already benefited most from Knight's introductory lectures!

The puzzler has 'absorbed' rather than merely memorized his various sources. It is therefore difficult for him to cite them all, and doubly difficult for him to give a fair account of them if he were to attempt it. An anecdote of Hayek's illustrates the problem; in discussing his lectures on the history of thought, he remarks that he enjoyed the imaginative reconstruction of the lives of early economists, but that he taught 'essentially what I had learnt from those writers and not what they chiefly thought, which may have been something quite different' (Hayek, 1978, p. 52). It may be for this reason that many great authors describe earlier writers either in terms of what they *ought* to have said (for example, Marshall in the *Principles of Economics*) or in terms of what they never said at all (for example, Keynes in the *General Theory*).

Knight opted to cite none of the previous work on the social problem. Because he makes no attempt to relate his own work to previous work on the subject, it is difficult for the reader to integrate Knight's views with the opinions that are already familiar to him. The reader who is not so well read as Knight (which includes practically everyone) cannot easily discern where Knight merely restates someone else's views and where he is saying something new.

Knight often writes as if his ideas about human nature were taken directly from observation of life, but it is possible to detect in some of his ideas the probable influence of other writers, notably Veblen and Marshall. Knight's method of presentation, therefore, makes the cost of assimilating his ideas extremely high. As Buchanan notes, most economists have to discover Knight's ideas for themselves before they can rediscover them – expressed with greater precision – in Knight's own work.

The puzzler's personal devil is intellectual pride. He relies on his own moral values to decide what questions need to be asked and he relies on his own resources to answer them. Problem solving becomes the principal means by which he asserts himself. He comes more and more to emphasize his personal autonomy in problem solving and develops a bias against the idea that he is influenced by other people's thinking to any significant extent. His critical powers make him contemptuous of the 'masters of the subject' who are regarded with such authority by the world at large and expect such regard as of right. His criticisms of ideas become personal criticisms of their advocates, and the more prestigious the people concerned, the more venomous the criticisms become. As the critic is forced gradually into professional exile, he adopts the pose of a detached spectator of a human comedy. His shafts of criticism are sharpened with wit and irony and give considerable offence to the bemused victims. Marshall's humourless pomposity, for example, attracted quite undeserved criticisms from puzzlers such as Cannan, and indeed Knight himself. Given the similarity in the ethical and economic positions of Marshall and Knight, it is difficult otherwise to explain the *ennui* in Knight's attacks on Marshall and on his successor Pigou. Knight was a natural wit, a master of epigrams, paradoxes and proverbs, and it is a pity that he occasionally wasted his talents in this way.

Although the puzzler faces numerous problems, most puzzlers have had more success than Knight in overcoming them. Although Hayek, for example, spent the early post-war years in the 'academic wilderness', he remained an effective controversialist and successfully seized the opportunity to promote his brand of classical liberalism when disillusionment with democratic socialism set in. The comparison is highly relevant, because there are strong similarities between some of Knight's ideas and those that have become closely associated with Hayek – hardly surprising, perhaps, when one recalls that both were professors at Chicago in the 1950s.

Knight's rather negative attitudes on a number of subjects may have reinforced his problems of communication. His emphasis on the abstract nature of economic theory led him to attack people from other disciplines who imputed to economics various empirical laws (see, for example, Knight, 1941). He admitted that to many economic theorists he appeared to be an institutionalist, whilst to institutionalists he appeared as a vigorous exponent of conventional theory (Knight, 1960, p. 82). He viewed with particular distaste any attempt to apply the methods of the natural sciences in the social domain. He saw them as anti-liberal, since he believed that the only motive for social prediction was social control. He therefore attacked Dewey's educational principles, held scientific management in low regard and was inclined to dismiss technological innovation as a significant source of progress compared to advances in ethical thought.

On balance, however, it seems that Knight was simply too much of a puzzler for his own good. The special vices of intellectual arrogance and excessive critical detachment appeared very early in his academic career. It is surely unusual for a doctoral student to refer, in the revision of his thesis, to 'discontent with loose and superficial thinking, and a real desire, out of sheer intellectual self-respect, to reach a clearer understanding of the meaning of terms and dogmas which pass current as representing ideas'. It is similarly unusual to brazenly admit in a thesis that 'my obligations to various economists through their published work are very inadequately shown by text and footnote references, but are too comprehensive and indefinite to express in detail'. In terms of Knight's own theory, we may say that Knight played the academic game according to his own rules and made few concessions to the rules followed by others.

3.8 KNIGHT AND CHICAGO ECONOMICS

Knight never turned his scheme of thought into a system. Even if he had been able to do so, it is doubtful if he would have been willing to go through with it. Intellectual systems are achieved by drastic simplification of a complex reality. The system builder succeeds through imposing spurious precision on a narrow field of study. Knight never found a system of thought that he could believe in to the exclusion of all others. His vision of the universe was a multi-faceted one. He was interested more in the problem of appraising the relative merits of alternative systems than in formalizing any one of them.

Most people, however, need a system of thought within which to work. If only trivial ones are available, then it is one of those that they will choose. Moreover, the elaboration of an existing system creates a well-defined research agenda, with a range of limited tasks which can be accomplished individually within a reasonable time by people with a modicum of technical competence; it is ideally suited to the needs of the professional career-minded researcher (Katouzian, 1980). It is almost essential to have a system in order to found a school of thought.

Knight occupies an unusual place in the history of economics in the sense that, while he founded no school himself, his students established an extremely powerful one. Students such as Stigler and Friedman are naturally assumed to know what their master taught, and their interpretation of Knight has therefore become the conventional one. There is, however, a natural tendency for the student to take selectively from the master and to hear only the teachings which he wants to hear. There is also the temptation to suggest that controversial views are endorsed by the authority of the master, and perhaps to concoct an 'oral tradition' when this claim cannot be supported in writing.

As a result of these tendencies, Knight is often identified with the post-war Chicago school. While there are undoubted similarities, there are also important differences. Many of these differences are clarified by remarks by Stigler, who has attacked Knight's arguments in *The Ethics of Competition* for their sweeping empirical generalizations and the intrusion of arbitrary ethical judgements. According to Stigler,

> Four charges are made by Knight against the claims of the competitive system to be just:
> 1. An economic system molds the tastes of its members, so the system cannot be defended on the ground that it satisfies demands efficiently.
> 2. The economic system is not *perfectly* efficient: there are indivisibilities, imperfect knowledge, monopoly, externalities, etc.
> 3. The paramount defect of the competitive system is that it distributes income largely on the basis of inheritance and luck (with some minor influence of effort). The inequality of income increases cumulatively under competition.
> 4. Viewed (alternatively) as a game, competition is poorly fashioned to meet acceptable standards of fairness, such as giving everyone an even start and allowing a diversity of types of rivalries.
>
> When I first read this essay a vast number of years ago, as a student writing his dissertation under Professor Knight's supervision, you should not be surprised to hear that I thought his was a conclusive refutation of 'productivity ethics'. When I reread it a year or so ago, I was shocked by the argumentation. Knight made a series of the most sweeping and confident empirical judgments (such as those underlying the first and third charges) for which he could not have even a cupful of supporting evidence. Moreover, why was it even relevant, with respect to his second charge, that real-world markets are not perfectly competitive in his special sense: one can define a perfect standard to judge imperfect performance, and assuredly real-world performance under any form of economic organization will be less than perfect by any general criterion. Knight kept referring to the objections to competitive results under any 'acceptable ethical system' but never told us what such a system contained in the way of ethical content. His own specific judgments do not seem compelling, as when he asserted that 'no one contends that a bottle of old wine is ethically worth as much as a barrel of flour'. Dear Professor Knight, please forgive your renegade student, but I do so contend, if it was a splendid year for claret. (Stigler, 1982, pp. 18–19)

Five observations seem to be called for.

(1) Stigler is incorrect in saying that it is the economic system that models the tastes of its members: according to Knight, it is the social system that does this. Stigler confounds Knight's crucial distinction between economic man – the economizer – and social man – who chooses his ends in accordance with the ethical values of his group.

(2) Stigler accuses Knight of judging the free-enterprise system by comparing it with an ideal alternative, whereas in fact he never used this method. He judged the free-enterprise system against its practical alternatives and he found most of the practical alternatives worse. He was, however, concerned that the rules of the free-enterprise game, as reflected in the laws of society, should as far as possible be deemed fair by the prevailing ethical standards. He therefore supported, for example, government control of natural monopolies because the private abuse of monopoly power was a potentially greater evil than political control of the industry. He was opposed to trade union monopoly power on similar grounds.

(3) The charge that Knight did not have an ethical system – in the sense that the Ten Commandments constitute an ethical system – is certainly correct, but it may be questioned whether students should look exclusively to their economics teacher for ethical instruction of this kind. It is in the spirit of Knight's teaching that his pupils should consult the ethical values of their society and accept personal responsibility for deciding which of these values command their personal commitment.

(4) To say that Knight's ethical system has no known content is incorrect, however. One of its central tenets is that ethical values can function effectively in guiding behaviour only if they are regarded as absolutes. Whether there really are any absolutes, however, seems to have remained an open question for Knight. The system of absolutes with which a society functions may be regarded as being provisional, until ethical criticism reveals its shortcomings. If there are any absolutes, therefore, it is evident that we can discern them only to a limited extent, although this discernment may evolve through ethical criticism. This belief in ethical evolution means that Knight is opposed to erecting tolerance of other people's ethical systems into an ethical absolute of its own. His belief that the most important values must be regarded as absolute also means that he is opposed to moral relativism. On these grounds he rejects the attitude of *de gustibus non est disputandum* (see also Stigler and Becker, 1977).

(5) Stigler alleges that Knight made confident judgements for which he had little supporting evidence. Knight contended, however, that decisions on most crucial issues rely heavily upon judgement: he developed this point in his analysis of entrepreneurship and continually re-emphasized it later. The need for judgement applies both in the field of ethical criticism and in the interpretation of historical evidence. Knight was not inclined to regard a collection of numerical data as decisive against a particular hypothesis; in other words, he was not a falsificationist. Even if one accepts the falsificationist standpoint, however, Stigler's criticism of Knight seems to miss the point. A falsificationist should search for disconfirming evidence of Knight's hypotheses, and not condemn him for the lack of *supporting* evidence. There is no reason, therefore, why Knight's hypotheses should not receive serious attention until a convincing

refutation is presented. Instead of attempting to test Knight's hypotheses by finding disconfirming evidence, his Chicago pupils have chosen merely to make a different judgement about these fundamental issues.

Given this difference in outlook between master and pupil, it seems that the influence of Knight on Chicago economics is less than is sometimes suggested. It appears to have been confined to the spirit of criticism he engendered, the importance he attached to the grasp of abstract economic principles and, as a corollary of this, his belief that economic principles could be applied in all areas of life, wherever means were being chosen to accomplish given ends. Reder (1982) remarks that his contribution to the Chicago tradition was that of sage and oracle, rather than initiator of research programmes, and Buchanan (1982) confirms his role of sage by quoting the Chicago saying, 'There is no God, but Frank Knight is his prophet' – an epigram worthy of the master himself.

3.9 APPRAISAL

It is difficult to know from what standpoint to appraise Knight's theory of society. To those who measure success by the ability to discover certainties, and who measure achievement by the creation of a system of thought that commands popular assent, Knight was a failure. This, however, is to apply criteria different from those of Knight himself. For, according to Knight, all knowledge is provisional and all unified systems ultimately rest on oversimplification. In the social sciences all situations are essentially unique. There are certain fundamental issues which recur in various situations, but these issues have no solution in the form of universal rules of conduct or principles of organization. This uniqueness means that a situation can be handled only by the exercise of judgement in trading off one thing against another. Uncertainty about the appropriate means calls for the exercise of judgement in economic life, and uncertainty about the ultimate ends calls for the exercise of judgement in social and moral life (Knight, 1956, p. 256). The exercise of judgement about means is the role of the entrepreneur, while the exercise of judgement about ends is the role of the philosopher. In a truly democratic society, everyone participates in the exercise of judgement to some extent. Every individual is, to a degree, a philosopher–entrepreneur. If this interpretation is correct, then any appraisal of Knight must be a provisional assessment, reflecting the prejudices of the assessor as much as the subject of his assessment.

Notwithstanding this qualification, it is instructive to consider exactly why it was that Knight failed to find a solution to the 'social problem'. The explanation seems to lie in three of his beliefs which, taken together, both define the problem and deny any solution. They are (i) the fallibility of man, (ii) the need for social progress, and (iii) the absence of a personal morality that can withstand criticism.

Conservative religious teachers accept the fallibility of man, but since they deny the need for social progress there is no problem for them. They preach that peace of mind comes with acceptance and resignation in the present life, and emphasize the prospect for improvement in the life hereafter.

Utopians believe, like Knight, in the progress of society, but they also believe in the perfectibility of man. Given Knight's scepticism, it may be asked why he believed in progress at all. His belief may reflect the influence on him of nineteenth-century philosophical literature, in particular, German romantic idealism. This idealism influenced several Anglo-Saxon philosophers, including F.H. Bradley and A.N. Whitehead, and social thinkers such as T.H. Green. It was also an ingredient in Alfred Marshall's eclecticism. According to Marshall, social progress is feasible because human behaviour will become more ethical as poverty diminishes. The 'growing earnestness of the age' will be reflected, not only in greater deliberation about the choice of means, but also in greater altruism within the realm of ends.

Marshall's emphasis on the moral factor is often dismissed by modern liberals, who argue that minimal rules, such as respect for property and freedom of contract, are sufficient. This appears to ignore the fact that, since compliance with the law in such a society rests purely on the pursuit of personal advantage, the power of punishment is essential to achieve success. Ultimately those who control punishment hold positions of very considerable power. Who, then, will punish the punishers if they abuse their power?

One way out of this difficulty is for individuals to legislate for their own behaviour. They may, for example, accept the Kantian moral imperative to will for oneself only what can reasonably be willed by all. The more people legislate for themselves, the less society has to do it for them, and hence the less need there is to rely upon the regular exercise of punishment. Personal morality, therefore, promotes a climate of political freedom by reducing the need to concentrate power for the purpose of punishment.

Although Knight faces up to this issue, he denies himself the moral solution because he does not believe that any moral system currently known can withstand criticism. He notes that one important aspect of a liberal order is that ethical criticism itself becomes democratized. He may have in mind that popular education, coupled with the declining relevance of traditional religious symbolism in industrial societies, undermines the fear and conformity on which much popular morality is based. But Knight appears to go further and to assert that all the ethical systems known to him are untenable. His arguments on this point are somewhat unconvincing and the criticisms are often of a superficial nature. He seems unduly severe on the ethical systems of the world's leading religions – and particularly on the Christian ethic (Patinkin, 1973, p. 806).

It is not necessary, on logical grounds, that discussion of the social problems be premised on Knight's own beliefs, and he may therefore be criticized for having set up the problem in a rather unhelpful way. If the first of his premises – human fallibility – is accepted, then it appears that we may either dispense with the concept of progress or accept that morality is essential for a progressive and truly liberal society. On the latter view, the fact that *some* morality is necessary might then form the basis upon which a *particular* morality could acquire popular justification. This advances discussion of the social problem a little, though it by no means constitutes a solution. It does, at least, liberate us from some of the 'dyspeptic' pessimism that is so characteristic of Knight himself.

ACKNOWLEDGEMENTS

I am grateful to James Buchanan, Peter Buckley, John Creedy, Geoff Harcourt, Geoff Hodgson and Denis O'Brien for their comments on an earlier draft of this chapter. I have also benefited from discussion of the chapter in staff seminars at Reading and Edinburgh. I alone bear the risks arising from errors of judgement contained in the chapter.

REFERENCES

American Economic Association (1973) In Memoriam: Frank H. Knight, 1885–1972, *American Economic Review*, **63**, 1047–8.

Blaug, M. (1978) *Economic Theory in Retrospect*, 3rd edn, Cambridge: Cambridge University Press.

Blaug, M. (1980) *The Methodology of Economics, or How Economists Explain*, Cambridge: Cambridge University Press.

Buchanan, J.M. (1968) Frank H. Knight, in D. Sills (ed.) *International Encyclopaedia of the Social Sciences*, Vol. 8, New York: Macmillan and Free Press, 424–8.

Buchanan, J.M. (1982) Foreword to F.H. Knight, *Freedom and Reform*, reprinted Indianapolis: Liberty Press, ix–xiv.

Bulmer, M. (1984) *The Chicago School of Sociology: Institutionalisation, Diversity and the Rise of Sociological Research*, Chicago: University of Chicago Press.

Edgeworth, F.Y. (1881) *Mathematical Psychics, An Essay on the Application of Mathematics to the Moral Sciences*, London: C. Kegan Paul.

Emmett, R.B. (1990) The Economist as Philosopher: Frank H. Knight and American Social Science during the Twenties and Early Thirties, PhD thesis, St. John's College, Winnipeg, Manitoba.

Gonce, R.A. (1971) Frank H. Knight on Social Control and the Scope and Method of Economics, *Southern Economic Journal*, **38**, 547–58.

Hayek, F.A. (1978) *New Studies in Philosophy, Politics, Economics and the History of Ideas*, London: Routledge and Kegan Paul.

Hirschman, A.O. (1970) *Exit, Voice and Loyalty*, Cambridge, Mass.: Harvard University Press.

Johnson, A. (1952) *Pioneer's Progress*, New York: Viking Press.

Katouzian, H. (1980) *Ideology and Method in Economics*, London: Macmillan.

Knight, F.H. (1921) *Risk, Uncertainty and Profit*, Boston: Houghton Mifflin.

Knight, F.H. (1935) *The Ethics of Competition, and Other Essays*, London: Allen and Unwin.

Knight, F.H. (1941) Anthropology and Economics, *Journal of Political Economy*, 49, reprinted in M.J. Herskovitz, *Economic Anthropology: A Study in Comparative Economics*, New York: Alfred A. Knopf, 1952, 507–23.

Knight, F.H. (1947) *Freedom and Reform: Essays in Economics and Social Philosophy*, New York: Harper and Brothers, reprinted 1982 (ed. J.M. Buchanan) Indianapolis: Liberty Press.

Knight, F.H. (1951) *The Economic Organisation*, New York: Augustus M. Kelley.

Knight, F.H. (1956) *On the History and Method of Economics*, Chicago: University of Chicago Press.

Knight, F.H. (1960) *Intelligence and Democratic Action*, Cambridge, Mass.: Harvard University Press.

Knight, F.H. and T.W. Merriam (1948) *The Economic Order and Religion*, London: K. Paul, Trench, Trubner.

Lakatos, I. (1978) *The Methodology of Scientific Research Programmes, Philosophical Papers*, 2 vols (ed. J. Worrall and G. Currie), Cambridge: Cambridge University Press.

Mises, L. von (1933) *Epistemological Problems of Economics*, new edn (trans. G. Reisman), New York: New York University Press, 1976.

Patinkin, D. (1973) Frank Knight as Teacher, *American Economic Review*, 63, 787–810.

Reder, M.W. (1982) Chicago Economics: Permanence and Change, *Journal of Economic Literature*, 20, 1–38.

Robbins, L. (1932) *An Essay on the Nature and Significance of Economic Science*, London: Macmillan.

Schultz, T.W. (1973) Frank Knight as Colleague, *Journal of Political Economy*, 81, 516–17.

Seligman, B.B. (1962) *Main Currents in Modern Economics: Economic Thought since 1870*, New York: Free Press of Glencoe.

Stigler, G.J. (1973) Frank Knight as Teacher, *Journal of Political Economy*, 81, 518–20.

Stigler, G.J. (1982) *The Economist as Preacher*, Oxford: Blackwell.

Stigler, G.J. and G.S. Becker (1977) 'De Gustibus non est Disputandum', *American Economic Review*, 67, 76–90.

Vining, R. (1984) *On Appraising the Performance of an Economic System*, Cambridge: Cambridge University Press.

von Neumann, J. and O. Morgenstern (1944) *The Theory of Games and Economic Behavior*, Princeton: Princeton University Press.

Wick, W. (1973) Frank Knight, Philosopher at Large, *Journal of Political Economy*, 81, 513–15.

PART II

Entrepreneurship in a Cultural Context

4. Entrepreneurship and business culture

4.1 INTRODUCTION

This chapter employs the methodology set out in Chapter 2 to derive a mutually consistent set of hypotheses about entrepreneurial behaviour. The hypotheses can, in principle, be tested using comparative data derived from case-studies at the individual, corporate, industry or even national level. The most rigorous theories of the entrepreneur are within the domain of economics, but their practical relevance is often impaired by very restrictive assumptions about human motivation and decision making. This chapter relaxes some of these assumptions – objectivity of information, autonomy of preferences and costless optimization – in order to accommodate insights derived from other social sciences. To retain predictive power, however, it replaces these assumptions with specific postulates about the way people handle information within a social environment.

The chapter begins by reviewing the basic concepts in the modern economic theory of the entrepreneur. It discusses some of the main forms which entrepreneurship takes in a market economy. It shows that the firm represents a natural institutional response to the problems of implementing entrepreneurial ideas in an economy where property rights are incomplete and insecure. There is not just one entrepreneur per firm, though. A large firm may operate as a coalition of entrepreneurs.

The main part of the chapter establishes a crucial link between entrepreneurship and business culture. With highly subjective information, the quality of entrepreneurship depends crucially on the quality of business culture. Different kinds of business culture favour different kinds of industry because different industries require different types of entrepreneurial skill. In all industries, however, the most important aspect of business culture is the extent to which it promotes trust. Trust facilitates cooperation between entrepreneurs, which is just as important as competition in achieving efficiency.

Finally, the question of how banks mediate the supply of funding to entrepreneurs is addressed. It is argued that such mediation incurs high transaction costs, which reflect a potential mismatch between the culture of the banking community, on the one hand, and the culture of the entrepreneurial borrowers, on the other. The greater the cultural distance, the higher will be the transaction costs and the poorer the performance of the economy.

4.2   ENTREPRENEURIAL JUDGEMENT

The analytical starting-point is a modern economic theory of the entrepreneur which synthesizes fundamental writings on the subject going back to Cantillon (1755). It defines the entrepreneur as *someone who specializes in taking judgemental decisions about the coordination of scarce resources* (Casson, 1982).

In this definition, the term *someone* emphasizes that the entrepreneur is an individual. It is the individual and not the firm that is the basic unit of analysis. A full analysis of entrepreneurship must explain the internal structure of the firm as well as its external competitive strategies. It cannot be assumed that membership of the firm is so cohesive that the firm has a 'will of its own'.

Judgemental decisions are decisions for which no obviously correct procedure exists: a judgemental decision cannot be made simply by plugging available numbers into a scientific formula and acting on the basis of the number that comes out. This defines judgement by what it is not, namely the routine application of a standard rule. What it is can best be explained by describing when it is most likely to be required. Judgement is most important in improving the quality of decisions that must be taken urgently in novel and complex situations where objectives are ambiguous. It is best defined in terms of the properties of the model that would be required to describe the situation accurately. This approach shows that complexity is associated with long-term decisions taken in uncertain and evolving situations where the potentially adversarial reactions of other people must be taken into account (Casson, 1990, ch. 3).

Judgement is required in decisions as diverse as choosing a marriage partner or a career. An emphasis on *scarce resources* confines attention to decisions of an economic kind. Reference to the *coordination* rather than the allocation of resources emphasizes the dynamic aspect: coordination *changes* the allocation in order to improve the situation (though entrepreneurship does not always improve the situation from everyone's point of view).

In principle, judgemental decision making could be a once-for-all rather than a continuing process. In an economic system, where everything depends on everything else, each individual faces a single integrated lifetime problem, namely how best to allocate their time, their wealth and their effort over the rest of their life. To cope with uncertainty, each individual could develop a contingent intertemporal plan which would specify how every moment of the remainder of his (or her) life would be spent. All reactions to new events would be preplanned, by calculating in advance the best response to every situation that could possibly occur. Provided all possibilities are considered at the outset, all decision making can be telescoped into the present.

In practice, of course, such planning is prohibitively costly, and so many decisions are deferred on the basis that the situations to which they relate may never materialize. Plans are therefore always liable to revision in the light of new information that makes these situations more probable. In the volatile environment in which entrepreneurs operate, change is endemic and so information of this kind regularly filters through. Thus entrepreneurship becomes a continuing process.

4.3   THE MENTAL DIVISION OF LABOUR AND INTELLECTUAL COMPARATIVE ADVANTAGE

An integrated problem may be decomposed into constituent parts. In certain cases the logic of the problem may permit exact decomposition, but this is fairly unusual. Decomposition normally involves ignoring some of the interdependencies. This introduces errors which would be unacceptable if information were not a scarce commodity. But because of information costs the net efficiency of decision making may actually improve. This is because it is far cheaper, in practice, to take a sequence of simple decisions than a single complex one. Thus short-term problems are often artificially separated from the long-term context by replacing a long-term strategic objective with a sequence of short-term tactical ones. Tactics can then be altered without changing the entire strategy.

The sub-problems generated by decomposition can usually be specified more precisely than the integrated problem from which they have been derived. Moreover, they tend to be of a standard type. Thus, whilst an overall strategic problem may be idiosyncratic, it may simply be an unusual permutation of tactical problems, each of a common type. When a problem has been decomposed in this way, different sub-problems can be allocated to different people. Because different types of integrated problem can generate the same kind of sub-problem, several different people may call upon the same person to solve a given sub-problem. By concentrating his effort on a particular sub-problem, the person concerned may acquire considerable expertise. Efficiency therefore dictates that problem solving should be concentrated on specialists.

This is a particular manifestation of the *division of labour* – albeit applied to the intellectual task of problem solving rather than the physical tasks of production. The related principle of *comparative advantage* implies that people with particular aptitudes should concentrate on particular types of problem. Specifically, some problems call for greater judgement than others – and it is people who specialize in judgemental decision making that become entrepreneurs. Thus, while everyone takes judgemental decisions from time to time, it is only entrepreneurs that *specialize* in doing so.

4.4   DELEGATION

The division of labour in problem solving can be effected either by *referring* problems or *transferring* them. Referral involves delegation: someone is instructed to solve the problem on someone else's behalf. Shareholders, for example, delegate corporate managers to solve the problem of how the wealth they have invested in the firm is to be used. The senior managers may in turn delegate some responsibility to junior managers. For example, the problem of factory management may be decomposed functionally into a production planning problem, a personnel problem and a financial problem, each of which is delegated to a different manager. Since the solutions to these sub-problems must complement each other, those involved must work as a team.

In a managerial division of labour the chief executive is responsible for synthesizing the overall solution. The chief executive's role normally requires the greatest judgement and so carries the main entrepreneurial responsibility. Whether other managers share this responsibility depends on whether they are given discretion to exercise their judgement. If so, the team is a coalition of entrepreneurs; if not, it is a hierarchy in which the members obey instructions on information processing dictated by a solitary entrepreneur.

Delegation must not be confused with subordination: in some cases subordinates may be deemed to have delegated decisions to their superiors. Thus workers may collectively delegate managers to coordinate workers' efforts so that they can operate effectively as a team (Alchian and Demsetz, 1972). This approach is particularly useful in analysing worker-cooperatives, where the workers may bear the financial risks and take responsibility for recruiting the manager, rather than the other way round.

A problem is transferred when the resources to which the problem pertains are allocated to someone else. Problems can be transferred either *between principals* or *between delegates*. The first involves an arm's-length transaction between two ownership units. Consumers, for example, pay producers for solutions to problems. These solutions are embodied in consumer goods and services. Problems relating to the production of those services are entirely the responsibility of firms. Producers may also pay other producers for solutions: a firm may sell off a component factory, for example, and buy back components at arm's length from the subcontractor. In this case the assembly firm has transferred problems of component manufacture to another firm.

The transfer of a problem between delegates is effected by an internal transaction. Assuming both delegates work for the same principal, the transfer occurs within the ownership unit. In a vertically integrated production sequence, for example, responsibility for the quality of intermediate products may be transferred from an upstream division to a downstream division as the products flow down the chain. Under long-term corporate restructuring, an entire facility may be transferred from one division to another, as when a central research laboratory is 'captured' by one of the application-centred divisions.

4.5 SUCCESSION

If the division of labour is organized on a purely person-to-person basis then it will be disrupted every time someone retires or moves to some other kind of work. To perpetuate the division of labour it needs to be specified in terms of roles in which individuals can succeed one another so as to maintain continuity. The management of succession in an enterprise is normally the responsibility of the chief executive, but difficulties can arise when the chief executive post itself is involved. A chief executive may not wish to resign even if his subordinates believe he should – because, for example, he has forfeited their confidence and trust. One advantage of joint stock ownership is that the chief executive can be removed by a coalition of shareholders. In an owner–managed firm this mechanism is not available, and it is quite possible for a senile owner–manager to run his firm into bankruptcy. Even in a family firm, dynastic custom may dictate that if the incumbent chief executive is replaced it must be by his eldest son (or the first in 'line of succession') irrespective of his talent. Although it is argued elsewhere in this chapter that family ties, in common with shared religious affiliation, can be an important advantage to an entrepreneur, when it comes to succession, the disadvantages of the family firm are all too evident.

4.6 INTERPERSONAL SUBJECTIVITY

In an evolving economy, the division of labour will adapt as new problems arise and existing ones are solved. Environmental change is endemic because of population ageing, resource depletion, wars, and so on. But it is the *perception* as well as the reality of problems that is important. Information lags mean that real problems may not be immediately perceived, while cultural changes mean that new problems may be perceived even if the underlying reality is unchanged. At the root of this is the subjectivity of problems (Shackle, 1979). This pertains both to their identification and solution.

Identification is subjective because people have different objectives and different norms. Conventional economics stresses that objectives differ because of differences in tastes. But the problem goes deeper than this. People also need to morally legitimate their wants, so objectives are affected by personal morality too (Casson, 1991). Differences in taste and morality mean that in the same situation one person may perceive one problem and another person another. Differences in norms are important too. In economic problems efficiency considerations are paramount and so the emphasis is on performance norms. A person with high norms may perceive a problem where a person with low norms does not.

Solutions are subjective because of both the information available and the model (or 'mental map') used. Because information sources are localized, different people have access to different information, but, even where access is similar, opinions may differ as to reliability. No item of information can authenticate itself, and so one person may dismiss as false and misleading information which someone else regards as true. People capable of synthesizing information from diverse sources are the best judges of truth because they can use different items to corroborate each other.

The interpretation of information requires a model. Models are typically very simple in relation to the environment they claim to represent, and so in many situations – particularly complex ones – there may be several models representing different aspects of the situation. At the other extreme, in an unprecedented situation there may be no adequate model at all. The decision maker may have to rely on very crude analogies instead. People who have been educated in a different way may be biased towards particular types of model or analogy and so interpret information very differently.

Thus a consumer products industry, which involves the continuous innovation of novel designs, may require entrepreneurs who are good at taking decisions without a carefully specified model and with only limited information. A mature process industry, by contrast, may require entrepreneurs who are good at reconciling different models which deal with complementary aspects of a very complex production system. The principle of comparative advantage applied to subjective decision making therefore implies that people with different personal qualities will gravitate to different industries. Individuals who are good at coping with ignorance due to shortage of data will incline to innovative industries, whilst those who are good at synthesizing different models will opt for mature industries with complex technologies.

4.7   INNOVATION AND ARBITRAGE

In a free-enterprise economy anyone can devote their time to identifying and solving any kind of problem they wish, provided they are willing to pay the opportunity cost involved. Profit opportunities provide the material incentive to use their time in this way.

Profit opportunities are exemplified by innovation (Schumpeter, 1934) and arbitrage (Kirzner, 1973, 1979). The most dramatic forms of innovation are those concerned with infrastructure, notably transport, communication, and the distribution systems associated with utilities (electricity grids, gas mains, and so on). These innovations solve crucial problems relating to the movement of people and freight, the exploitation of scale economies in energy generation and so on. Also significant, but less dramatic, are ordinary product and process innovations. A consumer product innovation, for example, may be based on the solution of a common household problem. The solution is embodied in the design of an ingenious durable good. The production and marketing of this good may form the basis of profitable corporate activity.

Innovation usually involves the entrepreneur in the active management of resources under his control. Arbitrage, on the other hand, does not. Arbitrage deals with problems which lie purely in the domain of ownership. For example, one party may require resources urgently to resolve a pressing problem, but the relevant resources may initially belong to someone else. Alternatively, someone may be mismanaging resources which would be better placed under someone else's control. A single transaction can solve problems of this kind, and recognition of this solution provides an opportunity for arbitrage. When the problem lies in the future rather than the present, the opportunity becomes a speculative one instead.

The successful appropriation of profit depends upon maintaining a monopoly of the solution until the appropriate contractual arrangements have been made. Competition from other entrepreneurs exploiting a similar solution will drive up the prices of resources it is planned to acquire, and depress the prices of resources which are to be sold.

Even with a monopoly, however, the appropriation of profit may be impeded if a key resource required to implement the solution is monopolized by someone else. To avoid being held to ransom, the entrepreneur must understate his valuation of the resource – withholding relevant information as a secret – so that the other monopolist underestimates his own market power. Negotiation skills of this kind are very important to the entrepreneur.

Because the economy is in a continual state of flux there is always uncertainty about whether any particular solution is really the best. The prudent entrepreneur will ask himself whether the problem is really as easy to tackle as he believes, and whether his solution is really the best available. Has he really discovered something that other people do not know, or has he merely overlooked some aspect of the problem that they have recognized? This issue can never really be resolved until the outcome is known. Indeed, even then it can never be fully resolved, for what seems in immediate retrospect to have been a failure may turn out even later to look like a success. Nevertheless, the entrepreneur must be prepared for the fact that the consensus of opinion, acting on hindsight, may condemn the judgement that underpinned his solution.

The entrepreneur therefore needs to be not only optimistic that the problem can indeed be solved, but also confident that his optimism, even though it is not shared by others, is still justified. He must also be able to tolerate the stress of waiting for the outcome to materialize and wondering if he can find a suitable excuse if it is a disaster. Indeed, it is because of his optimism and confidence that the entrepreneur is likely to have a monopoly of the opportunity: there is a subjective 'barrier to entry' into the exploitation of the solution created by the relative scepticism of the other people involved.

4.8   CAPITAL REQUIREMENTS AS AN ENTRY BARRIER

When the resources required to exploit a solution are large, however, the entrepreneur may himself become the victim of an entry barrier, namely lack of funds. To capitalize an enterprise properly, the funds must be sufficient to meet contractual obligations in the event of failure as well as in the event of success (see Chapter 5). These funds may be quite large in relation to the entrepreneur's personal wealth. Because of subjective differences in the perception of risk, potential financiers will be less optimistic than the entrepreneur. There is, moreover, a 'Catch 22' problem, because if the entrepreneur presents potential backers with convincing evidence for his optimism then they may decide to invest directly themselves. Since they have the funds and he does not, they can cut him out altogether. The evidence must therefore be presented with some crucial information withheld.

The success of the solution may also depend on the effort supplied by the entrepreneur after the funds have been made available. To provide a suitable material incentive, the backers may insist that the entrepreneur place some of his own personal wealth 'on the line'. It is in this way that the entrepreneur becomes an uncertainty bearer (Knight, 1921). The backers may also insist on powers of supervision, exercised by making the entrepreneur an employee. So far as gaining access to funds is concerned, therefore, the entrepreneur must have limited risk aversion and be willing to share responsibility with others.

The entrepreneur may, however, be reluctant to submit to supervision, or to share authority for implementation. An entrepreneur who values autonomy may confine his backing to family sources. Relatives may interfere less because they trust the entrepreneur more than do other people. In cases where the older generation of the family are lending to a descendant, the entrepreneur is effectively taking a loan against his own inheritance. In the absence of family sources, the entrepreneur may be able to tap the resources of a local business elite (see section 4.11) or borrow from the wealthier members of a religious group to which he belongs (see section 4.12). Otherwise, he will have to realize other assets – taking a second mortgage on his house (particularly useful if he has obtained capital gains), selling his second car, and so on. Apart from this he will have to rely on savings out of income from work.

4.9 INTERMEDIATION AND THE ENTREPRENEURIAL FIRM

The flexibility of a private enterprise economy owes much to the individual initiative of the entrepreneur. The decentralization of initiative is, in turn, promoted by specific institutional arrangements, in particular, money and markets. Money is important because it allows complex multilateral networks of trade to be resolved into separate bilateral arrangements. These are sufficiently loosely coupled that any one of them can normally be renegotiated without simultaneously changing all the others. Markets are important because they facilitate switching between trading partners – switching which can be informed by price comparisons obtained at convenient central places.

In a market economy a good deal of entrepreneurial effort is normally devoted to the problem of improving trading arrangements, that is to reducing transaction costs. Transaction costs are incurred in seeking out a partner (including advertising), specifying requirements, negotiating terms, transferring title (and exchanging physical custody of goods where appropriate), checking compliance and sanctioning defaulters. Two transaction cost-reducing strategies are particularly important for the entrepreneurial firm, namely *intermediation* and *internalization*. Both involve a significant measure of building trust.

Intermediation is exemplified by entrepreneurial activity in retailing and commodity broking, which is finely tuned to reducing customer's transaction costs. Reputation is very important to an intermediator. An intermediator with a reputation for integrity can establish a chain of trust between a buyer and seller who do not directly trust each other. The gains from reputation are such that, even if the intermediator is not particularly moral, it is in his own interests to maintain any reputation that he has incidentally acquired because of the profit it will yield in the long run. Thus the customers' collective trust in the intermediator has a self-validating property.

An intermediator with a widespread customer base will also wish to establish a reputation for taking a hard line in negotiations – quoting a firm price and sticking to it – particularly where low-value items are involved. Otherwise the time costs of negotiation will become prohibitive. Intermediation is particularly entrepreneurial when it involves buying and reselling goods on own account, rather than simply charging customers a fee, because it affords opportunities for speculation as well.

Some of the inputs into intermediation are of a very specialized nature. Since transactions normally involve the transfer of legal title, lawyers have an important role. Monitoring the timeliness of payment and managing the associated cash-flow problems is the prerogative of accountants. The demand for transaction cost savings therefore creates a derived demand for specialist employees.

The hiring of specialists in turn creates its own transaction cost problems, in particular assessing individual competence, which is very difficult for the layman to do. Professional accreditation, backed by examination and peer group review, has emerged as an important mechanism for guaranteeing quality. It is financed by professional membership fees paid by licensed practitioners out of the economic rents that flow from their accredited status. When one organization has a monopoly of accreditation these rents can be enhanced by the strategic limitation of entry to the profession and the regulation of professional fees. The employment of qualified professionals is an important feature of large-scale entrepreneurial activity, and the integration of different professions into a harmonious management team is a potential source of problems which require considerable judgement to resolve.

4.10   INTERNALIZATION

Internalization is another important strategy for reducing transaction costs. Internalization is effected by bringing the buying activity and the selling activity under common ownership and control (Coase, 1937). It is most appropriate when there are regular flows of intermediate products between two or more activities in the business sector. Internalization is particularly useful in a low-trust environment as it eliminates the incentives to haggle and default.

Internalization of the market in innovative solutions (see section 4.3) is particularly important for the entrepreneur. An entrepreneur can assure the technical quality of the solution most easily if it is generated by employed inventors working under his supervision. He therefore integrates backwards into R & D. Given the limitations of the patent system, it is often difficult to appropriate rents effectively by delegating exploitation to a licensee. He therefore integrates forward into production too. Economies of scale in transport and in wholesale and retail facilities normally discourage full forward integration into distribution, but nevertheless most entrepreneurs employ their own sales force to monitor the distribution channel and ensure adequate point-of-sale promotion. Thus transaction costs are minimized by establishing a firm which embraces several functional areas, rather than by simply arbitraging in an intellectual property market for innovations.

Some ideas have very wide applicability. For example, a knowledge of how low-income households can improve their status by conspicuous consumption of certain types of product may have implications for the marketing of an entire range of mass-produced goods. Such general concepts, exploited through internalization, can lead the firm to develop a diversified product range. Similarly, concepts which are general in a geographical sense – for example, pharmaceutical treatments – can lead to exporting and multinational production.

4.11   CULTURE

Subjectivity has hitherto been discussed as an individualistic phenomenon, as in the Austrian literature (Hayek, 1937; Mises, 1949). But subjectivity can also be collective. Culture may, indeed, be usefully defined (from an economic standpoint) as a collective subjectivity: a shared set of values, norms and beliefs. Many cultural elements are implanted during childhood, with those subjected to similar religious training and secular education within a particular community acquiring broadly similar values and beliefs. Because culture deals with values and beliefs to which everyone in a group conforms, individual members are often not aware of its influence. This in turn means that they are not naturally critical of these beliefs. This approach to culture is a useful antidote to the view that culture reflects a mystical 'collective will'.

Values are reflected in the legitimation of objectives; for example, one culture may see scientific progress as an important collective endeavour, another may see it as a purely utilitarian exercise, whilst a third may recognize only its adverse consequences in undermining traditional beliefs. At a prosaic personal level, one culture may endorse eating a certain kind of meat which another culture proscribes. Since different values legitimate different objectives, and different objectives generate different kinds of problem, societies with different cultures will tend to focus on distinctive types of problem solving. 'Learning by doing' is an important aspect of problem solving and so learning effects will give each culture a distinctive kind of problem-solving expertise. This may show up in the industrial pattern of comparative advantage between different cultural groups.

Absolute advantage as well as comparative advantage is important to a group. Absolute advantage confers high productivity on the comparatively advantaged sectors, thereby raising the standard of living. A culture that establishes high norms will keep group members 'on their toes', and so develop the high-level expertise that underpins absolute advantage of this kind.

Values and norms are also reflected in the relative status accorded to different roles. A culture that promotes industrial progress effected through structural change will confer high social status on entrepreneurs. Conversely, a culture that promotes stability maintained by formal authority will accord high status to politicians and bureaucrats instead.

It is beliefs about the social environment, rather than the natural environment, that are of greatest moment for the entrepreneur. Such beliefs can affect the political choice of the economic system within which the entrepreneur has to work. A belief that only a few people of a certain type are well-informed tends to support centralized decision making by the state, as in socialist planned economies, whereas a belief that potentially anyone may be well-informed tends to support decentralization through private enterprise based on individual property rights. In the centralized state entrepreneurial activity is concentrated on the planners, whereas under private enterprise it is much more widely diffused. In the intermediate case of a 'mixed economy', culture can affect the amount of bureaucratic intervention and market regulation to which private enterprise is subject.

Beliefs about genetics can be important too. Non-scientific beliefs may lend support to traditional systems of authority – kingship at the state level, paternalism in the family, and so on. Tradition often favours hereditary systems such as primogeniture, which is important to entrepreneurship because it maintains the personal concentration of wealth within family dynasties (see section 4.8). Tradition can also reduce social mobility by discouraging trade or inter-marriage between different classes or castes.

It is not just the choice of system, but the distribution of rights within the system, that can be affected (Sen, 1987). Belief in the inequality of intelligence, for example, may be used to support the persistence of an unequal distribution of property rights. Values interact with beliefs in this context: for example, the legitimation of equality of opportunity (which is closely associated with belief in private enterprise) has very different distributional implications than the legitimation of equality of income. The former, for example, tends to promote low marginal rates of taxation – to encourage saving, risk taking and effort – whereas the latter encourages higher rates, not only to narrow post-tax income differentials by taxing the rich but also to help finance social security programmes which benefit the poor. Entrepreneurs who share egalitarian social values may be quite happy to pay high taxes, but those that do not will tend to be discouraged by what they perceive as a hostile fiscal regime.

Perhaps the single most important set of beliefs, however, relate to the question of who can be trusted (see section 4.9). When few people can be trusted, transaction costs become very high. This affects relations both between firms and within them. Inter-firm relations are undermined because licensors cannot rely on licensees, assemblers cannot rely on subcontractors, or vice versa. In response to this, internalization becomes a widespread strategy. Industrial activities become divided up between a small number of large integrated firms.

Unfortunately, however, internalization encounters its own problems of distrust within the firm. To discourage slacking, complex and intrusive monitoring systems have to be established using a formal hierarchy supported by accountants, work study specialists and the like.

In a high-trust culture, by contrast, complex interdependencies between firms can be sustained by arm's-length contracts and within each firm the owner can rely on the loyalty and integrity of employees. One important implication of this is that it is a high-trust culture rather than a low-trust culture that sustains an industrial structure based on a large number of small, highly productive firms.

The high-trust culture and the low-trust culture are, of course, the two extremes of a continuous spectrum. In the middle of this spectrum culture influences perception of where exactly trust should be placed. Some authoritarian cultures suggest that subordinates must trust their superiors irrespective of their personal qualities, thereby allowing superiors to exercise moral suasion purely by virtue of their role. Other cultures require superiors to win the respect of their subordinates by 'getting alongside them' – reducing 'power distance' in Hofstede's (1980) terms. Management is clearly much easier in the first situation than in the second, though arguably good management, when available, can achieve much more in the second situation than in the first.

One of the characteristics of the Industrial Revolution in Britain seems to have been the emergence of high-trust cultures amongst regional business elites. As the front line of technological advance shifted around between Shropshire, Cornwall, the West Midlands, Teesside and the various Pennine areas (Pollard, 1981) so elite groups of businessmen emerged in these areas who were willing to collaborate in funding infrastructure improvements such as canals, turnpikes and railways. They also helped to develop supporting industries by extending credit to their suppliers (Hudson, 1986) and gave each other support through informal cartels and employers' associations.

In regions where cooperation between independent businesses was intense, regional economic performance will almost certainly have been better than it would have been had larger-scale business prevailed. Apart from the problems of succession encountered by small family businesses (noted earlier) there is no reason to believe that market forces promoted the survival of the wrong kind of firm. Large scale does not normally promote a high-trust environment within the firm. Indeed, formal hierarchies are often justified by their facility for supervising employees who cannot otherwise be trusted. Cooperation between family firms, which use paternalism for internal coordination and reciprocity for external coordination, may achieve better results than a merger which integrates the firms within a larger managerially controlled enterprise. It is the quality of the culture rather than the form of organization which is crucial.

4.12   RELIGION, CLASS AND ENTREPRENEURSHIP

The basic cultural unit is the social group. Each group typically has a leader whose role is to engineer the values and beliefs to which members conform. Large groups comprise subsidiary groups, which may themselves be further subdivided. Each member of a large group typically has several sub-group affiliations. A citizen of a nation, for example, is also a member of a family and a local community, and may be affiliated to a church, school, club or trade union as well.

The firm is the basic social unit for work, although it may comprise various sub-groups based upon patterns of social contact in the workplace. It has been argued above that the firm does not necessarily consist of a single entrepreneur, but rather a coalition of entrepreneurs. Nevertheless, one of the entrepreneurs may well have a dominant personality and so become responsible for the corporate culture of the firm. In other words, even if entrepreneurship is not unitary, leadership is.

Because the entrepreneur is a citizen of the nation state, the corporate culture may well 'free-ride' on the national culture. There is a complication, however. The national culture may be fragmented – the nation may be little more than a collection of factions subdued by a dominant faction that has acquired control of the state.

Two common bases for faction are religion and class. Religion deals with the most fundamental values and beliefs and is therefore a key influence on culture (Ekelund and Hébert, 1992; Lipford, McCormick and Tollison, 1993). Religions that stress freedom of conscience and the subduing of nature are most likely to sustain entrepreneurship. 'Middle-class' attitudes that endorse social competitiveness, wealth accumulation and upward mobility are more likely to encourage entrepreneurship than 'working-class' values of conformity and solidarity with fellow-employees. Thus within a nation entrepreneurs are likely to be recruited selectively from particular religious groups and social classes.

To some extent the individuals may be self-selected, as when certain groups opt for self-employment and others do not. In other cases they may be screened out from other groups because of the reputation for entrepreneurship enjoyed by the group as a whole. Finally, favouritism may lead successful members of the group to select subordinates or successors from the same group as themselves.

The division of labour in problem solving thus becomes organized with reference to cultural sub-groups. While individual personality remains important, the cultural affiliation of the individual becomes significant too. The cultural pattern of the division of labour may have considerable inertia, for when a particular group begins to dominate a particular industry or functional area, favouritism in recruitment may make that group difficult to dislodge. This can be a serious difficulty if environmental change alters role requirements, so that the culture is no longer appropriate, given the different kind of judgement now required.

The influence of religion on regional business elites can be seen in the role of church membership as a mediating influence, bonding individual members together in a manner analogous to family ties. It is not just that religion can promote entrepreneurial attitudes, as in the alleged tendency for Protestant dissent to foster confident individualism and hard work. Even more significant in the present context is the role of religion in inducing moral conformity and providing a ritual focus around which social contacts can be developed. Sects which encourage a sense of 'apartness' have particularly strong bonding qualities; the Quakers, in particular, seem to have been successful in exploiting these bonds for the cooperative financing of industry (Corley, 1988; Kirby, 1984).

4.13 CORPORATE CULTURE: THE MANIPULATION OF LOYALTY AND INTEGRITY

The 1980s have witnessed a surge of interest in corporate culture (Schein, 1985). The engineering of corporate culture is claimed to hold the key to long-run corporate performance. Much of the analysis has centred on the large enterprise, where considerable discretion may have to be delegated to managers of functional areas. Since managerial effort, being mental rather than physical, is difficult to monitor, managerial motivation cannot easily be achieved by supervision alone. Moral manipulation may be more effective. By creating a corporate ethic of integrity and dedication, the owner of the firm may encourage employees to punish themselves emotionally for lack of effort. External supervision is replaced by internal monitoring by the individual himself, and from an information-handling point of view this is much more effective.

Moral manipulation thus provides a useful complement to supervision. While supervision is helpful in discouraging gross misconduct, because such misconduct is easily observed, manipulation is valuable in eliciting that extra degree of effort of which only the employee himself is immediately aware. It may be suggested that it is a capacity for moral manipulation that distinguishes the true 'business leader' from a mere 'entrepreneur' .

A skilful corporate leader may be able to engineer a culture specifically adapted to the industrial and social environment in which his firm operates. The culture may borrow eclectically from various sources. It will probably resonate with certain dominant themes in the national culture (or with themes common to several national cultures in the case of a multinational firm). It is also likely to draw upon the leader's own personal commitments, for example his religious upbringing, and his own personality – in the sense of whether moral or material incentives are most heavily used. The strength of this culture and its suitability to the environment will then govern long-run corporate performance.

Cultural factors can also work against the entrepreneur, however. An absentee owner or employer is likely to convey an impression of indifference which may create a vacuum so far as moral leadership is concerned. Other people – such as a trade union leader – may then step in and exploit the situation by organizing collusion against the employer himself.

4.14   DEMAND AND SUPPLY OF ENTREPRENEURS

The market for entrepreneurship equates demand and supply. The demand for entrepreneurship determines the number and nature of the entrepreneurial roles that need to be filled. Supply factors govern the availability of suitable candidates to fill these roles.

It has been stressed throughout this chapter that the demand for entrepreneurship is highly subjective. This means, firstly, that the roles created reflect a perceived need for solutions to problems rather than any underlying reality. Secondly, and more importantly, it means that some roles may be specifically created by individuals who believe that it is their mission to occupy them. This is typically the situation of the self-employed entrepreneur, who has created his own demand for the role he plays.

The overall intensity of entrepreneurial demand will reflect the level of norms in the population for, as noted in section 4.6, high norms generate problems that low norms do not. Coordination problems are particularly intense when there is a perceived need for structural change. Structural change requires a pervasive reallocation of resources from declining industries into growth industries, and generates substantial profit opportunities for the entrepreneur. It is, therefore, amongst a population with high norms that perceives a far-reaching need for structural change that there is likely to be the most intense demand for entrepreneurs.

The supply of entrepreneurs is governed by occupational choice. The options include manual work as well as intellectual work and, within intellectual work, the rule-governed as well as the judgemental. Other options include unpaid work (housework, charitable work) and no work at all (unemployment, leisure). It follows that, for a given distribution of entrepreneurial aptitudes, recruitment to entrepreneurship depends upon the entire spectrum of rewards to alternative uses of time.

These rewards may contain a significant non-pecuniary element, such as a moral element (as in the case of charitable work). Negative moral attitudes to profit seeking – especially low-level activities such as arbitrage – may inhibit entry into entrepreneurship. The social dimension can be important too. Some roles carry a much higher status than others. Status may be particularly important in choosing between a professional career as a lawyer or accountant or a more broadly-based entrepreneurial career.

It has been emphasized that entrepreneurs must continually put their personal judgement to the test, and that in doing so they must also place some of their own resources, and their personal reputation, at risk. They must also be able to work in partnership with other risk bearers. The supply of entrepreneurs is therefore influenced by the level of confidence, tolerance of stress, moderation of risk aversion and willingness to share responsibility – all factors which have been mentioned earlier.

Occupational choice will also reflect educational background. Basic education increases the supply of entrepreneurs by inculcating basic literacy and numeracy. Further education has a more ambiguous effect. On the one hand, it can help to refine entrepreneurial judgement – for example, by providing historical awareness of the endemic nature of change – and so increase the rewards to entrepreneurship. On the other hand, it can open up artistic and scientific careers that can entice people away from business.

Early specialization in education can also reduce entrepreneurship by encouraging other people to enter narrowly defined professions instead. Although these professions support entrepreneurial activity indirectly, the support they give is often limited by the inability of complementary specialisms to coordinate with each other under the direction of the entrepreneur (see section 4.9).

Finally, the regulatory environment can influence the supply of entrepreneurs. Powerful vested interests (statutory monopolies, cartels, trade unions, guilds and so on) may obstruct entry into certain industries unless an active competition policy is in force. The absence of patents may discourage entrepreneurship in high-technology industries because vulnerability to imitation makes it difficult to recover the sunk costs of development work. National culture is important here because it affects the perceived legitimacy of the market system (see Chapter 8). Some cultures will accept income inequality as the price that must be paid for market efficiency and others will not. Those that do will adopt a pro-competitive policy stance, whilst those that do not may tolerate vested interests that oppose innovation on the grounds that they help to sustain a more desirable distribution of income.

The market for entrepreneurship will tend to adjust to equilibrium through changes in the pecuniary rewards offered to entrepreneurs. These rewards may be in the form of profits for owner–entrepreneurs or salaries for employee–entrepreneurs. It is, of course, anticipated rather than actual rewards that are important: expected profits may not materialize and even expected salaries may not get paid if the employer goes bankrupt. Because anticipations are liable to change even when there is no change in the underlying situation, the market for entrepreneurs is potentially volatile. The tendency to equilibrium is, therefore, only a fairly weak one in the short run. In the long run the underlying situation, too, is liable to change, and so the equilibrium to which the market tends is itself a moving target.

Subject to these reservations, though, certain predictions about market behaviour can be deduced using the method of comparative statics. A real resource shock, for example, such as a substantial oil price increase, will create a perceived need for structural change which stimulates the demand for entrepreneurs. Although the initial impact of this may be modified through macroeconomic effects caused by wage and price rigidities, the profit opportunities created by potential substitution possibilities will stimulate entrepreneurial demand in new and growing industries. The anticipated reward to entrepreneurship will rise, and new recruits will be attracted to these industries. While there may be some transfer of entrepreneurs from obsolescing industries, this will be limited by the industry specificity of many people's skills. Many of the new recruits will therefore be people drawn away from non-entrepreneurial occupations.

The increased pressure on a limited supply of competent entrepreneurs will reduce the average quality of judgement amongst practising entrepreneurs. Thus while there will be more entrepreneurs earning a higher reward for a given quality of judgement, many new recruits, though earning more than they would in some other occupation, may not earn anywhere near as much as the more able and experienced entrepreneurs.

Entry into entrepreneurship will be effected most smoothly when new recruits have an accurate perception of their own quality of judgement. If they overestimate this quality, however, then too many people of poor quality will enter. Mistakes will be made because of poor judgement – and as expectations fail to be realized, confidence will be undermined and entrepreneurs will withdraw from the industry in an atmosphere of crisis. In certain cases the effect may be severe enough to precipitate a macroeconomic recession (Schumpeter, 1939).

A similar analysis can be provided for shifts in supply. This shows, for example, that a shift to greater breadth in further education, by stimulating entrepreneurial supply, will lead to a greater number of people entering business because their potential productivity in more specialized work has been reduced. This will lead to greater entrepreneurial activity, but lower anticipated rewards for each entrepreneur because of greater competition between them.

Because state education is subject to government policy shifts, a public perception of rising demand for entrepreneurs may indirectly induce an increase in supply. Because the supply response refers to a flow of newly trained entrants, however, it will take a long time to make a significant impact upon the total stock of entrepreneurs. By the time the supply effect works through, demand may have changed, and so this lagged response may generate a 'cobweb' cycle in the market for entrepreneurs.

4.15 THE ROLE OF FINANCIAL INSTITUTIONS

The preceding analysis was silent on the crucial question of how exactly the market for entrepreneurs adjusts towards an equilibrium. It followed a long tradition amongst economists of fudging this issue. According to Adam Smith (1776), the market works through an 'invisible hand' – a concept which later economists attempted to formalize in terms of the hypothetical Walrasian auctioneer. Austrian economists have rightly criticized the Walrasian notion and stressed that the market is a process. They emphasize the decentralized nature of the process and tend to suggest that the market generally 'gets it right'. This view is dubious, however. Few markets get it right in the short run, and there are special reasons for believing that the market for entrepreneurs is one of the least efficient in the economy. While entrepreneurial activity may well improve the functioning of other markets, it has only a limited impact on the market for entrepreneurs itself.

One reason is that, like other labour markets, the market for entrepreneurs is a market in people and, in the absence of slavery – or transferable long-term employment contracts generally – opportunities for intermediators to arbitrage within it are limited. The main potential for arbitrage lies in identifying able entrepreneurs who are in the wrong job and offering them the right job for only a little additional pay. If the entrepreneur is loyal to his new employer he may refrain from demanding increased pay and so allow the employer to retain the arbitrage profit generated by his 'headhunting' activity. There is only limited scope for exploiting this approach, however, because of the problem of adverse selection: those who are most easily enticed to quit their present job are likely to turn out to be disloyal in the future.

Another problem with the market is that it is difficult to screen accurately for entrepreneurial qualities. Indeed, until recently, the backward state of entrepreneurial theory has meant that it was not even clear what the desirable qualities were. Because of these difficulties, intermediation in the market is confined mainly to the activities of financial institutions. There are grounds for believing that these institutions may systematically select inappropriate people for entrepreneurial roles. Key decisions are concentrated in the hands of a few institutions operating behind substantial barriers to entry, and the decisions of these institutions may well reflect shared – and possibly inaccurate – culturally specific values.

Pension funds are major shareholders in large corporations and can influence the selection of chief executives, while clearing banks and venture capitalists can regulate start-ups by potential self-employed entrepreneurs through their procedures for approving loan applications. The agglomeration of financial decision makers in major financial centres (see section 4.16) facilitates the formation of a distinctive culture based on frequent social interaction within the centre. This culture may evolve stereotypes of other social groups, which influences financiers' decisions whether to place financial resources under the control of members of particular groups. An inappropriate financial culture can therefore undermine performance at the micro-level even though at the macro-level the underlying demand and supply conditions are favourable.

If true, this proposition has important implications for economic performance. It suggests that good economic performance is not just the consequence of an intense demand for entrepreneurship driven by high norms, sourced by an abundant supply of able entrepreneurs, but also depends on the micro-level efficiency with which individual entrepreneurs are matched to particular roles. Are potentially good entrepreneurs overlooked and incompetents appointed in their place? Are entrepreneurs who would be good at managing innovation in high-growth consumer product industries mismatched to jobs managing complexity in mature process industries, and vice versa? Are young entrepreneurs who lack experience promoted too soon to positions of responsibility, and are old entrepreneurs allowed to stay on when they should be retired?

An economy that has a good supply of entrepreneurs, but serious inefficiencies in the domestic market for entrepreneurs, may find that entrepreneurs emigrate to exploit opportunities overseas. In addition, foreign capital may enter the country to employ the able entrepreneurs that domestic institutions are unwilling to support. Thus international migration and capital flows may emerge to compensate (partially) for the inefficiencies of the domestic market.

4.16   THE SPATIAL DIMENSION

The division of labour has an important spatial dimension. This applies both to the physical division of labour in production and the mental division of labour in problem solving. So far as production is concerned, activities are concentrated in plants, and these plants tend to agglomerate around hubs on a freight transport network. Entrepôt centres built upon freight traffic may evolve, however, to concentrate on passenger traffic instead. Markets initially created for the physical display and exchange of products may become administrative and financial centres dealing only in paper claims. Industry moves out to the hinterland as banks and hotels take over the central places.

Economies of internalization mean that many production plants may be branch plants of large integrated firms. The headquarters of these firms will be drawn to financial centres because of the importance of face-to-face contact in communicating with financiers, and with professional specialists such as international lawyers, tax advisers and so on. Access to government for lobbying, and to major corporate clients for marketing intermediate goods, may also be important. The agglomeration of headquarters activities around major financial centres means that most high-level judgemental decisions will be taken by people living within commuting distance of the centre. Only lower-level decisions will be taken in other places.

The most important centres may become international service centres and play an important role in cross-cultural communication. Merchants, bankers and businessmen from different cultures meet there to make contracts. For a city to achieve the status of an international service centre the local culture must support religious and ethnic toleration. Respect for business confidentiality, and impartiality in the legal enforcement of contracts, are important too.

Such centres are attractive to frustrated foreign entrepreneurs who cannot get backing from their own domestic financiers. They are also attractive to exiles. At any one time, civil wars and persecutions create refugees who need to re-establish their culture overseas. Exiled people, though dispersed, often maintain contact amongst themselves, creating channels of international communication along which commercial as well as personal and domestic information can flow. These channels are particularly well adapted to developing the international trade of the entrepôt, and to speculation and arbitrage in international financial markets.

Certain exile groups – 'wandering Jews', 'sojourning Chinese' and so on – have very strong business-oriented cultures which can survive persecution and take root in new locations. The creative intellectual tension generated by the arrival of these groups can transmit, through parental influence and schooling, a strongly entrepreneurial culture to the next generation of both indigenous and immigrant people. In this way the international service centre may be able to maintain its economic base even though the original rationale, such as port activity, goes into decline as a result of the geographical restructuring of trade.

4.17　THE LIFE CYCLE OF THE ENTREPRENEUR

The coexistence, within the division of labour, of high-level and low-level problems is important for the career structure of the entrepreneur. High-level problem solving typically requires a broader range of relevant experience and hence calls for older people to take it on. These people should have 'spiralled upwards' in their careers through a variety of more functionally specialized roles. Senior professionals who have remained within the same functional area all their life are not well-suited to these roles. They may be important as advisors to the high-level entrepreneurs (as noted above) but are not capable of filling the roles themselves.

Those who occupy high-level roles also require personal skills to elicit relevant information from delegates. They need team-building skills to handle their subordinates, and an extensive network of contacts to allow them to gain access to a wide variety of consultants. This suggests that the successful high-level entrepreneur will typically have followed a career path which begins with a fairly routine functionally specialized role ('learning the business' in his twenties) and switches to a more responsible innovative role (in his thirties). This role, as it expands, gives him team-building experience and brings him into contact with a wider group of people. He can then move, in his forties, to a leadership role, acting as an exemplar to an increasing number of subordinates and representing his organization to other institutions. He can retain this role until it becomes increasingly symbolic rather than executive (in his sixties). Finally, he retires and functions purely as an 'elder statesman' of business in a consultative and counselling capacity.

In exceptional circumstances the entrepreneur's responsibilities may grow along with the firm he has founded, so that his career development is also the biography of the firm. More usually, though, where high-level entrepreneurs are concerned, he will have acquired his initial experience of the industry as an employee of a large firm. In some cases he may remain with this firm throughout his career. In other cases he may quit to found his own business at the innovative stage of his career. When the innovation becomes successful, and the scale of operations grows, the entrepreneur may then sell out to a larger firm in return for a seat on the board, and pursue his rise to the top by internal promotion at board level. On this analysis, those most likely to reach the top are people who are willing, when necessary, not merely to share responsibility with, but even to subordinate themselves to, others and are willing to move geographically around production locations to learn the business and then transfer to the metropolis to take up a high-level post. The most successful entrepreneur, therefore, is unlikely to be the ruggedly independent self-employed individual of popular myth.

4.18 SUMMARY

The preceding analysis has used a fairly conventional economic methodology to generate an unconventional synthesis of insights derived from various social sciences. The entrepreneur has been defined as someone who specializes in judgemental decision making. Judgement is required in finding urgent solutions to novel, complex and ambiguous problems. Within a private enterprise economy, specialization is normally effected in two distinct stages. Firstly, problems are decomposed and allocated to separate ownership units. The coordination of problem solving between ownership units is then effected by the market mechanism. Further decomposition of problems can then be carried out within the ownership unit if desired.

The firm itself is an institutional product of the first stage of the specialization process. It takes over from consumers the problem of finding solutions to common household problems. It takes over from wealth holders the problem of how to manage the resources they own. It takes over from workers the problem of how to organize themselves as a team. The second stage of specialization is exemplified by the delegation of decisions to functional roles within the firm. Because delegates can enjoy considerable discretion, entrepreneurship is not necessarily confined to the owner or chief executive of the firm.

Even if the entrepreneur is a salaried employee, however, he is still exposed to risk. His reputation for good judgement – on which his future earning power depends – is always 'on the line'. His value lies in the fact that his judgement differs from that of other people and, since he is called upon to back his own judgement with his reputation, he needs to be confident that his judgement is correct. He must not become unduly anxious when the outcome of his decision is delayed, or when the risk he is bearing is relatively large.

Innovation is a judgement-intensive activity, particularly where infrastructure investments are concerned. Arbitrage and speculation require a rather different kind of judgement since they are concerned, not with the management of resources, but merely with the transfer of resources between one ownership unit and another. Internalization economies explain why innovation leads to managerial involvement: problems of insecure intellectual property rights and difficulties in quality control encourage backward integration into technical research and forward integration into production.

The demand for entrepreneurship is partly created by entrepreneurs themselves who perceive opportunities that they believe they are personally well-equipped to exploit. A culture that emphasizes high norms will stimulate this perceptual process. Another source of demand arises from people who perceive a need for economic restructuring but who wish to hire entrepreneurs to take decisions on their behalf. While the first source of demand leads to self-employment, the second source leads to the recruitment of entrepreneurial employees.

The supply of entrepreneurs depends upon natural abilities, the nature of the educational system (in particular the degree of specialization) and the relative status of entrepreneurial careers, and the regulatory environment. Demographic factors are important because few entrepreneurs acquire the breadth of experience needed for high-level entrepreneurship until early middle age.

Entrepreneurial rewards, in the form of profits for the self-employed or salaries for employees, tend to adjust to balance overall supply and demand. Adjustment is subject to substantial disequilibrium fluctuation, however, because it is anticipated rewards rather than real rewards to which supply and demand respond. Inefficiencies are even more serious where the matching of people to specific roles is concerned. Thus consumer product industries may require individuals who can take urgent and novel decisions of a fairly simple kind, while mature process industries may require people who can cope with complexity instead. Because it is difficult to screen for the necessary qualities, suitable placements can often be found only by trial and error.

The matching process is typically intermediated by financial institutions. Cultural stereotyping may result in group affiliation being used as a surrogate for personal qualities in deciding whether entrepreneurs are to receive financial backing. If the financial community has its own culture, then the stereotyping may merely reflect one culture's views of other cultures, and the outcome of the process may be quite poor.

The international competitiveness of an economy will depend crucially on entrepreneurial factors. The norms and values of the domestic culture will determine the types of problems that are researched and hence the industrial structure of the expertise that is developed. This expertise can be exploited internationally through either exporting, licensing or foreign direct investment. Education policy and the social ranking of occupations will govern the supply of indigenous entrepreneurs, while toleration and impartiality will govern the supply of immigrant entrepreneurs. A combination of buoyant demand, abundant supply and efficient matching will sustain international competitive advantage through entrepreneurship.

The theory of entrepreneurship has enormous potential for practical application. This chapter has shown that, unlike the conventional neoclassical theory of the firm, it has the ability to predict systematic differences in the behaviour of firms in different social environments. Differences in behaviour in turn have implications for the competitive performances of firms. By relating behaviour and performance to a wide range of cultural parameters, rather than just to narrowly economic variables, the theory considerably extends the power and scope of economic methods within the context of case-study research. Entrepreneurship theory is particularly appropriate to comparative studies relating to different types of firm (large and small, managerial and family, and so on) operating in different cultural environments (for example, religious conformity or non-conformity, efficiency- or equity-oriented social values, high-trust or low-trust attitudes to business partners). It is to be hoped that the availability of suitable theory will stimulate more research of this kind.

ACKNOWLEDGEMENTS

This chapter was originally prepared as a paper for the Lancaster–Reading Business History Conference on Entrepreneurship and the Growth of the Firm held at the University of Lancaster, April 1991. I am grateful to Mary Rose and Geoff Jones for their written comments, and to the other participants for oral comments.

REFERENCES

Alchian, A.A. and H. Demsetz (1972) Production, Information Costs and Economic Organisation, *American Economic Review*, **62**, 777–95.

Cantillon, R. (1755) *Essai sur la Nature du Commerce en Général* (ed. H. Higgs), London: Macmillan, 1931.

Casson, M.C. (1982) *The Entrepreneur: An Economic Theory*, Oxford: Martin Robertson.

Casson, M.C. (1990) *Enterprise and Competitiveness: A Systems View of International Business*, Oxford: Clarendon Press.

Casson, M.C. (1991) *Economics of Business Culture: Game Theory, Transaction Costs and Economic Performance*, Oxford: Clarendon Press.

Coase, R.H. (1937) The Nature of the Firm, *Economica* (new series), **4**, 386–405.

Corley, T.A.B. (1988) How Quakers Coped with Business Success: Quaker Industrialists 1860–1914, in D.J. Jeremy (ed.) *Business and Religion in Britain*, Aldershot: Gower, 164–87.

Ekelund, R.B. Jr and R.F. Hébert (1992) The Economics of Sin and Redemption: Purgatory as a Market-pull Innovation? *Journal of Economic Behavior and Organisation*, **19**, 1–15.

Hayek, F.A. von (1937) Economics and Knowledge, *Economica* (new series), **4**, 33–54.

Hofstede, G. (1980) *Culture's Consequences*, Beverly Hills, Cal.: Sage.

Hudson, P. (1986) *The Genesis of Industrial Capital: A Study of the West Riding Textile Industry*, Cambridge: Cambridge University Press.

Kirby, M.W. (1984) *Men of Business and Politics: The Rise and Fall of the Quaker Pease Dynasty of North-East England, 1700–1943*, London: Allen and Unwin.

Kirzner, I.M. (1973) *Competition and Entrepreneurship*, Chicago: University of Chicago Press.

Kirzner, I.M. (1979) *Perception, Opportunity and Profit*, Chicago: University of Chicago Press.

Knight, F.H. (1921) *Risk, Uncertainty and Profit* (ed. G.J. Stigler), Chicago: University of Chicago Press.

Lipford, J., R.E. McCormick and R.D. Tollison (1993) Preaching Matters, *Journal of Economic Behavior and Organisation*, **21**, 235–50.

Mises, L. von (1949) *Human Action: A Treatise on Economics*, London: William Hodge.

Pollard, S. (1981) *Peaceful Conquest: The Industrialization of Europe 1760–1970*, Oxford: Oxford University Press.

Schein, E.H. (1985) *Organisational Culture and Leadership*, San Francisco: Jossey-Bass.

Schumpeter, J.A. (1934) *The Theory of Economic Development*, Cambridge, Mass.: Harvard University Press.

Schumpeter, J.A. (1939) *Business Cycles: A Theoretical, Historical and Statistical Analysis of the Capitalist Process*, New York: McGraw-Hill.

Sen, A.K. (1987) *On Ethics and Economics*, Oxford: Blackwell.

Shackle, G.S.L. (1979) *Imagination and the Nature of Choice*, Edinburgh: Edinburgh University Press.

Smith, A. (1776) *An Inquiry into the Nature and Causes of the Wealth of Nations* (ed. R.H. Campbell, A.S. Skinner and W.B. Todd), Oxford: Clarendon Press, 1976.

5. Modelling entrepreneurship

5.1 INTRODUCTION

This chapter examines the possibilities of formally modelling entrepreneurial behaviour. Historically, economists have found entrepreneurship to be a rather elusive subject. Because of this elusiveness, entrepreneurship has usually been analysed in purely qualitative terms. The most significant attempt to build a formal algebraic model is that by Kihlstrom and Laffont (1979) who focus on the role of the employment contract in allocating risk between the employer (the entrepreneur) and the employee. They borrow this idea from Knight (1921), although it is more appropriately attributed to Cantillon (1755), as indicated below.

This chapter develops a model which synthesizes this risk-bearing idea with other long-established insights, notably those of Schumpeter (1934, 1939) on innovation and the Austrian school on the market process (Hayek, 1937; Kirzner, 1973, 1979; Mises, 1949). Other insights are also incorporated, including some of those discussed in Chapter 4.

The model offers theoretical advances in three main directions. First, it provides an exact method of measuring the economic rents that accrue to the entrepreneur. Secondly, it integrates transaction costs into the theory of the entrepreneur. Finally, it demonstrates the crucial importance of capital constraints on the intensity of entrepreneurial activity. The analysis of capital constraints helps to elucidate the influence of the banking system on long-run structural change in the economy.

5.2 A REVIEW OF THE THEORY

From an economic point of view entrepreneurship is best considered as a function. The entrepreneur *is* what the entrepreneur *does*, in other words. The contractual status of the entrepreneur, whether he is owner, manager or middleman, can then be analysed in terms of a division of labour which specializes this function on certain roles. The problem is that the traditional literature suggests several quite distinct functions, as indicated below.

Risk Bearing

Cantillon, an Irish economist of French descent, was the first to demonstrate that contracts reallocate risk. A merchant who purchases supplies at a price which is fixed independently of resale value insures the seller against subsequent fluctuations in price. If the merchant could resell the product forward at the same time that he purchased it then risk could be avoided, but as a service to customers sales are normally effected spot, at the customer's convenience, from goods held in stock. Thus the merchant becomes a specialized bearer of risk. A manufacturer can also become a bearer of risk (Azariadis, 1975) by purchasing a worker's labour before he sells the product of that labour. In this way Cantillon's scheme of thought divides society into two main classes, the risk-taking entrepreneurs and the non-entrepreneurial consumers and workers.

Arbitrage

For Austrian economists the entrepreneur is the key figure in the market process. In a continually changing environment he moves the economy towards equilibrium through speculation and arbitrage. From a subjectivist standpoint, markets provide individuals with information on what other people think resources are worth. This allows people to buy or sell according to whether their own subjective valuations are greater or less than the weight of opinion, as reflected in the market price. The price discovery function is specialized with entrepreneurs who pass on their information through free price quotations. Their motivation for price discovery is the prospect of a temporary monopoly gain from arbitrage. Freedom of entry ensures that the marginal entrepreneur receives only a normal rate of profit, once his costs of discovery are allowed for. The most alert entrepreneurs may attain positive rents because of the scarcity of this attribute, however.

Innovation

Schumpeter's heroic vision of the entrepreneur combines a romantic view of human motivation with technological optimism and an unconventional view of monetary economics. The Schumpeterian entrepreneur is an innovator who carries out new combinations: introducing a new technology or product, discovering a new export market, exploiting a new source of raw material supply, or creating a new type of institution, such as a joint stock company, cartel or trust. The entrepreneur is not an inventor – he does not generate technology himself – but merely identifies its commercial potential. Nor does he carry financial risk – that is the role of the banks. Banks extend credit to new ventures by sacrificing liquidity to expand advances. The resultant expansion of bank deposits stimulates a mild inflation which raises the costs of traditional producers competing with the innovation and hastens their obsolescence. The innovation, if successful, encourages imitators who eventually overexpand the new industry and create a crisis of confidence which precipitates depression, as a result of which further innovation is postponed. The entrepreneur's role is to persuade the bank to back the new technology. His motivation is not primarily pecuniary. He is driven by 'the dream and the will to found a private kingdom', 'the will to conquer' and 'the joy of creating'. Nevertheless, the realization of the dream depends on convincing hard-headed bankers that the project will be a commercial success.

5.3 JUDGEMENTAL DECISION MAKING

The most sophisticated literary analysis of entrepreneurship is due to Knight, who extends Cantillon's insights using a subjectivist Austrian perspective. His starting-point is a distinction between risk and uncertainty. Risk, according to Knight, is measurable, because it relates to situations which have many precedents and where, as a consequence, the odds of success can be calculated quite accurately. Many individual risks are statistically independent of one another and hence insurable. Knight regards the joint-stock conglomerate corporation as an important device for providing individual insurance through the pooling of risks.

Situations without precedent create uncertainty. The decision maker must employ subjective probabilities rather than objective relative frequencies in this case. Different people may form different probability estimates. A confident individual who recognizes that his own beliefs differ from the common view may perceive an opportunity for speculation. In particular, if he is more optimistic than others then he can exploit an opportunity that others do not recognize. Their pessimistic evaluation discourages them from competing with him. From his own point of view, their ignorance acts as a barrier to entry, though of course if their beliefs turn out to be right then it is his overconfidence that leads him into losses instead.

Knight's ideas may be extended by noting that there are many issues that cannot be decided by objective methods, in the sense that there is no obviously correct decision rule that can be implemented given available information. Decisions of this kind call for judgement (see Chapter 4). Judgement may be defined by exclusion: it is a service which enhances the quality of decisions in novel, complex and ambiguous situations which require an urgent decision.

Schumpeterian innovation is a classic example of a judgemental decision. The synthesis of incomplete data on product demand, factor supply and technological possibilities calls for a high level of judgement. A lower level of judgement is involved in Austrian type speculation and arbitrage too. The concept of judgement, applied to the discovery of monopolistic opportunities, is thus a common theme in both Austrian and Schumpeterian theories. There is a difference of emphasis, of course – the Schumpeterian entrepreneur typically creates a new market through large scale investment in a long-run monopoly protected by patents, whilst the Austrian entrepreneur equilibrates an established market through small-scale arbitrage of an essentially transitory nature. But once they are adjusted for the degree of novelty, the scale of activity and the time period involved, the underlying phenomenon is the same.

It is important to note that successful judgement does not necessarily imply accepting every proposal. Innovation and arbitrage are not always the right decisions to make. Sometimes it is important not to innovate or arbitrage because the opportunity is illusory: it is the 'fools that rush in' where the more deliberate decision makers fear to tread. Focusing on judgement therefore emphasizes that it is the responsibility for the decision, rather than the outcome of the decision, that is crucial.

5.4   OWNERSHIP, MANAGEMENT AND THE PLACE OF THE ENTREPRENEUR WITHIN THE FIRM

A firm may be regarded as a nexus of contracts established by an entrepreneur to facilitate the exploitation of his ideas. While an entrepreneur could, in principle, subcontract every aspect of the implementation of a project, it is not normally economic to do so. Transaction costs are minimized by substituting long-term open-ended contracts for explicit spot contracts (Coase, 1937). For example, interlocking employment contracts can be created in which the occupant of one role is subordinated to the occupant of another role in respect of a particular class of decisions. The relations between different roles create a hierarchy which is governed by the entrepreneur in accordance with the constitution of the firm (Aoki, Gustafsson and Williamson, 1990).

The differentiation of roles within the firm reflects the application of the principle of the division of labour to the function of decision making. It is a special case of the division of *intellectual* labour envisaged by Babbage (1832). This division of labour creates a problem, however, of identifying where exactly entrepreneurship is located within the firm.

There are three aspects to this problem. The first is to tackle the entrenched but misleading view that entrepreneurship is unitary, in the sense that there can only be one entrepreneur per firm. Kaldor (1934) suggests, for example, that entrepreneurship is a fixed factor in every firm because there can only be one brain which ultimately makes any decision. But when a committee makes a democratic decision, for example, it is clear that everyone participates in the decision by deciding how to cast their vote.

The idea that entrepreneurship is unitary is a special case of the more general belief that where there is a division of labour the entrepreneur should be distinguishable from other people by his *complete* specialization in the function concerned. If judgemental decision making is taken as the defining function, however, it is clear that few business people do nothing but take decisions all day. But, on closer examination, it turns out that, although the actual time involved in taking a decision may be quite brief, a large amount of time is devoted to the complementary activity of gathering relevant information – consulting colleagues in committee, being briefed by subordinates through reading their reports, and so on. Moreover, most organizations effect a quite clear distinction between those roles where decision making is primarily judgemental, because no decision rule is prescribed, and those where it is purely routine. It is those roles where decision making is relatively more judgemental than others that are the entrepreneurial ones, and typically these roles will be found close to the top of the hierarchy.

The third problem is whether the entrepreneur is the owner or the manager of the firm. Clearly this problem does not arise with small owner-managed firms, where it is natural to regard the owner–manager as the entrepreneur. But the separation of ownership and control in the modern large corporation has led Knight and others to take the view that a choice must be made between the competing claims of owners and managers.

According to Knight, no-one who bears financial responsibility for a situation will voluntarily allow someone else to take a decision that affects the outcome. Since the shareholders carry financial responsibility, they must therefore take the key decisions. The key decision is to select the chief executive, argues Knight. By choosing a person who will implement appropriate management procedures, all other decision making is rendered routine. The shareholders bear the risks and take the only decision that matters, and so are the entrepreneurs.

There is clearly something unsatisfactory about the idea that the thousands of small shareholders in a large firm collectively act as an entrepreneur. The flaw in Knight's argument is his view that decision making cannot be delegated. Delegation is perfectly feasible if the delegate can be trusted. Both the competence and integrity of the delegate are important in this respect. The chief executive is the shareholders' delegate, and he in turn can delegate to board members, and indeed much further down the pyramid of authority. At each stage confidence in the delegate can be reinforced by incentives. Thus in the long run a manager's salary will reflect his opportunity earnings, which in turn reflect his reputation in the capital market. A good track record of stewardship and judgement will bring its own pecuniary rewards, and there may be non-pecuniary emotional satisfactions too. Wherever decision making is delegated, together with discretion to exercise judgement, both the delegator (the 'principal') and the delegate (the 'agent') can share the entrepreneurial role. Contrary to Knight's argument, it may be noted that the shareholders have only an intermittent role in the selection (normally the annual reselection) of the chief executive, while the chief executive himself has daily involvement in judgemental decisions on the shareholder's behalf, so that on normal criteria it is the chief executive who is best regarded as the entrepreneur.

5.5   A SIMPLE MODEL

Key aspects of the theories reviewed above can be encapsulated in a simple model. In this model entrepreneurial activity leads to the creation of a new industry. Entrepreneurship therefore involves innovation and structural change, as emphasized by Schumpeter. The outcome of investment in the new industry is uncertain, so there is risk in the sense of Cantillon. Only the other (traditional) industry yields a certain output. In later versions of the model there are divergent opinions about the probability of success, so that there is Knightian uncertainty too. Finally, one entrepreneur may have a temporary monopoly of information about the opportunity, so that Austrian insights are encapsulated as well.

Consider therefore an economy comprising two categories of people: merchants and workers. There are a fixed number of each type. Workers are totally risk-averse. They are initially all attached to the risk-free traditional industry, where they are self-employed. Production in the traditional industry is risk-free. Workers will only move into the new industry if they are fully insured against risks relating to the new product.

The new product is a perfect substitute for the old one. Everyone knows that if the new product industry is successful then one unit of the new product will exchange for $p > 0$ units of the mature one; this is because everyone's tastes exhibit the same constant marginal rate of substitution between old and new products. If the new product is unsuccessful, however, because of technical or design failures, for example, or for whatever other reason, then it is worthless. All the new product produced in any time period achieves the same success, so that the elimination of individual risks through pooling is not possible: in other words, all risk is essentially systematic risk.

Workers obtain insurance through a contract of employment offered by merchants in the new industry. The contract guarantees each worker a fixed wage $w > 0$, independently of whether production is successful. There is such a large number of workers that each worker constitutes an infinitesimal proportion of total labour supply. It is assumed for simplicity that each worker has the same physical productivity in the new industry (so that the number of workers is effectively measured in units of labour supplied to this industry).

Workers differ in their personal comparative advantage; a worker's physical productivity in the old industry is given by the worker-specific parameter a, which is uniformly distributed amongst the working population between the limits a_1 and a_2 in accordance with the distribution function

$$F(a) = (a - a_1)/(a_2 - a_1) \qquad 0 \leq a_1 \leq a \leq a_2 \qquad (5.1)$$

Each worker's utility is directly proportional to the value of consumption (measured in units of mature product). Maximizing utility subject to the no-risk constraint shows that workers will move to the new industry if and only if

$$w \geq a \qquad (5.2)$$

It follows from (5.1) and (5.2) that the supply of labour to the new industry, n^s, is

$$n^s = (w - a_1)/(a_2 - a_1) \qquad (5.3)$$

A merchant's utility depends upon both the expected return from the new industry and the standard deviation of the return. Although tolerant of risk, the merchant is more averse to it than he is disposed towards it, so that while the expected return carries a positive weight in his utility function the standard deviation carries a negative one. For simplicity the coefficient on the expected return is normalized to unity. This gives the utility function

$$u = (\mu - b\sigma)n^d \qquad (5.4)$$

where μ is the expected value of profit per worker in the new industry, σ is the corresponding standard deviation, $b \geq 0$ is the coefficient of risk aversion shared by all merchants, and n^d is the merchant's demand for labour, as reflected in the employment contracts offered. With a perceived probability of success $\pi(0 \leq \pi \leq 1)$,

$$\mu = p\pi - w \qquad (5.5)$$

$$\sigma = p(\pi(1 - \pi))^{1/2} \qquad (5.6)$$

With homogeneous perceptions of π, and free entry, competition between merchants will eliminate economic rents,

$$u = 0 \qquad (5.7)$$

giving a total demand for labour n^d which is infinitely elastic at the wage

$$w_0 = p\pi - b\sigma \qquad (5.8)$$

Substituting (5.8) into (5.3) and using the equilibrium condition

$$n^d = n^s = n^e \qquad (5.9)$$

gives the equilibrium outcome

$$w^e_0 = w_0 \qquad (5.10.1)$$

$$n^e_0 = (p\pi(1 - b((1/\pi) - 1)^{1/2}) - a_1)/(a_2 - a_1) \qquad (5.10.2)$$

Suppose that the true probability of success is π^*. *Ex post*, all uncertainty relating to the new industry is resolved. Thus the true expected value of *ex post* utility is the true expected value of profit which, when normalized with respect to the number of employees, is

$$\mu^*_0 = p(\pi^* - \pi) + b\sigma \qquad (5.11)$$

This suggests that, *ex post*, innovating merchants benefit from group pessimism ($\pi < \pi^*$) and from a high perception of risk, as measured by σ. Merchants as a group do not benefit to the same degree, however, because pessimism and subjective uncertainty discourage some merchants from participating altogether.

If one merchant alone is optimistic of success then that merchant will enjoy monopsony power over labour entering the new industry. Suppose for simplicity that all merchants except one are totally pessimistic. Maximizing utility (5.4) subject to (5.3), (5.5) and (5.9) gives the new equilibrium

$$w^e_1 = a_1 + (a_2 - a_1)n^e_1 \qquad (5.12.1)$$

$$n^e_1 = n^e_0/2 \qquad (5.12.2)$$

where n^e_0 is given by (5.10.2). Comparing (5.10) and (5.12) shows that both the wage rate and employment are reduced by the exercise of monopsony power.

The competitive equilibrium is illustrated in Figure 5.1 and the monopsony equilibrium in Figure 5.2. The real wage is measured vertically and employment horizontally. The total size of the labour force is indicated by the width of the horizontal axis ON. If merchants were risk-neutral their demand for labour in the new industry PP' would be infinitely elastic at the real wage OP, equal to the expected value of the new product, but because of risk aversion demand is shifted down to WW', whose intercept OW measures the risk-adjusted expected value of the product. The upward slope of the labour supply curve for the new industry, A_1A_2, reflects the increasing comparative disadvantage of additional labour drawn into the new industry.

Equilibrium is at the intersection E_0 of WW' and A_1A_2, giving a wage OW and employment ON_0. The area of the quadrilateral $OA_1E_0N_0$ measures the opportunity earnings of labour in the new industry, while the area of the triangle A_1WE_0 measures workers' economic rent. The shaded area of the rectangle WPQ_0E_0 measures the expected profit accruing to merchants, which is their reward for risk bearing, and corresponds to the merchant's profit described by Cantillon. The output of the traditional industry is measured by the area of the quadrilateral $E_0A_2NN_0$. The total value of economy's output is reduced by the area of the triangle $E_0Q_0R_0$ on account of merchants' risk aversion.

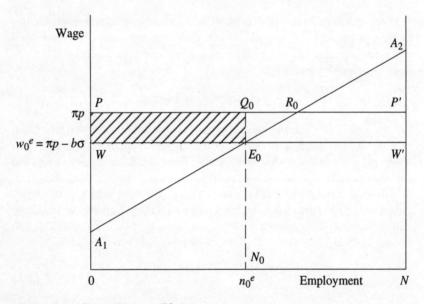

Figure 5.1   Competitive equilibrium

In the monopsonistic equilibrium illustrated in Figure 5.2 the solitary active merchant faces a marginal cost of labour schedule A_1B, whose slope is twice that of the supply curve A_1A_2. The steeper slope reflects the fact that a monopsonist incorporates the rising supply price of labour into his calculation of marginal cost, whereas a competitor does not. There is no corresponding market power in the product market because, by assumption, the old product is a perfect substitute for the new one. Equilibrium is where the risk-adjusted expectation of marginal revenue, OW, is equal to the marginal cost, as measured by the height of A_1B: that is, at the intersection F of WW' and A_1B.

The monopsonist's expected profit is measured by the area of the rectangle PQ_1E_1X. After deducting the compensation for risk, this leaves a pure monopsony profit equal to the area WFE_1X. By restricting employment in the new industry to $ON_1 < ON_0$, the exercise of monopsony power reduces social welfare (measured in units of the traditional product) by the area of the triangle E_0E_1F.

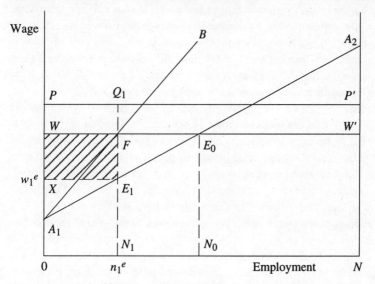

Figure 5.2   Monopoly equilibrium

An Austrian would argue, however, that the relevant comparison is not with the competitive equilibrium, which represents an unattainable ideal, but rather with the absence of any innovation at all. Were it not for the optimism of the monopsonist no innovation would have occurred, and all labour would have remained allocated to the traditional industry. From this perspective the monopsonist increases social welfare (after adjustment for risk) by the area of the quadrilateral A_1WFE_1. The monopsonist appropriates some of this as pure profit and the rest, measured by the area of the triangle A_1XE_1, accrues to employees in the new industry as economic rent.

5.6   SUPERVISION AND THE SIZE OF THE FIRM

The preceding model affords only a limited role to the firm. Because a merchant may simultaneously employ several workers, the merchant himself qualifies as a 'nexus of contracts' in the sense of section 5.4. But what exactly determines the number of employees? While the size of the industry is determinate, the allocation of employees between merchants is not, except in the case of monopsony, where industry and firm coincide. In particular, the model above cannot predict, for a competitive industry, how many firms of what size will operate in the industry.

An important influence on the size of firm is the cost of supervision. The demand for supervision arises in the present model because of the nature of the employment contract. When workers are insured against variations in the value of their output, they have an incentive to slack. If a positive cost of effort is introduced into the worker's utility function, his rational response to a fixed wage will be to slack. (This incentive does not exist in the traditional industry because, by assumption, workers are self-employed there.)

There are two main methods by which a merchant can motivate workers' effort. One is familiar to economists and the other is not. The familiar approach is to monitor the workers by appointing one of them as a supervisor to report on the others. Those who slack are fined by loss of pay. The merchant himself does not supervise, it is assumed, but appoints a supervisor for this task. The merchant's role is simply to 'supervise the supervisor' and since the merchant has only a single supervisee it is assumed for simplicity that this is a costless task.

The average cost of supervision varies according to the span of supervision, which is determined by the number of workers in the production team. It is assumed that the productivity of each worker is independent of the size of team. Thus team size is governed solely by the cost of supervision. Each team has a single supervisor, and so the supervisor constitutes an indivisible resource. It is assumed for simplicity that any worker can be appointed a supervisor and in this capacity receives the same wage as his supervisees. As team size $z > 0$ increases so the effectiveness of supervision declines (team size is measured exclusive of the supervisor himself). The proportion of time each worker is idle under supervision is

$$g = \alpha_1 z / (1 + \alpha_1 z) \tag{5.13}$$

which is increasing in z for $\alpha_1 > 0$. Each unit of output now requires $1 + \alpha_1 z$ workers, in addition to an imputed proportion $1/z$ of the supervisor's time.

Supervision is a labour-intensive activity with a standardized technology and so the average cost of supervision is simply the sum of these two cost components, namely

$$c = w(\alpha_1 z + (1/z)) \tag{5.14}$$

In a free-entry competitive industry a firm must minimize (5.14) in order to survive.

The new industry expands by the replication of teams of optimal size. It is assumed that each merchant operates a single team (that is, all firms are single-plant) and that there are sufficient merchants to sustain all the replication required. Dividing industry output by optimal team size determines the number of firms involved.

Differentiating (5.14) with respect to z and equating to zero shows that the optimal team size is

$$z^e = \alpha_1^{-\frac{1}{2}} \tag{5.15}$$

so that the minimum attainable average cost is

$$c^e = 2w\alpha_1^{\frac{1}{2}} \tag{5 16}$$

The break-even condition (5.7) implies that wages will be bid up to

$$w_2^{\ e} = (p\pi - b\sigma)/(1 + 2\alpha_1^{\frac{1}{2}}) \tag{5.17}$$

whence from (5.3)

$$n_2^{\ e} = (w_2^{\ e} - a_1)/(a_2 - a_1) \tag{5.18}$$

Equilibrium employment $n_2^{\ e}$ is divided between supervisors and supervisees in the ratio $1: z$.

The equilibrium is illustrated in Figure 5.3. The left-hand quadrant determines the minimum average cost of supervision and the optimal size of team, while the right-hand quadrant feeds these results into the determination of employment in the new industry as a whole. The height of the average cost curve in the left-hand quadrant reflects the wage rate determined in the right-hand quadrant. It is this that ensures the cost factor OS in the left-hand quadrant coincides with the cost factor XW in the right-hand quadrant.

In the left-hand quadrant the average fixed cost due to the supervisor's wage is indicated by the hyperbola FF', while the increasing average cost of slacking is indicated by the straight line OV. Overall average cost TT' is minimised at J, which determines the optimal team size z^e.

In the right-hand quadrant the risk-adjusted value of new industry output, net of slacking cost $OS = WX$, is given by OX. The infinitely elastic demand for labour XX' intersects the labour supply schedule A_1A_2 at E_2, giving employment ON_2. This consists of OY workers and YN_2 supervisors. The cost of supervi-

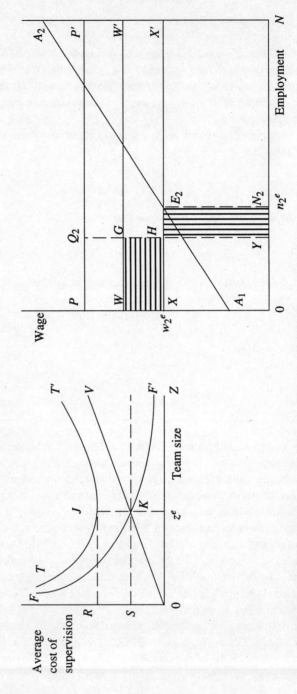

Note: The scale of the team size axis OZ is much enlarged compared to the scale of industry employment ON.

Figure 5.3 Competitive equilibrium with supervision costs

sion is measured by the area of the vertically hatched rectangle E_2N_2YH, while the cost of output lost from slacking is measured by the area of the horizontally hatched rectangle $WGHX$. Given the assumed pattern of slacking (5.13), the cost of optimal supervision is equal to the cost of the optimal degree of slacking, as reflected in the fact that the hatched areas are equal. Given the reduced level of employment, the risk premium accruing to merchants is reduced to the area of the rectangle PQ_2GW. Workers' economic rent is reduced to the area of the triangle A_1XE_2.

5.7 LEADERSHIP AND THE ENTREPRENEUR

An alternative to supervision is leadership. Leadership, though widely used in practice, is largely ignored by economists. It involves influencing workers' preferences in order to neutralize the cost of effort. The leader's personal example, backed by his moral rhetoric, emphasizes the importance of commitment to the task (see Chapter 2). Workers anticipate self-inflicted non-pecuniary penalties – guilt, loss of self-esteem and so on – if they slack. When these emotional penalties outweigh the material benefits of slacking, workers will work hard even though they are not supervised.

It is assumed that, while anyone can act as a supervisor, only a few people are capable of exercising leadership. The potential leaders are all merchants in this model, though in real life many workers (notably trade union leaders, and industrialists with shop-floor origins) have leadership qualities too. It is assumed that exercising leadership (for the few who have the necessary qualities) is no more difficult than supervising the supervisor, which in the present model makes it a costless activity.

Leadership, it is assumed, is most effective in small groups. The incidence of slacking increases faster with the span of control under leadership than it does under supervision. The ability of the leader to influence workers by personal example, and to relate his rhetoric to the personal attitude of each worker, requires more face-to-face contact than does the relatively impersonal method of supervision.

The incidence of slacking under leadership is measured by

$$g_2 = \alpha_2 z/(1 + \alpha_2 z) \qquad \alpha_2 > \alpha_1 \tag{5.19}$$

and so, with no fixed costs associated with a supervisor's wage, the average cost of leadership is simply

$$c_2 = \alpha_2 wz \tag{5.20}$$

Substituting

$$\mu = w - c_2 \tag{5.21}$$

into (5.4) and maximizing utility gives the demand curve for labour

$$z = (((p\pi - b\sigma)/w) - 1)/2\alpha_2 \tag{5.22}$$

Two types of equilibrium are possible. In the first there are sufficient leaders to replace supervisors entirely. Given a fixed number of leaders, m, the total demand for labour is then mz, and equilibrium with supply is achieved at the wage

$$w^e_3 = k_1 + (k_1^2 + 4k_2)^{\frac{1}{2}} \tag{5.23}$$

where

$$k_1 = \alpha_1 - ((m/2)(1 - (\alpha_1/\alpha_2))) \tag{5.24.1}$$

$$k_2 = (m/2)(1 - (\alpha_1/\alpha_2))(p\pi - b\sigma) \tag{5.24.2}$$

The corresponding level of employment in the new industry is

$$n^e_3 = (w^e_3 - a_1)/(a_2 - a_1) \tag{5.25}$$

and the optimal team size is

$$z_e = n^e_3/m \tag{5.26}$$

It can be shown that both wages and employment vary directly with the number of leaders m and inversely with the incidence of slacking under leadership α_2. Because the number of leaders influences the wage rate, the optimal size of team depends on the wage rate too.

A somewhat more interesting and relevant equilibrium occurs when specialization in leadership is incomplete. This typically occurs when the number of leaders is very small. When leaders and supervisors operate side-by-side in the industry the wage and employment levels are determined by the marginal costs of supervision, in accordance with (5.17) and (5.18) above. Substituting (5.17) into (5.22) shows that the optimal size of team is

$$z^e = \alpha_1^{\frac{1}{2}}/\alpha_2 \tag{5.27}$$

Thus the optimal size of team under leadership depends on the relative and absolute incidence of slacking under leadership and supervision and is independent of the expected value of output and the wage.

The ability of a leader to avoid the cost of supervision allows him to obtain an economic rent. The total profit per leader under incomplete specialization is

$$u^e = (p\pi - b\sigma)((1 + \alpha_1^{1/2})/(1 + 2\alpha_1^{1/2}))\alpha_1^{1/2}/\alpha_2 \qquad (5.28)$$

Thus the leader's profit varies directly with the incidence of slacking under supervision and inversely with the incidence of slacking under leadership.

The determination of leadership rent in this second case is illustrated in Figure 5.4. The demand for labour under supervision is infinitely elastic at a wage OX, as in Figure 5.3. The leader's demand for labour is indicated by the downward-sloping schedule WL. The downward slope arises because under leadership both marginal and average cost rise continuously with team size, and it is impossible to replicate additional teams of optimal size. The intersection D of WL and XX' determines the numbers of workers operating under leadership, OM. Total employment in the industry is determined at the intersection E_3 of XX' and A_1A_2, exactly as in Figure 5.3. Employment under supervision is MN_3.

Supervisory firms earn no economic rent, whereas leaders do. The expected rent, net of risk, is given by the shaded area WXD. This rent reflects the fact

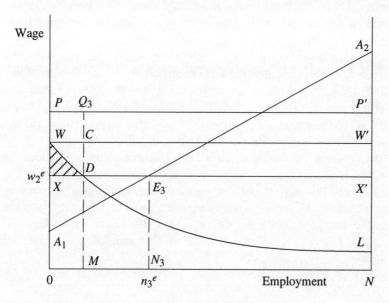

Figure 5.4   Competitive equilibrium with leadership as well as supervision

that leadership avoids the fixed costs of supervision incurred by the other firms. Leadership does not avoid slacking problems, however; the value of output lost by slacking under leadership is measured by the area *WCD*.

5.8   CAPITAL CONSTRAINTS

It is the merchant's doubts about the effort of workers that creates the demands for supervision and leadership noted above. But the converse is also possible: workers may doubt the merchant's promises as spelt out in the contract of employment. There is the question of integrity – will the merchant actually pay up when wages are due (net of any fines for slacking)? – and also the question of competence – will the merchant be able to pay up, even if he wants to, if production turns out unsuccessfully? It is this second question of competence that is the focus of attention here.

Workers who are totally risk-averse will need to be assured that the merchant can meet his wage obligations in the 'worst case' scenario. If the worst case is that the output is, say, worth only half the wage bill, then the other half of the wage bill must be covered by the merchant's own capital. In the present model the worst case is that the output is completely valueless, which means that the entire wage bill must be covered by merchant's capital. Thus workers' demand for insurance creates a demand for capital which means that, if merchants are capital-constrained, the expansion of the new industry may be impaired.

If the capital is actually paid out in advance of production, and production takes time, then it is equivalent to 'working capital' or a 'wages fund' (Cannan, 1893). In the analysis here, however, capital is merely kept in reserve and paid out at the same time that revenues (if any) are generated. This eliminates analytical complications arising from the role of time preference and the influence of the real rate of interest on the overall cost of production.

Assume for simplicity that the capital of the economy consists of stocks of the mature product. This is a totally durable good. It does not assist production (as capital does in conventional multi-factor production functions) but mainly exists for future consumption. The capital is distributed between merchants and workers in the proportions $s: 1 - s$. Being totally risk-averse, the workers will not make the capital available to merchants except through banks (whose role, for the moment, is ignored).

Given a wage w, and total wealth y, the sustainable level of labour demand is

$$n^{d'} = sy/w \qquad\qquad (5.29)$$

This constraint need not be binding, in which case the equilibrium is determined exactly as before. But where it is binding, the equality of (5.3) and (5.29) gives the equilibrium

$$w^e_4 = (a_1 + (a_1^2 + 4(a_2 - a_1)sy)^{1/2})/2 \qquad (5.30)$$

$$n^e_4 = sy/w^e_4 \qquad (5.31)$$

which, in the special case $a_1 = 0$ reduces to

$$w^e_4 = (a_2 s)^{1/2} \qquad (5.32)$$

$$n^e_4 = (sy/a_2)^{1/2} \qquad (5.33)$$

The equilibrium is illustrated in Figure 5.5. To simplify the figure, monitoring problems connected with supervision and leadership have been ignored. This is not a serious omission for, although supervision costs may determine *whether* the capital constraint is binding, they do not determine wages or employment *given that it is*. The equilibrium is determined at the intersection E_4 of the capital constraint YY' and the supply of labour schedule A_1A_2. The equilibrium wage is OL and equilibrium employment ON_4. A pure economic rent, measured by

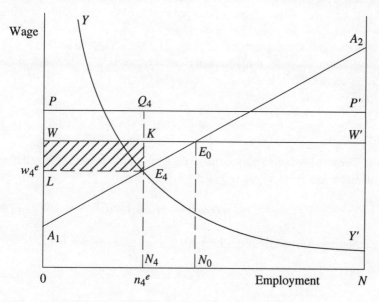

Figure 5.5   Competitive equilibrium with capital constraints

the area of the shaded rectangle WKE_4L, accrues to the merchants as owners of capital. This is in addition to the reward they receive for risk bearing (measured by the area of the rectangle PQ_4KW). The pure rent to capital confirms the popular view (refined by Marxist economists) that access to capital, as well as tolerance of risk, explains the profits earned by the entrepreneur.

5.9   HETEROGENEOUS EXPECTATIONS

The preceding analysis does not really do full justice to the subjectivity of expectations emphasized by Hayek and Knight. When expectations differ it is the most optimistic, as well as the least risk-averse, who are inclined to innovate, and the ultimate distribution of income between individuals will be governed by whether or not this optimism is justified.

To capture the effect of optimism as clearly as possible it is useful to abstract from risk aversion by assuming that all merchants are risk-neutral ($b = 0$). To further simplify the analysis, supervision issues and bank lending are again ignored. Thus merchants are obliged to rely upon their own capital in guaranteeing wage payments.

With heterogeneous expectations, different merchants evaluate employment contracts using different values of π. The distribution function $F(\pi)$ specifies the proportion of all merchants whose perception of the probability of success is less than π. It is assumed that the degree of optimism, as reflected in the value of π, is distributed independently of personal wealth. This means that $F(\pi)$ can also be interpreted as the proportion of all merchant wealth in the hands of those who perceive the probability of success to be less than π.

Each merchant for whom

$$\pi \geq w/p \tag{5.34}$$

will offer employment contracts up to the limit of his wealth. Hence the total demand for labour at wage w will be

$$n^d = (sy/w)(1 - F(w/p)) \tag{5.35}$$

Assuming, for simplicity, a uniform distribution of subjective beliefs,

$$F(\pi) = \pi \tag{5.36}$$

the demand for labour reduces to

$$n^d = sy((1/w) - (1/p)) \tag{5.37}$$

Equating demand to supply using (5.3) and (5.37) gives a rather complex expression for the equilibrium, but setting $a_1 = 0$ (that is, the labour supply schedule has zero intercept) gives the simpler results

$$w^e_5 = j((1 + (2p/j))^{1/2} - 1) \tag{5.38}$$

$$n^e_5 = (sy/2p)((1 + (2p/j))^{1/2} - 1) \tag{5.39}$$

where

$$j = a_2 sy/2p \tag{5.40}$$

This equilibrium is illustrated in Figure 5.6. The downward-sloping demand for labour DD' reflects the heterogeneity of merchants' beliefs and the amount of wealth at their disposal. The vertical intercept of the demand curve OD is given by the price of successful output, p. Demand intersects supply OA_2 at E_5, where the marginal merchant is just sufficiently optimistic to offer the marginal worker employment in the new industry.

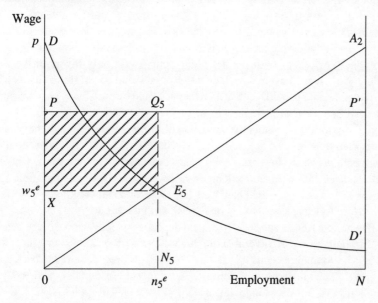

Figure 5.6   Equilibrium with heterogeneous expectations

If optimism is justified then *ex post* the optimists earn a profit measured by the area of the rectangle PQ_5E_5X, whereas if pessimism is appropriate then the optimists make a loss measured by the area of the rectangle OXE_5N_5. The value of non-participation is, of course, zero in either case.

Let π^* once again represent the true probability of success; then it pays, on balance, to participate if

$$\pi^* \geq (j/p)((1 + (2p/j))^{1/2} - 1) \qquad (5.41)$$

Thus optimists gain *ex post* if (5.41) is satisfied, but otherwise they lose. It then pays to be pessimistic simply to avoid being lured into a loss-making situation.

5.10   QUALITY OF JUDGEMENT AND THE SCREENING ROLE OF BANKS

It was noted in section 5.3 that in the long run entrepreneurial reward will reflect quality of judgement because it is judgement that is the ultimate scarce input where decision making is concerned. A simple case of reward to judgement was illustrated in Figure 5.2, where the monopsony reward to the innovator reflects a rent to superior assessment of the probability of success. The example in section 5.9 also demonstrates the point by showing how a positive reward can be obtained by relatively optimistic people whose optimism is, on average, justified.

Neither of these examples considers the most sophisticated form of judgement though. A merchant with perfect judgement would only invest in the new industry when he knew in advance that success would occur. If merchants with perfect judgement could be identified then it would be possible to channel funds selectively in their direction.

One possibility is that banks have a skill of this kind. If they do have such skills then they may be able to mobilize workers' wealth to fund the sophisticated entrepreneurs. In particular, if banks have perfect judgement of who is a sophisticated entrepreneur, bank investments become effectively risk-free. This means in turn that, provided banks are honest, even totally risk-averse workers can afford to leave their money on deposit with the banks.

The rent accruing to perfect judgement depends crucially upon the uniqueness of this judgement. If several individuals have perfect judgement they will always be competing against each other for the resources required to back their judgement, and the rents will accrue to the owners of resources (specifically to the owners of resources in inelastic supply) instead. This point is emphasized in Casson (1982), where it is shown that, when rents accrue to superior judgement, bargaining skills are needed to maximize the rents involved.

Suppose, therefore, that there is a single sophisticated merchant who has been identified by several banks, and that they compete to lend to him. The merchant is not constrained by problems relating to supervision and leadership so his demand for funds is limited only by the influence of the wage on his cost of production. It is assumed that he has no personal wealth of his own. Because the merchant is competing for labour against unsophisticated merchants, he does not have absolute monopsony power. Nevertheless, he is a sufficiently 'big player' for him to be able, in principle, to influence the wage. But when the capital constraint set by bank lending is quite tight, he may not wish to exploit this monopsony power. In other words, his demand for labour is constrained by the size of the 'wages fund' to below the level to which it would be reduced, in the absence of capital constraints, in order to exercise monopsony power. The size of this wages fund is determined by the workers' wealth which is on deposit with the banks.

When the capital constraint is binding the merchant will need to be sure to exercise monopsony power against the banks, though. It is assumed for simplicity that, when the banks compete, the cost of borrowing, as measured by the real rate of interest, will be bid down to zero. This zero cost reflects the fact that the merchant's perfect judgement eliminates normal business risk. It also reflects the complete confidence of the banks (and their depositors) in their judgement about the borrower's qualities. It also means that the banks are unconcerned about the fact that, in lending to someone with no personal wealth, they are fully insuring him against the consequences of a bad decision. This implies that either they have complete confidence in the borrower's integrity as well as his judgement or they believe that the quality of his judgement is independent of the amount of deliberation and effort involved.

To exercise his monopsony power against the banks, the merchant must restrict his demand for borrowing to no more than the maximum the banks are able to lend. Otherwise he will begin to compete against himself. The rate of interest will rise until the cost of capital is so high that the merchant only just breaks even, and all the merchant's economic rent is dissipated. When the banks are in turn competing for workers' deposits, the rent will accrue to the workers instead.

The simplest case to analyse algebraically is one in which the supply of labour is infinitely elastic at a wage w^*:

$$a_1 = a_2 = w^* \tag{5.42}$$

Provided capital constraints prevent the sophisticated merchant from hiring everyone (so that the inelastic economy-wide supply of labour constrains him) the infinite elasticity of labour supply eliminates any monopsony power. His demand for labour is determined simply by his capital constraint. He exploits his monopsony power against the banks simply by requesting no more funds than they actually have available. This means that, in effect, he voluntarily restricts his demand for funds to the value of workers' wealth.

The unsophisticated merchants, it is assumed, have heterogeneous expectations, as in section 5.9, which they back using their personal wealth. Banks do not lend to unsophisticated merchants, and unsophisticated merchants do not put wealth on deposit with the banks. (It is easy to relax this assumption by supposing that those who choose not to participate at the wage w^* will deposit their funds with the banks instead.) The profitability of merchants' participation is not affected by the option of investing in bank deposits so long as bank deposits earn a zero return, so the demand for labour from unsophisticated merchants is exactly the same as before.

Given the elastic labour supply, the total demand for labour is also the equilibrium employment. It is readily deduced that equilibrium employment is

$$n_6^e = (s(1 - (w^*/p)) + (1 - s)\beta)(y/w^*) \tag{5.43}$$

where $\beta = 1$ if the next new industry project will be successful and $\beta = 0$ otherwise. The first component of (5.43) represents the familiar demand from unsophisticated merchants with heterogeneous expectations and the second component the demand from the sophisticated one.

The equilibrium is illustrated in Figure 5.7. (If the new industry is going to be unsuccessful then the sophisticated merchant does not participate and so the equilibrium is the same as in Figure 5.6.) When the sophisticated merchant does participate, he enters the labour market with a demand D_2D_2' determined by his borrowing constraint. (In the absence of a borrowing constraint his demand would be infinitely elastic at a wage OD_1, as indicated by the schedule D_1F.) His demand is superimposed on the demand from unsophisticated merchants D_1D_1' (corresponding to the schedule DD' in Figure 5.6) giving an aggregate demand for labour, obtained by horizontal summation, D_2D_3.

The infinitely elastic labour supply to the new industry is represented by the schedule A_1A_2. Equilibrium employment is determined at the intersection E_6 of D_2D_3 and A_1A_2. Employment offered by unsophisticated merchants is ON_u and by the sophisticated merchant ON_s. Profit per employee for the sophisticated merchant is measured by QM and his total profit is measured by the area of the shaded rectangle D_1QMA_1.

Given an expected frequency of successful outcomes π^*, the ability to avoid all loss making through perfect judgement produces an expected reward per employee $\pi^*(p - w)$, compared to the equivalent reward $\pi^*p - w$ earned by an ordinary optimist and a zero reward earned by a pessimist. The premium attributable to perfect judgement compared to ordinary optimism is therefore $w(1 - \pi^*)$ per employee.

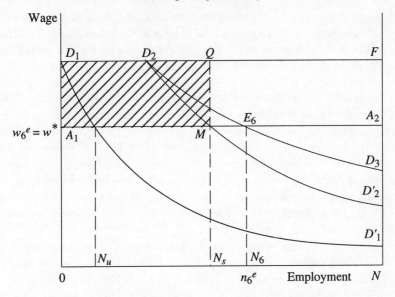

Figure 5.7 Equilibrium with a sophisticated merchant financed by the banking system

5.11 THE WIDER ISSUES

In the analysis of banking it was assumed that banks have a reputation for selecting entrepreneurial projects with unerring judgement. This implies that only those individuals with demonstrably perfect judgement can borrow from banks because banks can screen out everyone else. This in turn implies that entrepreneurial failures occur only because merchants who have personal wealth can avoid screening by banks. This is, of course, a very extreme view, which is untenable in practice. Banks do, of course, lend to entrepreneurs with less than perfect judgement, and occasionally serious banking failures do occur. The analysis nevertheless highlights some significant issues. In particular:

1. What determines the quality of entrepreneurial judgement? Are some entrepreneurs systematically better than others, or is better than average performance simply the result of a run of good luck?
2. If there are systematic factors promoting good judgement, then is it possible to identify these factors in order to single out talented entrepreneurs? Can entrepreneurial potential be developed through suitable training and life experience?

3. Is there any reason to believe that banks are better at making lending decisions than ordinary individuals? Is it really advantageous for individuals to deposit funds for banks to relend, rather than to lend themselves: for example, through direct investment in equities?

Casson (1982) argues that good judgement is partly a product of life experience. A wide range of employment experience, based on a career 'spiral' through varied jobs of increasing difficulty, is useful in giving the entrepreneur practice in synthesizing information from diverse sources. Migration may also provide a similar kind of varied experience. Personality is important too. A high degree of confidence helps the entrepreneur to cope with the stresses of decision making, while perseverance and ascetic lifestyle may be useful in surviving setbacks. Where high-level entrepreneurship is concerned, a rational scientific 'systems view' is useful as well.

High norms encourage achievement. People with low norms may perceive few problems and so develop few skills in decision making. The moral content of norms is particularly important, as the discussion of leadership in section 5.7 indicated. An entrepreneur with a reputation for personal integrity is more likely to be looked up to as an employer and to receive information freely from his employees. He is also more likely to be trusted by leaders and to find access to capital easier.

This suggests that education can improve entrepreneurship both by providing technical instruction – showing how to cope with complexity by adopting a 'systems view', for example – and by instilling moral values. It is sometimes suggested that the cultivation of individualism is an important moral factor, but this needs to be qualified by the fact that entrepreneurs frequently need to operate in a group. They need not only to lead social groups, such as teams of production workers, but also to participate in groups alongside political leaders, bankers and other entrepreneurs: for example, in coordinating national industrial policies. Excessive individualism can disrupt such group behaviour. What really seems to be required is an ethic of *voluntary association*, a willingness to choose between alternative group affiliations, but to develop commitment and loyalty to a group once it has been joined.

It is quite possible, in principle, to screen for qualities of this kind. Life histories can be obtained and checked (a common recruitment procedure), attitudes can be sampled through interview, and even participation in simulated problem situations can be invoked. The main danger is that the candidate knows the qualities being screened for and can outwit the assessor. Such astuteness is by no means universal, however. Moreover, the problem may not be as acute as it seems, since the ability to discover and then impersonate the qualities other people want is a kind of entrepreneurial ability itself.

One obvious reason why banks may develop expertise in screening is that they have a wide range of relevant experience. Although a bank may lack technical expertise in the area in which the entrepreneur has formulated his project, it may be able to substitute personality assessment for assessment of the project itself (Harper, 1990). Repeated use of personality assessment may allow bank managers to form quite sophisticated judgements about borrowers. Equity investors, by contrast, normally have to rely on media commentaries and annual reports for their information, although professional investors may use stock-brokers' reports as well. Thus the view that bank deposits are safer than equity investments because they benefit from access to greater expertise may well be true. Moreover, bank investments are more likely to be protected by government rescue in the event of failure than are personal equity stakes.

5.12 CONCLUSION

Some of the greatest thinkers in the social sciences – Cantillon, Hayek, Knight and Schumpeter, amongst others – have contributed to the development of the economic theory of the entrepreneur. Until recently the theory has been artic-ulated mainly in verbal terms. This chapter has attempted to show how many of the insights can be captured in a simple model. Like all economic models, drastic simplifications are made in order to purify the analysis of all but the key effects. The model is nevertheless sufficiently versatile to encompass several important dimensions of entrepreneurship.

It has been argued that the key service supplied by entrepreneurs is quality of judgement. A capacity for absolutely correct judgement is often unique, and affords monopoly or monopsony rents to the entrepreneur. Other successful entre-preneurs may simply be individuals disposed to optimism in a situation where optimism is on balance appropriate.

Even where expectations are homogeneous, entrepreneurs can earn a reward because of their greater tolerance of risk. In the model above, the expected reward of the marginal entrepreneur is just sufficient to compensate him for the risk involved.

In an idealized world, entrepreneurial ideas could simply be licensed through competitive bidding to other people who would exploit them. But the limita-tions of the patent system are such that the licensing of ideas is impracticable. Entrepreneurs must exploit their own ideas, and this draws them into the management of teams. The firm comes into being as a nexus of contracts – notably, though not exclusively, contracts of employment. The entrepreneur must choose between leadership and supervision as a method of motivating the firm's employees. The entrepreneur becomes more than just a speculator or arbitrager; he becomes a leader and a manager as well.

It has been emphasized that the model developed in this chapter is a very flexible one. It is, therefore, a suitable tool for the entrepreneurial academic who wishes to adapt it to analyse issues besides the ones addressed here. It is particularly suitable for researchers in the recently revitalized areas of small-firm growth, industrial policy and international competitiveness, as well as for scholars seeking stronger intellectual foundations for business and economic history. It is therefore to be hoped that further extensions of the model will be developed in due course.

REFERENCES

Aoki, M., B. Gustafsson and O.E. Williamson (eds)(1990) *The Firm as a Nexus of Treaties*, London: Sage.

Azariadis, C. (1975) Implicit Contracts and Underemployment Equilibria, *Journal of Political Economy*, **83**, 1183–1201.

Babbage, C. (1832) *On the Economy of Machinery and Manufactures*, London: C. Knight.

Cannan, E. (1893) *A History of the Theories of Production and Distribution in English Political Economy from 1776 to 1848*, London: Percival.

Cantillon, R. (1755) *Essai sur la Nature du Commerce en Général* (ed. H. Higgs), London: Macmillan, 1931.

Casson, M.C. (1982) *The Entrepreneur: An Economic Theory*, Oxford: Martin Robertson.

Coase, R.H. (1937) The Nature of the Firm, *Economica* (new series), **4**, 386–405.

Harper, D. (1990) The Process of Interpersonal Criticism with the External Capital Market, mimeo, New Zealand Institute of Economic Research, Wellington.

Hayek, F.A. (1937) Economics and Knowledge, *Economica* (new series), **4**, 33–54; reprinted in F.A. Hayek, *Individualism and Economic Order*, London: Routledge and Kegan Paul (1959), 77–91.

Kaldor, N. (1934) The Equilibrium of the Firm, *Economic Journal*, **44**, 60–76.

Kihlstrom, R.E. and J.J. Laffont (1979) A General Equilibrium Entrepreneurial Theory of Firm Formation based on Risk Aversion, *Journal of Political Economy*, **87**, 719–48.

Kirzner, I.M. (1973) *Competition and Entrepreneurship*, Chicago: University of Chicago Press.

Kirzner, I.M. (1979) *Perception, Opportunity and Profit*, Chicago: University of Chicago Press.

Knight, F.H. (1921) *Risk, Uncertainty and Profit* (ed. G.J. Stigler), Chicago: University of Chicago Press (1971).

Mises, L. von (1949) *Human Action: A Treatise on Economics*, London: William Hodge.

Schumpeter, J.A. (1934) *The Theory of Economic Development*, Cambridge, Mass.: Harvard University Press.

Schumpeter, J.A. (1939) *Business Cycles: A Theoretical, Historical and Statistical Analysis of the Capitalist Process*, New York: McGraw-Hill.

6.   Cultural factors in innovation

6.1   INTRODUCTION

The economic significance of culture has been widely recognized in historical and institutional economics, but almost totally ignored in neoclassical economics (see Chapter 2 and Chapter 4). Pioneering economic sociologists such as Weber (1978) and Pareto (1916) were acutely aware of the cultural framing of individual decisions. They recognized, for example, that the preferences revealed in the demand for goods represent notions of what is right and wrong, and not just of what is desirable and what is not. They appreciated that the factual information on which people act is seriously incomplete, and that the gaps are filled by beliefs acquired from society as a whole (Giddens, 1987). Many of the beliefs which frame an individual's perceptions of constraints are fundamental untested beliefs based on tradition and revelation rather than scientific proof. Their authority derives from the social elites who espouse them rather than from the critical judgement of the individuals concerned.

The marginalization and eventual exclusion of culture from neoclassical economic models can be explained in both ideological and instrumental terms. The political conflict between socialism and liberalism, and between interventionism and *laissez-faire*, polarized early twentieth-century intellectuals between individualist and collectivist views of society. Collectivists embraced culture to give substance to their analysis of conflict between socioeconomic classes, whilst individualists rejected it as superfluous, given the harmonious coordination of anonymous individuals effected by the impersonal market process. Culture was useful to the collectivists in explaining how the 'free-rider' problem was overcome in sustaining group solidarity. But culture seemed to have no corresponding instrumental value in market models; indeed, the interdependence of preferences suggested by the cultural view seemed to be an unnecessary complication which should be avoided at all costs.

The growing intellectual dominance of the individualistic view in the post-war world thus relegated culture to a peripheral role in economics, a mere label to be applied indiscriminately to the residual effects that remained once simple 'economic' explanations of some phenomenon had been exhausted. But as the scope of market activity widened under the influence of individualistic attitudes, market failures became more conspicuous and transaction costs emerged as the main cause of the problem.

Transaction costs have an important cultural dimension. Formal contracts rely for enforcement on a legal system which is itself a cultural artefact. Informal contracts sealed with a handshake depend crucially on a sense of mutual obligation between the parties. The dilemma for those neoclassical economists who favour a totally rational view of human action is that, while it is obviously rational for an individual to defend their rights, it is not so obvious why they should uphold their obligations too.

To rationalize obligation it is necessary to take a more imaginative view of human motivation than that encapsulated in the conventional utility function, with its Benthamite emphasis on selfish and materialistic rewards. Emotional rewards engendered by moral integrity can be introduced as well (Etzioni, 1988). Utility analysis has already been generalized by Akerlof (1980), Frank (1985) and Jones (1984) to rationalize a wide range of social behaviour.

Culture can be regarded as a common factor weighting the various emotional rewards experienced by members of a social group. Culture can reinforce natural feelings of obligation – to be honest, to be loyal, to work hard – and so improve interpersonal coordination within a group. Individualists who wrongly dismiss culture as an unfortunate legacy of primitive customs ignore its potential as an economic asset. When culture is well adapted to the economic environment it improves economic performance by eliminating externalities and reducing transaction costs: it becomes, in fact, an intangible public good.

Culture can adapt to the environment through various mechanisms. Following earlier chapters, it is assumed below that each social group has a leader who makes a conscious decision to manipulate the preferences of his followers in order to maximize the performance of the group. He optimizes the functional characteristics of the culture by equating the marginal benefit of improved coordination between the followers with the marginal cost of manipulation involved. This is a simple, if rather contrived, way of making culture the subject of testable hypotheses. Not everyone who believes in the importance of culture will necessarily agree that this is the appropriate methodology to establish its economic relevance. But it nevertheless provides a rigorous framework within which to derive some plausible and interesting results.

6.2   SCHUMPETERIAN INNOVATION

The particular focus of this chapter is the impact of culture on innovation. Schumpeter was emphatic that non-hedonistic motives are important in innovation. He writes of 'the dream and the will to found a private kingdom, usually, though not necessarily, also a dynasty. (...) Then there is the will to conquer: the impulse to fight, to prove oneself superior to others, to succeed for the sake, not of the fruits of success, but of success itself. (...) Finally, there is the joy of creating' (Schumpeter, 1934, p. 91).

Schumpeter recognizes that such motives could, in principle, be included in the utility function, but does not believe that this would be very useful because he is thinking only of the role of utility in the derivation of demand. Were he thinking instead of the influence of utility on the supply of effort he might have decided otherwise, for he later remarks that the efforts which entrepreneurs dedicate to their businesses cannot be explained purely by expected material rewards.

Schumpeter also recognizes the influence of culture on these non-hedonistic motives. He notes

> that it is society that shapes the particular desires that we observe; that wants must be taken with reference to the group which the individual thinks of when deciding his course of action – the family or any group, smaller or larger than the family ... that the field of individual choice is always, though in very different ways and to very different degrees, fenced in by social habits or conventions and the like. (Schumpeter, 1934, p. 91)

Schumpeter feels, however, that the entrepreneur may well be different from this norm: the entrepreneur is more likely to set the culture of the group than to be influenced by it. He views the entrepreneur as having relatively autonomous preferences, and enjoying a high-profile role which allows him to influence the behaviour of the group.

This chapter amplifies this view in two respects. First, it argues that the entrepreneur's leadership role is logically quite distinct from his role in discovering opportunities and combining the resources required for innovation. This leadership role can be understood only by recognizing that, so far as employees are concerned, the firm is not only an economic unit but also a social group.

Secondly, the entrepreneur is seen, not as entirely autonomous, but as a product of a wider society in which social, political and religious leaders influence everyone's preferences. As a result, non-hedonistic motivations may vary quite significantly between countries. Schumpeter's approach emphasizes intra-country differences which lead some individuals to become entrepreneurs and others not. Inter-country differences, on the other hand, can explain why some countries generate a disproportionately large number of entrepreneurs and hence come to dominate other groups in the organization of trade and in the pace of technological innovation.

6.3 OTHER ISSUES IN INNOVATION

Professional Scientific Culture

Cultural factors are relevant to innovation even where it is not in the hands of traditional Schumpeterian entrepreneurs but in those of scientific employees.

Scientists and engineers have their own professional allegiances and share a sub-culture which needs to be respected by the top management of the firm (Buckley and Casson, 1992). Successful innovation in high-technology industries such as office equipment and pharmaceuticals depends crucially on reconciling the scientific cultures of the researchers with the corporate culture of the general management team (Casson, Pearce and Singh, 1991).

Cultures cannot be reconciled simply by standardizing everyone on a hedonistic culture which links pecuniary reward to hard objective measures of performance. Top scientists, like Schumpeterian entrepreneurs, do not do their best work just for the money, or even for the status, but for a curiosity-driven desire to solve a problem to their own satisfaction. A manager who believes that incentiviz-ing innovation is simply a matter of 'fine-tuning' monetary rewards is likely to be disappointed by the results.

Cartel Cheating

Another issue connected with Schumpeterian innovation is the role of informal cartels in assuring temporary monopoly profits. Schumpeter (1942, ch. 8) believed that investment in major new plant, new methods of organization and new product development benefited from some attenuation of competition. Price may need to be maintained above marginal cost even when imitation has occurred, and also in recession, where price warfare could eliminate the profits required to fund continuing R & D. In this way he perceived short run price stability generated by an informal cartel as promoting long-run competition.

Cartels can create a Prisoner's Dilemma, however, in which it pays to cheat whether or not the other members are honest. A culture which emotionally penalizes cheating may help to enforce the cartel price. Such a culture could involve a class-based ethic of loyalty to the business group. The advantage of the emotional mechanism in this context is that it can be self-enforcing. Cartel cheating is notoriously difficult to detect. Emotional penalties triggered by the cheat's self-knowledge work even if the cheating cannot be detected by other members of the cartel. This can avoid expenditure on a central sales organiz-ation and on regular factory inspections, which a distrustful cartel membership may otherwise require.

The Supply of Entrepreneurs

In a long-run context, entrepreneurship involves prospecting for profit oppor-tunities (Kirzner, 1979). If at any time there is a finite set of opportunities then an increase in the number of entrepreneurs increases the chances of multiple discovery. This has two implications. First, the marginal social benefit of entre-preneurship diminishes, even where entrepreneurs are of equal ability, because the probability that what the marginal entrepreneur discovers would have been discovered anyway increases. If multiple discoverers share the rewards then new entrants can effectively force incumbents to part with rewards that otherwise they would have kept for themselves. The private return to the marginal entrepreneur therefore exceeds the marginal social benefit, and so excess entry occurs.

The second implication is that, if entrepreneurs cannot fully appropriate the social value of their discoveries, then a compensating reduction in the supply of entrepreneurship may take place. This can occur either because the entrepreneur cannot bargain effectively with workers and consumers, or because of competition engendered by multiple discovery.

The supply of entrepreneurs may therefore be either above or below the social optimum. In theory taxes and subsidies, or a system of licensing entrepreneurs, could be used to tackle this problem, but in practice the administrative problems are too great. A system of emotional rewards and penalties is likely to be more effective, though. These rewards and penalties can be linked to the social status of an entrepreneurial career. They can be 'fine-tuned' to achieve optimal entry into entrepreneurship.

6.4 AN ECONOMIC THEORY OF BUSINESS CULTURE

Three key issues in innovation have now been identified: the motivation of salaried scientists and engineers, the maintenance of cartel solidarity and the supply of entrepreneurs. To analyse all these issues in a single chapter it is useful to embed them within the general model of cultural manipulation outlined above (see Chapter 2 and Casson, 1991). This model assumes that all individuals receive two sources of reward: conventional material rewards, typically derived from purchases in the market place, and emotional rewards derived from personal relationships within the group. Each individual maximizes the sum of material and emotional rewards. The intensity of emotional rewards can be manipulated by the leader of the group, whereas the intensity of material rewards cannot (see Table 6.1).

The principal emotional reward is respect. An individual who is respected enjoys peace of mind, as described in Chapter 1. Respect can be received from oneself (an inward-directed emotion), from peers within the group (an outward-directed emotion) and from the leader (an upward-directed emotion). In each case respect is earned by being seen to make choices which are endorsed by the leader. The stronger is the leader's endorsement, the greater is the emotional intensity experienced by a member of the group. A skilful leader may be able to extend the subjective boundaries of the group from which members derive respect. Future generations may be introduced, so that individuals become concerned with the magnitude of their bequests and the way that history will judge their actions. Past generations can also be imaginatively introduced: ancestors, and even tribal gods, may be visualized as passing judgement on one's actions. Finally, there is the influence of religion itself, and in particular the judgement of an all-seeing Calvinistic God (Weber, 1930).

Table 6.1   Nature of rewards in conventional and modified theories

	Causality	
Nature of reward	Autonomous	Manipulable
Material	Conventional hedonistic model	—
Emotional	—	Cultural model

By emphasizing emotional penalties as well as emotional rewards, a powerful system of sanctions can be developed. This emotional incentive system can promote innovation by placing an emotional tax on someone who cheats in a cartel, or fails to supply effort in an R & D team. Similarly, a sense of honour in the choice of an entrepreneurial career can subsidize the supply of entrepreneurs when material rewards are too low.

Emotional sanctions have a major advantage over conventional pecuniary sanctions enforced through a formal legal system, namely that they can be self-monitoring and/or self-enforcing. The various possibilities are illustrated in Table 6.2. Each cell in the table contains a pair of entries in which a positive emotion appears on the left and a corresponding negative emotion on the right. Other things being equal, the use of positive sanctions will generate higher levels of welfare than the use of negative sanctions. Emotions such as pride and guilt are based on self-observation; they do not require other people to know of one's actions in order for the emotion to be felt. By contrast, honour and shame reflect one's perception of what other people know and think about one's actions, but, like pride and guilt, they reflect a response to what is known, rather than to what is actually said. On the other hand, emotions aroused by congratulation and humiliation reflect what other people have actually said or done in response to one's action, rather than simply what they know.

Different cultures emphasize different sanctions. The most efficient from an economic point of view appear to be pride and guilt, because they do not require the intervention of other people at all. Compared to pecuniary incentives they avoid the need for another party to monitor actions and implement the penalties and rewards. Some sanctions may not be so intensely felt as others, though. For example, guilt may be more difficult to arouse than a sense of shame. If this is the case, shame may be more efficient than guilt, even though it depends on peer-group observation, because it is an easier emotion to arouse. A similar point explains why negative as well as positive emotions are employed. Other things being equal, positive emotions will generate higher levels of welfare, but if they are more difficult to arouse then on balance negative sanctions may be chosen because they are a stronger deterrent.

Table 6.2   Typology of emotional sanctions

	Observation by	
Enforcement of sanction by	Self	Others
Self	Pride, guilt	Honour, shame
Others		Congratulation, humiliation, bonus*, fine*

Notes:
Entries are (reward, penalty).

* Indicates a *monitoring* as opposed to manipulative approach.

The focus in this chapter is on the emotions of pride and guilt. Emotional incentives are contrasted with material incentives – bonuses and fines – as specified in contracts, policed through monitoring systems and enforced by law. It is shown that emotional incentives can be much more effective than material ones, particularly in small groups.

The leader manipulates the intensity of emotions on behalf of the stakeholders in the group. Where the social group in question is a firm, the traditional Schumpeterian entrepreneur appears as both stakeholder (an owner with a controlling equity interest) and leader (a manipulator of morale amongst his employees). By contrast modern industry has evolved a functional separation of these roles, at least in the large firm sector, so that the leadership role is carried out on behalf of the shareholders by a salaried chief executive. Since this separation gives both analytical clarity and contemporary realism, it is assumed to hold in the models below.

A further assumption is that a leader arouses emotions in his followers by conspicuously sacrificing resources to a worthwhile cause. This cause is promoted as the moral mission of the group. The sacrifice gives credibility to the leader's moral rhetoric and thereby elicits a sense of obligation in the followers. Individual actions which further the group's objective then carry a net emotional reward (relative to actions that do not). Thus the leader of a research team who commits resources to basic research of no commercial value emphasizes the intrinsic value of research work and thereby endorses a no-shirking strategy by researchers. The fact that the research is of no commercial value emphasizes the nature of the commitment. The resources are provided by the stakeholders because it is they that will benefit from the improved performance elicited by the researchers' emotional response.

6.5   MOTIVATING TEAMWORK IN R & D

The influence of leadership on the performance of a research team may be formally analysed as follows. Readers not interested in the mathematics should study the following paragraph and then proceed to the discussion of Figure 6.2 (p. 143).

Chain of Responsibility

A private firm employs a research team to generate a patentable innovation to be sold under licence. The profit-maximizing owner (that is, the stakeholder) can choose between two mutually exclusive methods of motivation: (i) manipulation: a leader is hired to endorse hard work amongst team members; (ii) monitoring: a supervisor is hired to monitor team members and ensure that they receive no pay if they do not work hard.

The owner decides which method to use. He also fixes the wage rate and employment level. The leader (if hired) decides the amount of resources committed to basic research. The leader also has a manipulative capability that the owners do not have. For simplicity the leader's salary payment is ignored. The situation is summarized in Figure 6.1.

Technology: Engineering and Effort

When everyone works hard there are constant returns to team size up to a maximum size N, after which marginal returns fall to zero. Thus a team size of $n^3 \geq 0$ generates an output of value

$$y = \left\{ \begin{array}{ll} an & 0 \leq n \leq N \\ aN & n > N \end{array} \right. \tag{6.1}$$

if each member works hard, and zero otherwise. The productivity parameter $a > 0$ is fixed. All team members have identical preferences and face identical incentives, and hence they either all work hard or all slack. Thus the crime rate q, which measures the incidence of slacking, takes only the values zero or one.

This means, incidentally, that it is of no consequence whether members' efforts are strictly complementary or not.

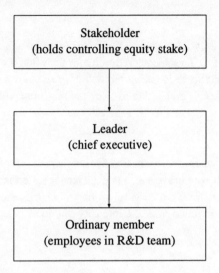

Figure 6.1 Chain of responsibility

Each member receives a wage $w > 0$ and incurs a cost of effort $e > 0$. The owner seeks to maximize expected profit

$$\pi = (1 - q)y - wn - h_1 \tag{6.2}$$

where $h_1 \geq 0$ is the cost incurred in controlling slacking. The subscript 1 is used to identify the ethic of pure research.

The Group Objective

The leader maximizes

$$v = \pi + \theta_1 z_1 \tag{6.3}$$

where z_1 is the quantity of pure research output of no commercial value and $\theta_1 \geq 0$ is the intensity of endorsement.

Pure research output can be generated only by hiring additional resources at a user cost $b_1 > 0$. These resources generate output under diminishing marginal returns, such that the total input required is equal to the square of the output. Thus the costs of pure research are

$$h_1 = b_1 z_1^{2} \tag{6.4}$$

The Leader's Decision

Employees assess the leader's commitment to the group objective by observing the chosen value of z_1. To achieve credibility for the value θ_1 that he is claiming, the leader must maximize v, *taking the values of q and w as given*. Substituting (6.1), (6.2) and (6.4) into (6.3) and using the first-order condition on z_1 gives

$$\theta_1^{e} = 2bz_1 \tag{6.5}$$

Thus the intensity of endorsement that the employees infer is directly proportional to the quantity of pure research that the leader undertakes. Using equation (6.5) to eliminate z_1 from equation (6.4) shows that the leader's manipulation costs are a quadratic function of the intensity of endorsement

$$h_1^{e} = \theta_1^{2}/4b_1 \tag{6.6}$$

Equation (6.6) can, if desired, be used on its own without the preliminary derivation from (6.3) – (6.5), since it is only (6.6) that affects subsequent results.

Note that, in equation (6.6), b_1 enters *inversely* into h_1^{e}: the more expensive the resource inputs, the smaller the expenditure required. This reflects the fact that, when making a gesture, such as a symbolic sacrifice, a small amount of something expensive has a more powerful effect than a large amount of something cheap.

Employee Preferences

Each employee values commitment to research, because when he feels part of the collective effort he receives an emotional bonus φ_1. The value of this bonus, in material equivalents, is

$$\varphi_1 = sj_1 l\theta_1/n \tag{6.7}$$

where $s > 0$ is individual sensitivity, and is a property of the population from which team members are drawn; $j_1 > 0$ is the relevance of the leader's ethic to the individual's commitment to hard work, and is a property of the specific ethic employed; and $l > 0$ is the leader's ability in terms of the intensity of emotion he can arouse from a given intensity of endorsement.

Team size n enters inversely into φ_1 on the grounds that identification with the collective effort diminishes as the size of the team increases. Taken as a whole, equation (6.7) shows that emotional rewards depend on the interplay of population-specific, leader-specific, ethic-specific and team-specific factors.

Employee Decisions: the Interaction of Occupational Choice and Shirking

The employee's best alternative employment offers a wage $w^* \geq 0$, and requires hard work. The employee's total utility is

$$u = \begin{cases} w - e + \varphi_1 & \text{from hard work} \\ w & \text{from slacking} \\ w^* - e & \text{from alternative employment.} \end{cases} \tag{6.8}$$

The optimal decision rule is to work hard if

$$\varphi_1 \geq e \tag{6.9}$$

and

$$\varphi_1 \geq w^* - w \tag{6.10}$$

where weak inequalities are used for mathematical convenience. Other aspects of the decision are of no interest, for reasons indicated below.

The Owner's Decisions: Setting the Wage

So far as a profit-maximizing owner is concerned, it is best to close down the firm if the employees will not work hard, and so the firm will operate only if condition (6.9) is satisfied. Since a positive θ_1 implies a sacrifice of profit, it is best to satisfy (6.9) exactly. Since high wages reduce profit it is also best to satisfy (6.10) exactly. Thus assuming the firm operates instead of closing down, the employer will set

$$\theta_1^e = en/sj_1l \tag{6.11}$$

$$w^e = w^* - e \tag{6.12}$$

giving (with $q = 0$),

$$\pi^e = (a - w^* + e)n - (e^2/4s^2j_1^2l^2b_1)n^2 \tag{6.13}$$

Comparative static analysis applied to (6.11) indicates that commitment to the group objective will be stronger the greater is the cost of effort and the larger the size of team. It will be lower the greater the sensitivity of the population, the more appropriate the ethic and the more able the leader. Equation (6.12) indicates that the wage is independent of the precise manipulation strategy and dependent only on alternative earnings and the cost of effort. This is because the emotional benefit of hard work is fine-tuned to just offset the cost involved.

The Owner's Decisions: the Monitoring Alternative

Supervision, it is assumed, incurs a constant marginal cost per employee $m \geq 0$. Unlike leadership, supervision affords no emotional benefits. A supervisor who catches an employee slacking imposes a fine, $f > 0$. It is assumed that detection of slackers is complete. Thus the employee's total utility is

$$u = \begin{cases} w - e & \text{from hard work} \\ w - f & \text{from slacking} \\ w^* - e & \text{from alternative employment} \end{cases} \tag{6.14}$$

The optimal decision rule is to work hard if

$$f \geq e \tag{6.15}$$

and

$$w \geq w^* \tag{6.16}$$

It is assumed that f is always sufficiently large for (6.15) to be satisfied. Since high wages reduce profits, it pays the employer to satisfy (6.16) exactly:

$$w^e = w^* \tag{6.17}$$

Using (6.17) it can be seen that, provided $w^* \geq e$ (that is, provided that the best alternative employment is at least as good as no employment), a fine equivalent to receiving no pay ($f = w$) will always be sufficient to deter slacking.

Under monitoring, profit is

$$\pi^e = (a - w^* - m)n \tag{6.18}$$

It is assumed that $m < a - w^*$, so that under monitoring team size will always expand to N. Comparing (6.13) and (6.18) shows that manipulation is preferred to monitoring if team size is less than the critical level

$$n^* = 4s^2j_1{}^2l^2b_1(m + e)/e^2 \tag{6.19}$$

If $n^* \geq N$ then manipulation will be preferred, and the owners will optimize the size of team by applying a first-order condition to (6.13), giving

$$n^e = 2s^2j_1{}^2l^2b_1(a - w^* + e)/e^2 \tag{6.20}$$

and

$$\pi^e(n^e) = [(a - w^* + e)/sj_1l]^2/b_1 \tag{6.21}$$

If $n^* < N$ then manipulation may still be preferred, but only if

$$\pi^e(n^e) \geq \pi^e(N)$$

that is, if and only if

$$N \leq (a - w^* + e)^2e^2/(a - w^* - m)s^2j_1{}^2l^2b_1 \tag{6.22}$$

Discussion

The solutions (6.19) and (6.20) are illustrated in Figure 6.2. The choice of optimal strategy for given team size depends upon whether monitoring or manipulation offers the lowest average cost. The average cost of manipulation AC_1 increases with team size whereas the average cost of monitoring AC_2 does not. The intersection F of AC_1 and AC_2 determines the critical team size n^*, below which manipulation is preferred. Note that when manipulation is preferred it is always for the smaller size of team. This is a direct consequence of the assumption that the intensity of emotional benefits diminishes with respect to the size of team. Thus, as research teams grow, formal methods of monitoring tend to replace informal methods of manipulation.

When manipulation is chosen, the optimal team size n_1^e is set at E, the intersection of the upward-sloping marginal cost of manipulation MC_1 and the discontinuous horizontal marginal revenue schedule MR. On the other hand, when monitoring is chosen the optimal team size n_2^e is set at G, the intersection of MR and the horizontal marginal cost of monitoring schedule MC_2. Provided the firm does not shut down, this implies the choice of the maximum size of team, N. Thus monitoring and manipulation are associated with different sizes of team.

The figure illustrates the case $n^* < N$, which means that manipulation will be chosen only if the gains associated with the lower wage rate, measured by the horizontally shaded area $JKLM$, outweigh the costs associated with using a smaller size of team, as measured by the vertically shaded area $EHGJ$. The higher are the costs of monitoring, the more likely it is that this condition will be satisfied.

Partial differentiation of the equations shows that under manipulation the optimal size of research team increases with the sensitivity of the population, the relevance of the ethic, the ability of the leader, the cost of pure research inputs and the value of patented output. It decreases with respect to the cost of effort and the market wage rate (but not because of diminishing marginal physical productivity, as in conventional theory).

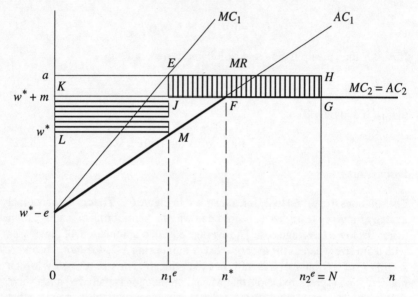

Note: 1 refers to manipulation strategy; 2 refers to monitoring strategy.

Figure 6.2   Simultaneous determination of motivation strategy and size of team

The same sort of results apply to the critical team size. As the optimal intensity of manipulation increases the costs of manipulation also rise and so monitoring is more likely to be preferred instead. The only new point is the obvious one that high costs of monitoring offset high costs of manipulation and increase the maximum size of team to which manipulation is applied.

6.6   CARTEL SOLIDARITY

Cartel solidarity is a general issue which just happens to have a bearing on innovation. Its particular interest is that it highlights the possibility that entrepreneurs not only manipulate their employees but also manipulate each other.

Chain of Responsibility

It is assumed that successful R & D effort has already generated a patented innovation which is to be exploited through licensing. The licensor's aim is to maximize the value of his licence by controlling spatial competition amongst licensees. The licensor, as stakeholder, can hire a charismatic leader who will preach an ethic of loyalty to the licensees' cartel. Credibility is achieved by a sacrifice of resources funded by the licensor. It is assumed that it generates a quadratic cost of manipulation as before (see equation (6.6)):

$$h_2 = \theta_2^2/4b_2 \tag{6.23}$$

where the subscript 2 means that now the ethic of loyalty is involved.

The Incentive to Cheat

The model of spatial competition used is the standard one, with two licensees located at either end of a unit line along which buyers are uniformly distributed (Tirole, 1988, ch. 7). The role of the licensees is fully symmetric: each has a constant marginal cost of production $c > 0$. Customers demand one unit of the product only, with reservation price p^*; they collect the product themselves, incurring a transport cost $t > 0$ per unit product and unit distance. For notational simplicity the number of customers is normalized to unity.

The licensor announces a price P which the licensees are supposed to implement. It is assumed that the price is set to 'cover the market': it is not so high that a customer mid-way between the licensees refuses to buy, that is,

$$P \le p^* - (t/2) \tag{6.24}$$

It is, on the other hand, set sufficiently high for either licensee to be able to afford to cover the market on his own:

$$P \ge c + t \tag{6.25}$$

Each licensee can cheat on the announced price without detection. It is easily shown that he has an incentive to do so. If the production cost c is very low, it may pay to drop the price so far that the other licensee is expelled from the market altogether. This possibility is ruled out by assuming that

$$P \le c + 3t \tag{6.26}$$

When the licensee located at $x = 0$ cheats his honest partner located at $x = 1$ then the marginal customer located at

$$x^e = (P - c - t)/4t \qquad (6.27)$$

pays a price

$$p^e = (P + c + t)/2 \qquad (6.28)$$

Equation (6.28) is the familiar Bertrand response function. The gross profits accruing to the licensees (both cheat and victim) are shown in Table 6.3. The bottom line of the table includes an adjustment for the guilt incurred by cheating, which is explained later on. It can be seen that, in the absence of guilt, the licensees face a Prisoner's Dilemma, in which it pays to cheat whether or not the opponent cheats. The only equilibrium is one of mutual cheating.

The equilibrium shown assumes that a cheat derives his strategy on the assumption that his opponent will be honest, an assumption which is, of course, falsified by the outcome. If a cheat correctly anticipates that his price will always be matched then price will converge on the Bertrand equilibrium instead:

$$p^b = c + t \qquad (6.29)$$

This is the rational consequence of mutual distrust.

Table 6.3   Rewards to the licensees

Strategy	Opponent's strategy	
	Honest	Cheat
Honest	$(P - c)/2$	$(P - c + t)/4 - ((P - c - t)^2/4t)$
Cheat	$(P - c)/2 + ((P - c - t)^2/8t) - \varphi_2$	$(P - c + t)/4 - \varphi_2$

Licensor's strategy

Suppose that the licensor can extract all the rents accruing to the licensees by setting an appropriate lump sum fee before they commence operation. The licensees' willingness to pay will be determined by their expectation of the actual price p, which is assumed to be correct. The licensor's revenue from fees is therefore

$$r = p - c \qquad (6.30)$$

The maximum revenue is obtained when both licensees are honest in upholding a price which is just sufficient to cover the market; that is,

$$p = P \tag{6.31}$$

where, using (6.24),

$$P = p^* - (t/2) \tag{6.32}$$

Applying (6.25) to (6.28) and (6.29) shows that

$$p^b < p^e < P \tag{6.33}$$

for any permitted value of P, so cheating dissipates total rent and should be avoided if possible.

Suppose that, in the absence of monitoring, the leader employed by the licensor can associate guilt with cheating. The intensity of guilt is determined, by analogy with equation (6.7), by

$$\varphi_2 = sj_2/\theta_2 \tag{6.34}$$

It is assumed that the penalty φ_2 applies whether or not the opponent cheats, because the ethic links guilt to the intention to cheat, independently of the outcome.

Referring to the one-shot game reported in Table 6.3, a level of guilt

$$\varphi_2 \geq (P - c - t)^2/8t \tag{6.35}$$

ensures that mutual honesty becomes an equilibrium, as well as mutual cheating. A credible leader may be able to engineer this equilibrium by announcing that, in his opinion, both licensees are honest for, given an expectation of the opponent's honesty, honesty is the best response.

If the licensor wishes to ensure that mutual honesty is achieved irrespective of whether the announcement is believed, the critical value of φ_2 is doubled. If

$$\varphi_2 \geq (P - c - t)^2/4t \tag{6.36}$$

then a licensee will prefer to be honest even if he is sure that he will be cheated, and so the honesty equilibrium becomes unique. The cost of ensuring that (6.36) is exactly satisfied can be deduced from (6.23) and (6.34):

$$h_2 = (P - c - t)^4/b_2(8 \, sj_2lt)^2 \tag{6.37}$$

The licensor maximizes profit

$$\pi = r - h_2 \tag{6.38}$$

where both r and h_2 depend upon P. The profit-maximizing manipulation strategy is obtained from the first-order condition with respect to P. The optimal value of the cartel price is

$$p^e = p^b + 2(2s^2 j_2^2 l^2 t^2 b)^{\frac{1}{3}} \tag{6.39}$$

which varies directly with the sensitivity of the licensees, the relevance of the loyalty ethic, the charismatic quality of the business leader and the cost of the resources he commits to the common cause. It also varies directly with the unit transport cost. The impact of these different variables can, in principle, be tested using cross-industry and cross-country comparisons of cartel pricing, although the difficulty of quantifying the determinants imposes a significant limitation.

Note that when manipulation is prohibitively expensive because, for example, sensitivity is zero, the price that prevails is the Bertrand price. This indicates that conventional theory is a special case of this more general one. The more general insight is that, in addition to production cost and transport cost, it is the quality of the business culture that determines the cartel price.

6.7   THE SUPPLY OF ENTREPRENEURS

The last of the three formal models concerns entrepreneurs prospecting for profit opportunities. It is a very naive model, in which in each period one idea of value $\pi > 0$ is hidden in one of several equally probable places. Each entrepreneur can search one place per period and has a probability $z(0 < z < 1)$ of finding it. The probability that a given entrepreneur will make a discovery is indicated in Table 6.4, while the implications of this result for a population of $n > 0$ entrepreneurs is indicated in Table 6.5. It can be seen that when z is small (as assumed here) the probability of multiple discovery depends (approximately) on the square of n, and hence rises sharply as the size of the population increases. When multiple discovery results in the total dissipation of profit through competitive exploitation of the idea, this has important incentive effects on the supply of entrepreneurs.

Table 6.4   Probabilities of discovery for an individual entrepreneur

Outcome	Probability
No discovery	$1 - z$
Unique discovery	$z(1 - z)^{n-1}$
Multiple discovery	$z(1-(1 - z)^{n-1})$

Socially Optimal Supply of Entrepreneurs.

Suppose that even with sole discovery only a proportion of λ_1 of the social benefit π accrues to the entrepreneur, while with multiple discovery only a proportion λ_2 of what a single entrepreneur would obtain is shared between the entrepreneurs ($0 \leq \lambda_1, \lambda_2 \leq 1$). The stakeholders, who are the political electorate, are assumed to agree on the maximization of the expected surplus

$$y = (\beta_1 + \beta_2)\pi - wn \qquad (6.40)$$

where β_1 and β_2 are the respective probabilities of single and multiple discovery as defined in Table 6.5, and the wage $w > 0$ represents the opportunity cost of becoming an entrepreneur. It is assumed that electors and entrepreneurs are risk-neutral and that entrepreneurs are all of equal ability and in perfectly elastic supply. Complications arising from the fact that entrepreneurs, as electors, have a vested interest are ignored.

Table 6.5   Probabilities of discovery for a population of entrepreneurs

Number making discovery	Probability	Quadratic approximation
0	$(1 - z)^n$	$\beta_0 = 1 - z(1 -(z/2))n - (z^2n^2/2)$
1	$nz(1 - z)^{n-1}$	$\beta_1 = z(1 + z)n - z^2n^2$
2 or more	$1-(1 + z(n - 1))(1 - z)^{n-1}$	$\beta_2 = z^2n(n - 1)/2$

Note: The quadratic approximation applies for small z and is based on ignoring terms involving powers of z greater than 2.

Maximizing (6.40) with respect to n using the information given in Table 6.5 shows that the socially optimal number of entrepreneurs is

$$n^* = \tfrac{1}{2} + ((z\pi - w)/z^2\pi) \qquad (6.41)$$

This has a positive value provided that, in the absence of multiple discovery, the expected benefit of entrepreneurship, $z\pi$, exceeds the opportunity cost, w. The optimal number of entrepreneurs varies directly with the value of an idea, π, and inversely with the wage w, as would be expected. It varies directly with the probability of discovery z when z is small ($z < 2w/\pi$) but inversely when z is large, because diminishing returns caused by multiple discovery are greater in this case. It should be stressed that n^* is socially optimal only with respect to the consensus objective (6.40) and not in any more profound sense (see section 6.9).

Manipulating the Supply of Entrepreneurs

As noted in section 6.3, there is an externality problem caused by the statistical averaging of returns to entrepreneurship across all entrepreneurs. The expected private reward to entrepreneurship is

$$r = ((\beta_1 + \beta_2\lambda_2)\lambda_1\pi/n) + \varphi_3 \tag{6.42}$$

where φ_3 is the emotional benefit inculcated by an enterprise culture. Comparing this expected reward with the opportunity cost w shows that in the special case where multiple discovery leads to competition ($\lambda_2 = 0$) and no enterprise culture is invoked ($\varphi_3 = 0$) the equilibrium number of entrepreneurs is

$$n^e = 1 + ((z\lambda_1\pi - w)/z^2\lambda_1\pi) \tag{6.43}$$

Comparing (6.43) with (6.41) shows that the restriction of supply induced by low appropriability just offsets the excess supply induced by statistical averaging if

$$\lambda_1 = 1/(1 + (z^2\pi/2w)) \tag{6.44}$$

In other words, even if multiple discovery dissipates rents, it will pay to restrict entrepreneurship, rather than promote it, provided that entrepreneurial appropriation in the case of sole discovery is sufficiently high. This is because the statistical averaging of returns has a relatively strong effect on entrepreneurial supply.

In the absence of manipulation costs, the ideal level of manipulation to compensate for violations of (6.44) is

$$\varphi_3^e = (1 - \lambda_1)w - (z^2\lambda_1\pi/2) \tag{6.45}$$

This is greater the higher is the wage rate and the smaller is the probability of discovering an idea, the smaller the proportion of the value of the idea that is appropriated and the lower the value of the idea itself. These results may seem counter-intuitive; they are explained by the fact that the actual supply of entrepreneurs is more sensitive to these factors than is the socially optimal supply, so that the role of culture is to eliminate overreaction rather than to increase the elasticity of response.

The situation is illustrated in Figure 6.3, which shows the average and marginal returns to entrepreneurship as functions of the number of entrepreneurs when $0 < \lambda_1 < 1$. Because of the diminishing returns induced by multiple discovery, the marginal social benefit schedule *MSB* is downward-sloping. There is a social optimum at E^*, where the marginal social benefit is equal to the social opportunity cost, as measured by the real wage w. This determines the optimal supply of entrepreneurs n^* given by equation (6.41).

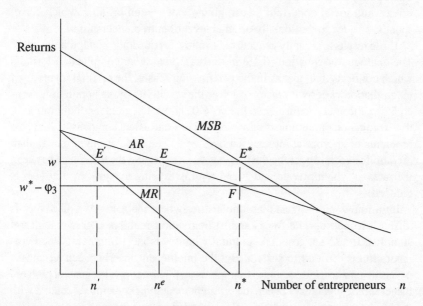

Figure 6.3   Determination of the supply of entrepreneurs

Individuals decide whether to enter entrepreneurship on the basis of the private average revenue, as indicated by the downward-sloping schedule *AR*. This has a smaller vertical intercept than *MSB* because even in the absence of multiple discovery entrepreneurs cannot appropriate all the rents from their activities. It also has a lower slope than *MSB* because it is an average rather than a marginal schedule. The corresponding marginal schedule *MR* has a steeper slope than *MSB*, as would be expected, because the replication of a discovery, which merely fails to increase the social benefit, actually eliminates some of the private rewards.

If entrepreneurship were controlled by a monopolist, from whom licences had to be obtained, then this monopolist would maximize profit at the intersection E' of *MR* and the horizontal supply schedule, thereby restricting the number of entrepreneurs to n'. Where no such restriction is enforced, the desire to share in the rewards of entrepreneurship expands the supply to $n^e > n'$, determined by the intersection E of the average revenue schedule *AR* with the corresponding supply curve. As noted earlier, E could in principle lie to the right of E^* although, as shown in the figure, it lies to the left.

When the supply of entrepreneurship is too low, as in this case, it can be corrected by an emotional subsidy $\varphi_3 > 0$. This subsidy compensates for the discrepancy between *AR* and *MSB* by creating a matching discrepancy between private and social opportunity cost, giving a new equilibrium F which corresponds, like E^*, to the socially optimal level of entrepreneurship n^*.

These results are readily generalized to allow for quadratic manipulation costs. The analogue of equation (6.45) in this case is a rather complicated formula which confirms that, just as in the two previous cases, the optimal intensity of manipulation varies with factors such as the sensitivity of the population. Generalizing the analysis further so that $\lambda_2 > 0$ shows that greater collaboration in the exploitation of multiple discoveries will to some extent compensate for basic problems of appropriability caused by $\lambda_1 < 1$. The compensation mechanism is complicated, however, by the fact that, as λ_2 increases, the difference between the rates at which private and social returns to entrepreneurship diminish is reduced.

Intuition would suggest that in industries where the value of a discovery is difficult to appropriate (λ_1 is small) innovation requires a greater cultural stimulus. It also suggests that cultural stimulus is most important when collaboration is difficult to sustain. But the interdependence between λ_1 and λ_2 means that matters are not quite so simple as this. This reflects the general problem that complex linkages between the different incentive problems associated with the innovation process make simple predictions rather difficult to obtain.

6.8   APPLICATIONS

While direct applications of the preceding formulae may have limited value, there are some important lessons to be learnt from the analytical exercises by which they are derived. The basic idea is to replace a complicated system of pecuniary incentives, which would be expensive to monitor and enforce, with simple emotional incentives based on self-monitoring and self-enforcement. Different populations have different sensitivities to different ethics, though, and also have different qualities of leader, and these lead to differences in chosen manipulation strategies.

Take the ethic of pure research, for example, which is familiar to most academics. This ethic was particularly strong in the British scientific elite of the late nineteenth and early twentieth centuries. Purity – in the sense of being untainted – is of course a very primitive idea, applied in all societies in the context of food hygiene. In the context of research the tainting is by commercial interests, representing the 'worldly' side of natural science. Worldliness may even come to be associated with practical applications, a view still exemplified by the low status of engineering compared with mathematics in British academic circles.

The subsidization of pure research in order to motivate applied research can, therefore, have an opposite effect to the one intended if it raises the status of pure research relative to applied research rather than the status of research as a whole. Problems of this kind are encountered not only in British research laboratories. In the 1970s, they became endemic in some major US central research laboratories, whose corporate owners were subsequently obliged to close them down or to transfer them to more 'near market' divisional work in order to restore viability. As part of this movement, an ethic of quality improvement and obligation to the customer replaced the 'pure research' ethic. R & D was integrated more closely with marketing and production management through the 'total quality management' movement, which took its inspiration from the achievements of post-war Japan.

In Japan itself quality management not only resonates with traditional values but also integrates well with the general emphasis on loyalty to the corporation. The leaders of the company conspicuously sacrifice resources to the welfare of their employees rather than to pure research and thereby avoid some of the possible distortions noted above. It is, however, doubtful if this ethic can elicit an equally great emotional response amongst the most creative research employees. The pure research ethic still has an important role to play in sectors of the economy committed to basic research, such as the pharmaceutical industry and, of course, higher education.

Now consider the cultural attitude to cartels. In Germany there has been a tradition of organizing industry-wide cartels in the national interest, together with implicit specialization agreements whereby different firms dominate different segments of each industry. In the United Kingdom cartels have tended to be more clandestine affairs, concentrating less on the development of export markets and more on 'orderly marketing' at home. They seem to have reflected

British culture in exploiting class solidarity to control cheating. Competition law exists, but is not enforced rigorously. This is in marked contrast to the United States, where vigorous enforcement reflects a culturally specific commitment to freedom of entry into almost all lines of business, allied to the view that such freedom must be formally guaranteed by law. However, hostility to collusion in the United States seems to have spilled over to make all forms of collaboration difficult. Distrustful regulators suspect that collaboration is merely a cloak for collusion. Indeed, distrust within the business community itself makes it difficult for firms to collaborate anyway (Casson, 1990, ch. 5).

The difficulty of collaboration in the United States implies that the private returns to entrepreneurship in that country may be particularly low relative to the social returns. This would provide a rationale for the strength of enterprise culture there. This interpretation, though speculative, squares with recent UK experience in which a stronger emphasis on competition between entrepreneurs has been associated with an improvement in the status of the entrepreneur as well.

The UK experience under Mrs Thatcher reflected a deliberate effort to eliminate an anti-entrepreneurial culture. Although the government attributed the problem to socialist influence, anti-entrepreneurial ideas can be traced back to a romantic concern with environmental issues which developed in the mid-nineteenth century (Wiener, 1981). Although class conflict may well have impaired entrepreneurship because of the vigorous efforts of trade unions to appropriate the rents from innovations, the emphasis on the external diseconomies of industry was shared by all sections of society and in particular by the political and bureaucratic elite. This attitude also supported the academic emphasis on pure rather than applied research, noted above.

In terms of the preceding models, it may be said that Britons held a culturally specific view that the private rewards to entrepreneurship significantly exceeded the social benefits (that is, $\lambda_1 > 1$) so that an anti-entrepreneurial culture was necessary to correct for the negative externalities involved. The existence of an open geographical frontier in the United States, and the Japanese preoccupation with catching up with the West, has meant that environmental concerns have taken a much lower priority in those countries (at least so far as their political elites are concerned). As anxieties over environmental degradation increase, however, it is quite possible that the anti-entrepreneurial view may regain ground at least so far as large-scale industry is concerned. Indeed the contemporary emphasis on small business growth in service industries may be interpreted as a cultural compromise between entrepreneurship and environmentalism so far as these issues are concerned.

6.9 LIMITATIONS OF THE MODELS AND POSSIBLE EXTENSIONS OF THE ANALYSIS

The preceding discussion invites a number of very obvious objections. The first concerns the rather heroic view of leadership that is presented, for history is full of dictators who united one group by attacking or persecuting others. The language in which the analysis is couched, and in particular the use of the term 'manipulation', has been chosen to alert the reader to the ever-present dangers of this kind. But even so, the preceding analysis could be used as an advisory manual by someone planning to misuse their power. Placing the information in the public domain may, however, help followers to distinguish between good leaders and bad ones, and also help responsible regulators who are trying to prevent abuses to understand the mechanisms of manipulation they are attempting to control. The view taken in this chapter is that manipulation is a fact of social life and that, while certain forms of manipulation are morally wrong, others are justifiable. People who join a group generally know that they are going to be manipulated through social pressures and may consent to it – it is not necessarily irrational to do so. It does seem important, however, that people should have a choice of group allegiance and be reasonably well-informed about what the consequences of their choice are likely to be.

Another objection would be that the full significance of culture cannot be appreciated within a neoclassical framework whose ideological role has been to support a *laissez-faire* approach to the market system. This objection would indeed be serious, were it not for the fact that the endogenization of preferences within a neoclassical framework undermines many of the familiar neoclassical policy implications. Welfare results need to be drastically revised. The conventional interpretation of Pareto efficiency is conditional on given preferences, so that when cultural influences are introduced direct comparisons of material rewards under different levels of manipulation cease to be valid. It is still valid to make welfare comparisons by imposing a social welfare function, although the result will depend crucially upon whether emotional as well as material rewards are included in it.

It is also viable to use a generalized Pareto criterion to assess whether the losers from an increase in manipulation could be compensated by the gainers. However, since the compensation would be mainly paid to cheats, to compensate them for increased feelings of guilt, it is not clear that the payments would be compatible with the leader's morality. Thus, once culture and morality are recognized as significant factors, the application of even this generalized Pareto criterion seems to lack practical validity. The whole approach of evaluating policy in utilitarian terms appears very questionable as a result. It seems more appropriate to evaluate performance in terms of the leader's own morality. If this is considered too relativistic, then the natural alternative is the imposition of a social welfare function, as noted above. An exercise of this kind will not provide the same general endorsement of *laissez-faire* as a conventional utilitarian Pareto criterion does. Thus endogenization of preferences through cultural manipulation subverts much of the traditional ideological role of neoclassical theory.

6.10   SUMMARY AND CONCLUSION

Schumpeter's account of entrepreneurial psychology is one of the most attractive aspects of his theory, but his approach has three shortcomings which need to be addressed. First, his somewhat elitist view of entrepreneurship tends to suggest that the kind of motivations he discusses are the prerogative of just a few. But in fact the entrepreneur's motivations differ in degree, rather than in kind, from those of other people.

Secondly, Schumpeter divorces his psychology from the utility function, despite the fact that in an economic model the psychology of motivation is most naturally expressed through the utility function. The formal model of culture developed in this chapter has addressed these issues by focusing not on the unique psychology of the entrepreneur but on the collective manipulation of preferences.

Schumpeter also tends to discuss entrepreneurial innovation as a single integrated function rather than as a sequence of related functions of the kind discussed above. For the purposes of formal modelling, however, it is important to consider these functions separately, since the incentive problems which arise are different in each case. This has been done using a sequence of formal models, all of which belong to the same general family. They can therefore be integrated with other models to provide a reasonably comprehensive account of the entire innovation process. It is hoped that future research will elaborate these models and generate new insights from the interactions between them.

ACKNOWLEDGEMENTS

I am grateful to Gerald Gunderson and Mark Perlman for comments on an earlier draft of this chapter.

REFERENCES

Akerlof, George A. (1980) A Theory of Social Custom, of Which Unemployment may be One Consequence, *Quarterly Journal of Economics*, **94**, 719–35.
Buckley, Peter J. and Mark C. Casson (1992) Organising for Innovation: The Multinational Enterprise in the Twenty-first Century, in P.J. Buckley and M.C. Casson (eds)

Multinational Enterprise and World Competition: Essays in Honour of John Dunning, Aldershot: Edward Elgar, 213–31.

Casson, Mark C. (1990) *Enterprise and Competitiveness: A Systems View of International Business*, Oxford: Clarendon Press.

Casson, Mark C. (1991) *Economics of Business Culture: Game Theory, Transaction Costs and Economic Performance*, Oxford: Clarendon Press.

Casson, Mark C., Robert D. Pearce and Satwinder Singh (1991) A Review of Recent Trends, in Mark C. Casson (ed.), *Global Research Strategy and International Competitiveness*, Oxford: Blackwell, 250–71.

Etzioni, Amitai (1988) *The Moral Dimension: Towards a New Economics*, New York: Free Press.

Frank, Robert H. (1985) *Choosing the Right Pond: Human Behavior and the Quest for Status*, New York: Oxford University Press.

Giddens, Anthony (1987) *Social Theory and Modern Sociology*, Cambridge: Polity Press.

Jones, Stephen R.G. (1984) *The Economics of Conformism*, Oxford: Blackwell.

Kirzner, Israel M. (1979) *Perception, Opportunity and Profit*, Chicago: University of Chicago Press.

Pareto, V. (1916) *Trattato di Sociologia Generale* (ed. N. Bobbio), Milan: Edizioni di Comunità, 1964.

Schumpeter, Joseph A. (1934) *The Theory of Economic Development* (trans. Redvers Opie), Cambridge, Mass.: Harvard University Press.

Schumpeter, Joseph A. (1942) *Capitalism, Socialism and Democracy*, 5th edn. (ed. Thomas Bottomore), London: Allen and Unwin, 1976.

Tirole, J. (1988) *Theory of Industrial Organization*, Cambridge, Mass.: MIT Press.

Weber, M. (1930) *The Protestant Ethic and the Spirit of Capitalism* (trans. T. Parsons), London: Allen and Unwin.

Weber, M. (1978) *Economy and Society: An Outline of Interpretive Sociology*, (ed. G. Roth and C. Wittich), Berkeley, Cal.: University of California Press.

Wiener, M.J. (1981) *English Culture and the Decline of the Industrial Spirit,* Cambridge: Cambridge University Press.

PART III

The Political Economy of National Culture

7. Cultural determinants of national economic performance

7.1 INTRODUCTION

The fact that culture is not well understood is often interpreted as an inherent limitation of the subject. It is certainly difficult to quantify cultural variables. It is also difficult for analysts to detach themselves from their own cultural prejudices. Culture is everywhere and 'the fish is the last to discover water'. Yet disciplines such as social psychology and social anthropology claim to have studied culture in depth. If this claim is accepted then clearly their studies have achieved only limited success. In particular, they have failed to evolve a dominant paradigm within which a cumulative body of research results can be assessed (Whitley, 1984). It is therefore entirely reasonable to argue that other methods of analysing culture should be tried as well. Economic methods are a plausible candidate because they have achieved reasonable success, not only in traditional areas such as price determination, but also in newer areas such as public choice, demography and criminology. Economic methods are also distinctive, because of their methodological individualism, and so are likely to generate new ideas rather than just reproduce existing ideas in a different form. Competition from new ideas may provoke a constructive response from the other disciplines too.

The chapter begins by reviewing basic concepts and definitions in sections 7.2 and 7.3. Culture is defined in a way that is compatible with the view that individuals optimize, and that their behaviour sustains an economic equilibrium. The equilibrium, it is shown, reflects the values and beliefs of the leader who establishes the culture of the group.

In sections 7.4–7.8 it is argued that the performance of the group will reflect five key cultural characteristics. Two of these aspects are primarily technical, and three primarily moral. Different groups have different characteristics and hence different levels of performance. It is the interaction between these characteristics, and not just their additive effects, that are important.

It is argued in sections 7.9 and 7.10 that a certain combination of characteristics is particularly common in the advanced Western countries of today, and that this is associated with a dominant ideology of competitive individualism.

Although the recent collapse of collectivism in Eastern Europe has reinforced belief in the triumph of Western societies and economies, it is suggested that contemporary Western culture is not, in fact, ideal from the standpoint of economic performance. The popular view that the West has much to learn from Japan is strongly supported. However, the cultural strengths of post-war Japan are by no means specific to the Orient: for example, some of them were once a feature of leading sectors of the Victorian British economy too. The key to success, it is argued in section 7.11, is to reconcile individual freedom with a high degree of trust, and this can only be achieved through effective leadership at the level of both the nation and the firm. Section 7.12 concludes the chapter by outlining the research agenda implied by this cultural approach to the explanation of economic performance.

7.2   BASIC CONCEPTS

In economic terms, culture may be defined as collective subjectivity (see Chapter 4). Subjectivity has two meanings in economics. The subjective theory of value emphasizes that individual preferences are not directly measurable: they are revealed only indirectly through behaviour. Interpersonal comparisons of welfare have no objective significance because absolute welfare cannot be inferred from behaviour. The second use of subjectivity is in the context of probabilities. In the absence of information about relative frequencies, an individual may attach a purely personal probability to an event. This probability cannot be directly measured, but, when an individual maximizes expected utility, changes in his behaviour may be attributed to the modification of his subjective probability.

What these concepts of subjectivity have in common is that the preference or belief on which the individual acts cannot be directly observed. It is also usual to associate subjectivity with individuality and to assert that these preferences and beliefs differ between individuals, too, but this overlooks the fact that subjectivity can also be collective. Individuals belonging to the same group may have similar preferences and similar beliefs. The most likely reason for such similarity is that preferences and beliefs are malleable, so that individuals exposed to the same influences tend to conform in these respects (Earl, 1986). These influences represent the culture of the group to which the individuals belong.

There are many different kinds of group, ranging from small groups such as the family, the workgroup and the local club to large groups such as churches, political parties, trade unions and the nation state. In each case, the culture of the group affects individual behaviour through its impact on preferences and beliefs. In particular it affects individuals' behaviour towards each other. This can affect both efficiency and equity within the group, as Table 7.1 shows. The table distinguishes between the moral aspects of a culture, which influence preferences, and the technical aspects, which influence beliefs (Casson, 1990, ch. 4), although the two aspects are often related, as the following discussion shows.

So far as efficiency is concerned, a culture that encourages a realistic and sophisticated view of the environment is likely to support better-informed and more successful decisions. This reflects the technical aspect of a culture. A culture that encourages good behaviour towards other people, honesty and integrity, for example, is likely to improve the coordination of different individuals' decisions: for example, by reducing transaction costs. This may be termed the moral aspect of a culture.

Table 7.1   Role of culture in enhancing the performance of a group

| | Aspect of group performance | |
Aspect of culture	Efficiency	Equity
Moral	1. Reduces transaction costs	1. Redistributes income to compensate for inadequate initial distribution of rights, or underinsurance against disaster, etc.
	2. Compensates for missing property rights	
		2. Promotes intergenerational altruism
Technical	1. Facilitates better decisions from better information or better model of the environment	
	2. Promotes improved technology through innovation	
	3. May improve monitoring and supervision systems	

Other impacts on efficiency are apparent too. For example, a culture may attach moral value to an important occupation whose practitioners find it difficult to appropriate material rewards. It may therefore boost recruitment to an occupation that would otherwise suffer from a serious shortage of supply. Thus the moral aspect of a culture may not only reduce transaction costs but also solve a wide range of externality problems.

Culture can also affect equity, both within generations and between them. Not surprisingly, it is the moral aspect of a culture that is most important here. For example, a culture that emphasizes the moral worth of every individual is likely to encourage altruism, not only towards those who are born into poverty, but to those who become poor through misfortunes against which they were inadequately insured. In the latter case, equity and efficiency considerations are closely linked, since inadequate insurance may reflect high transactions costs associated with moral hazard and adverse selection problems.

7.3   THE CULTURAL FRAMING OF OPTIMIZING BEHAVIOUR

A conventional economist is likely to inquire at this point how collective subjectivity can be reconciled with the assumption of rationality that underpins so much of economic theory. The short answer is that it is fully compatible so long as individuals are still assumed to optimize, subject to perceived constraints. It is just that their preferences are malleable rather than fixed, and that their constraints may not be correctly perceived (see Chapter 1).

This short answer leaves some loose ends, however, because it does not explain how preferences and beliefs are formed. The longer answer is that each group may be assumed to have a leader (see Chapter 2). For simplicity, the leader's preferences and beliefs are taken as given. The leader understands the interactions between other members of the group and can calculate, within his model, what kinds of equilibria will emerge within the group, conditional on various patterns of preference and belief among the followers. He then manipulates the followers' preferences and beliefs to select the desired equilibrium. Thus the preferences and beliefs of the followers are predicted by the model, once the leader's preferences and beliefs are specified. The model therefore provides a comprehensive account of the way in which the performance of the group depends upon the characteristics of its leader. The behaviour of the followers towards each other is also predicted, as it is the crucial link between the leader's attitude and the performance of the group. Culture becomes an endogenous factor, to be explained by the environment of the group and the quality of leadership within it.

But why, it may be asked, are the followers so easily led? Do not their own consumption experiences dictate the form of their preferences, and does not their own experience of life tell them the kind of constraints they face? The answer, it is suggested here, is that preferences need to be legitimized, and life experiences need to be interpreted. The former requires a moral system, and the latter a scientific theory of some kind. But both moral systems and scientific theories are difficult to develop and apply. A person who has comparative advantage in this area can become a leader and provide a moral system as a service to other members of society. By both presenting and interpreting the system the leader can legitimate certain kinds of action and denounce others.

If there were just one obviously correct morality, and one irrefutable set of scientific theories, societies could be expected to converge on these in the long run. It may well be the case that a uniquely correct morality and uniquely valid set of theories do indeed exist, but there is certainly no consensus at the moment on what they are, or even on whether they have been discovered yet.

There are several criteria by which a set of ideas can be judged, such as internal consistency, relevance and compatibility with the evidence. In the case of moralities these criteria are very difficult to apply. Internal consistency is difficult to judge when the philosophical status of moral statements is still hotly debated. It is also unclear what kind of evidence, if any, is relevant to the appraisal of moralities, although it is interesting to note that the present chapter provides an implicit ranking of moral systems by their instrumental contribution to material economic performance.

The appraisal of competing scientific theories is, on the face of it, a more straightforward task. However, the strongly positivist attitude to this issue favoured by many economists must be qualified in several ways, for example, by the theory dependence of empirical evidence. The most crucial limitation, from the present point of view, is that no theory can do full justice to the complexity of any real-world situation. All available theories, it is suggested, are far too simple to explain all the relevant phenomena satisfactorily. Thus no economic model, for example, is ever completely accurate in its predictions, as economists know to their cost. For some purposes it may be useful to assume that the agents in the model know the modeller's model to be correct, but for the purposes of analysing culture it is more useful to assume that agents choose between a set of oversimplified models instead. The correct model is just not in the feasible set.

When all available theories are unsatisfactory, individual judgements have to be made as to whether discrepancies reflect fundamental flaws in a theory or something innocuous, such as measurement error. One group may support one theory and another group another simply because their respective leaders are good at explaining away the shortcomings of their favoured theory and dismissing the attempts of other leaders to do the same for theirs. Theories that were not invented here, or whose policy implications are inconsistent with the leader's moral stance, may therefore be successfully dismissed.

7.4   CULTURAL PREREQUISITES FOR SUSTAINED DEVELOPMENT

A comprehensive economic theory of culture has not been worked out, but existing analysis makes it possible to identify with some accuracy the key characteristics of a culture that determine the economic performance of a group. The first of these is the differentiation of science and morals. In a sophisticated society, morality is concerned with the legitimation of ends, while science informs the choice of appropriate means. In more traditional societies the distinction is not always so clear. The religions of traditional societies sometimes mix accounts of the way things are with accounts of the way things ought to be. For example, they invoke a multiplicity of spirits who will cause bad events unless their cults are obeyed. Nature is viewed anthropomorphically: it is manipulated not by gaining understanding of scientific laws but by making offerings and sacrifices to the relevant spirits. Conversely, morality is confused with expediency; the aim is to do what the spirits desire even if they are manifestations of evil rather than good.

Sophisticated societies are not necessarily secular, they simply have religions within which the differentiation of science and morals is clear. In a monotheistic religion, for example, where a law-giving creator–God no longer intervenes on a day-to-day basis, science can be devoted to discovering the natural laws while society can be based on moral laws revealed through incarnation or prophecy. Such religion confers respectability on scientific inquiry while providing strong supernatural endorsement for morality. Societies with such religions are therefore quite sophisticated from an economic point of view.

The differentiation of science and morals opens up the route to economic development through technological advance. It is feasible to raise material aspirations to levels above subsistence. Objectives that previously centred exclusively on the reproduction of the family or the group can be supplemented by progressive missions that harness resources to more ambitious ends. These may include the building of great religious centres, the production of sophisticated works of art and craft, the colonization of new territories, and so on. Morality can be used to support higher standards of health and hygiene, and to encourage sexual restraint in the interests of population control. More generally, as material affluence increases, higher standards of self-restraint can reasonably be required, since the need to steal and so on in order to survive is reduced. There is scope for setting generally higher norms, in terms of both the efficiency and the equity of the society.

An emphasis on achieving ever-higher norms leads to what may be called a high-tension society. In this society people are continually engaged on projects designed to explore the limits of human capability. It can be compared with a low-tension society in which, once people have accomplished enough to survive, they relax until a problem next occurs. An important difference between high-tension and low-tension societies lies in their attitude towards aggression. Aggression is regarded more favourably in a high-tension society because it supports self-confidence and perseverance in achieving high norms. The important thing in a high-tension society is not to subdue aggression but to channel it in an appropriate direction, whereas in a low-tension society agression may be purely disruptive unless harnessed for collective defence.

7.5   ATOMISTIC AND ORGANIC SOCIETIES

The precise manifestation of high-tension depends, however, on the way that the society views itself. At one extreme is the atomistic view, favoured by neo-classical economists, in which the emphasis is on the potential of the individual and his self-fulfilment. Atomistic morality stresses the individual's rights rather than his obligations to society. It supports the private appropriation of resources and the alienability of such property through voluntary exchange (Putterman, 1990). Free competition is favoured as an efficient and impersonal way of distributing the gains from trade. Atomism encourages privacy in consumption and lack of interest in the behaviour, and perhaps even the welfare, of others.

At the opposite extreme is the organic view, favoured by many sociologists, in which the emphasis is on collective achievements such as the creation of a good society or a welfare state. Private ownership is discouraged, not only on the grounds that it lacks moral legitimacy, but that the unrestrained exercise of ownership rights by selfish individuals will impose negative externalities on others. Collective ownership or the sharing of common resources is recommended instead. Competition, on this view, is merely a manifestation of conflict: it rewards the strong (who are good at bargaining and physical appropriation) at the expense of the weak. Organic morality favours social obligation and conformity to eliminate this conflict at source.

The atomistic view suggests that individuals need as much freedom as possible in order to fulfil themselves. The organic view, on the other hand, suggests that too much individual freedom could subvert the group. It could become so loosely coupled that it splits into factions. Even if sub-groups remained coupled, the most powerful sub-group might become even more powerful at the expense of the weaker ones. The organic view therefore tends to favour coercion in order to restrain factions.

Both the atomistic and organic views can support a strong ethic of work and a high level of saving, but the process of moral legitimation is very different. In the atomistic society, hard work is necessary in order to discover what one is really capable of. People who do not work hard lose reputation because they appear to have given up this personal adventure, presumably because they have already formed a low opinion of themselves in terms of what they are really capable of. In an organic society, hard work indicates dedication to the common cause. It is an expression, not merely of conformity, but of solidarity.

The attitude towards aggression is different too. In an organic society all aggression needs to be channelled outwards; it is useful for waging imperial wars on enemy groups, for example, but dreadfully divisive if channelled inwards, because a collectivist society has few mechanisms for internal conflict management other than repression. An atomistic society, on the other hand, has access to the market mechanism. Individual acts of aggression are channelled into competition for status between consumers and competition for profit between producers. Innovation is the key in both cases: the consumer innovator is at the forefront of fashion, while the producer innovator wins temporary monopoly profits. The atomistic society therefore has less need to channel aggression into external relations, and it is likely to be a more peaceable neighbour as a result.

7.6   THE LEVEL OF TRUST

The preceding analysis suggests that the high-tension organic society tends to be internally coercive and externally aggressive, while the high-tension atomistic society is internally free and internally aggressive. The reconciliation of internal freedom and internal aggression in the atomistic society hinges, as noted above, on the market mechanism, and in particular on the dynamics of competition. While competition between externally aggressive groups involves very few rules of the game, this is certainly not true of internal competition. Internal competition is institutionalized by markets that are subject to the rule of law.

When individuals consider the law more as a scientific instrument than a moral code, however, calculations will often reveal that it is advantageous for them to cheat on contracts. In this case, the market mechanism may break down because transaction costs are too high. The problems are well known (Milgrom and Roberts, 1992): monitoring contractual compliance is difficult as people may not realize they have been cheated; detecting the culprit may prove impossible because it is not always clear who is cheating; convincing evidence on the primary suspect may not be available and courts may reject uncorroborated testimony; penalties on defaulters may be small, and restitution or compensation difficult to obtain.

The question then arises as to whether people can be trusted to honour contracts even when it is not in their material interests to do so. This is a particular problem in the high-tension atomistic society because high-achieving individuals stake their material well-being on the outcome of the market process. They can gain short-run material advantage by supplying poor quality products, breaking confidences, competing unfairly for promotion, and so on. In some cases reputation mechanisms can discourage such behaviour; in repeated encounters long-run incentives may favour cooperative behaviour, but the conditions that must be satisfied are too strict for enlightened self-interest to support cooperation in every case.

In a highly mobile atomistic society many transactions will be one time affairs, and with an imperfect legal system markets must operate in an atmosphere of trust underpinned by moral forces. Trust requires an optimistic view of the other party's intentions and a moral commitment of one's own. If both parties have this trust then each will validate the other's beliefs and a successful equilibrium outcome will be achieved. Otherwise, it is likely that each will attempt to cheat the other, and trade will break down: a no-trade equilibrium will emerge instead.

An atomistic philosophy that takes a pessimistic view of human nature will therefore have difficulty in supporting trade. If other people are believed to be selfish and materialistic, rather than altruistic, then they will be expected to cheat. Moreover, since this belief about human nature applies also to oneself, it suggests that altruism is an unattainable goal. Thus a person's beliefs about human nature will affect both his own behaviour and his expectations of other people's behaviour. A pessimistic view of human nature can therefore precipitate self-validating distrust. An optimistic view of human nature is therefore required to make markets work.

This optimistic view can be difficult to reconcile with the individual aggression on which the high-tension atomistic society relies. A major theme of this chapter is the importance of channelling aggression into strong personal commitments to corporate goals – goals that lie beyond oneself and thereby give meaning to life. To be morally legitimate these goals must be non-selfish and the organizations through which they are pursued must not have someone's personal gain as their only goal. This does not prevent them from being efficient in respect of their own objectives, though (see section 7.10). Thus a society with energetic individuals pursuing non-selfish corporate goals may actually turn out to be more materially successful than a society based upon self-interest, because of, rather than in spite of, the fact that people are not working purely for their own material interests. Thus at the level of society, if not the individual, a paradox emerges: material wealth is the incidental reward for non-selfish behaviour, and the more material wealth is sought for itself, the less material wealth is actually obtained.

7.7 THEORY, PRAGMATISM AND JUDGEMENT

A high-trust society supports a sophisticated division of labour. People can afford to specialize because everyone is confident that the specialists on whom they rely will not let them down. It is not just a question of specializing in production, moreover, but of specializing in decision making too. In a high-trust society, people are happy to delegate decisions about the use of resources they own to other people, who will take the decisions on their behalf (see Chapter 4).

But how will the specialist decision maker arrive at his decision? Culture is important here, too, but now it is the scientific rather than the moral aspect that is paramount. Some cultures emphasize the importance of theory; it is important to understand the situation before acting, they maintain, and such understanding can only be provided by a theory of some kind. Other cultures are more pragmatic; they suggest that it is sufficient to know that, on the basis of experience, a certain course of action produces good results in certain circumstances without knowing exactly why this is the case.

Table 7.2 compares the theoretical and pragmatic cultures as they apply to scientific inquiry within a differentiated culture. Eleven key aspects of inquiry are used in this comparison. Examination of the table indicates, for example, that the culture of the economics profession, with its emphasis on rigour, formality and reductionism, would qualify as far more theoretical than the culture of the management and business administration profession, which is heuristic, informal and eclectic.

The difference between theoretical and pragmatic cultures will also be reflected in social organization. Prevailing views about the correct way to take decisions will be reflected in the criteria by which people are selected for specialist decision-making roles. Is a good grasp of theory, or relevant experience, the most appropriate qualification? Because many people have difficulty grasping the abstract elements of a theory, qualification in theory is often difficult for more than a few people to obtain. On the other hand, anyone is, in principle, capable of accumulating experience, although there are, of course, differences between people in their ability to learn from it. On the whole, though, emphasis on theory will tend to create a more elitist society because fewer people have the innate ability to acquire the qualifications.

Emphasis on pragmatism is more likely to establish age as a relevant criterion for seniority, since age will proxy the amount of experience that has been gained. Pragmatism will also favour variety of experience – breadth over depth – and therefore favour generalist rather than specialist decision makers. By contrast, since theory is intellectually difficult to grasp, an emphasis on theory tends to favour the specialist rather than the generalist. Thus in theory-oriented cultures decision makers will tend to be young elitist specialists, while in pragmatic cultures they will tend to be older generalists with a more versatile background. Elitism in theory-oriented cultures is likely to be centred on the alumni of prestigious educational institutions that employ competitive examinations. While pragmatic culture may also be promoted through prestigious educational institutions, there is likely to be more emphasis on socialization (the moral dimension) rather than intellectual achievement (the scientific dimension).

Table 7.2 Technical aspects of a culture

Aspect	Differentiated		Undifferentiated
	Theoretical	Pragmatic	
Perceived capacity to control environment	High	Moderate	Low
Method of inference	Deductive	Inductive	Mixed: interpretation of omens, oracles, books of wisdom and revelations
Type of experimentation	Use of controlled conditions to test theories	Tinkering, trial operation of practical devices	None
Quantification	High	Moderate	Low
Outlook	Reductionist	Eclectic	Holistic
Metaphor	System	Mechanism	Anthropomorphism
Reasoning	Rigorous	Heuristic	Elementary
Presentation	Formal	Informal	Artistic
Change	Radical	Incremental	None
Policy orientation	Progressive	Opportunistic	Survival
Method of control	Plan, design, organization	Improvization	Prayer, sacrifice

In practice neither pure theory nor pure pragmatism is likely to provide the most successful formula for decision making. Knowledge of theory is useful for the interpretation of evidence but, as noted earlier, no single theory is ever likely to be entirely adequate, and so some element of eclecticism needs to be invoked. Conversely, no pragmatist is ever really independent of theory, because theory is always needed for the interpretation of evidence. Thus the implicit theory of the pragmatist may actually be worse than an explicit theory because the weaknesses of the explicit theory can at least be more readily discerned and compensated for.

To combine theory and pragmatism successfully, considerable judgement is required. Judgement involves relying on theoretical formulae and prescriptions only when they seem to be supported, being willing to switch to new theories when the evidence warrants, and improvising decisions when no available theory seems appropriate. Judgement of this kind is the hallmark of the successful entrepreneur (see Chapter 4). It is a quality that can be deployed within any economic system, though there are considerable differences in the way that it is used. Some cultures regard entrepreneurship as a very scarce quality, possessed only by an elite who take key decisions in a centralized organization, whereas others regard it as an abundant quality which can readily be tapped by decentralizing decisions, typically within a market economy. This point is taken up later in the chapter.

7.8   SYNTHESIS: THE IMPACT OF CULTURE ON ECONOMIC DEVELOPMENT

The preceding discussion has identified five key factors that, it is claimed, are crucial for sustained economic development. These factors are itemized in the left hand column of Table 7.3. A crude application of this five-factor theory would relate economic performance to the number of these characteristics that are present in a culture. On the face of it, there is some justification for this. Table 7.3 considers four potential applications, and the results suggest a positive correlation between the number of factors and the level of economic performance. The second and third columns of the table present a simple stereotyping of two categories of country, the less developed country and the East European country, while the last two columns stereotype two major industrial powers, the United States and Japan. There is, of course, considerable cultural diversity, not only within categories, but also within individual countries, but notwithstanding this it seems reasonable to portray the salient differences in this way.

Table 7.3   A simple classification of national cultures

Factor	LDC	Eastern Europe	United States	Japan
Scientific differentiation	Weak	Strong	Strong	Strong
High-tension	Weak	Strong	Strong	Strong
Atomism	Weak	Weak	Strong	Weak
High trust	Weak	Weak	Weak	Strong
Judgement	Weak	Weak	Strong	Strong

Most LDCs seem to lack at least one of the two basic prerequisites for development, a clear moral system harmonized with a scientific world-view, and a high-tension culture in which aggression is channelled into attaining high social and economic norms. Their political organization often reflects an organic view of society in which dissent is identified with factionalism and suppressed in the interests of maintaining a fragile national unity. Networks of trust are confined to extended families and to religious groups, with considerable suspicion existing between members of different groups. Because scientific and moral issues are not clearly distinguished, the quality of judgement used in decision making is relatively poor.

Unlike LDCs, East European countries typically have the prerequisites for economic development; indeed, with certain qualifications, their nineteenth century cultural heritage is a Western European one (see Chapter 11). The separation of science and morals is not quite so clear as in some Western countries, however, because Protestantism has been a less significant force and Eastern religious influences are also present in some of the countries. (There are notable exceptions, of course: the Czech Republic is more Protestant than either France or Italy, for example, but on balance this generalization about Eastern Europe is probably no worse than any other.)

These East European countries have little more than the prerequisites, however. The system they are in transition from promoted a strongly organic view of the state. High-tension personal aggression was channelled into external defence against Western capitalist nations and into collective achievements in scientific research and in large-scale industrialization. Where individual achievement was sought, it involved building a political career within the Communist Party. Organic culture has now been rejected, of course, and indeed in many East European countries there is an uncritical and even fanatical devotion to the concept of an atomistic society within reformist groups. But the transition from organicism to atomism may be the only transition that can be easily accomplished. The transition to a high-trust culture exploiting good entrepreneurial judgement may prove much more difficult.

Low trust is a legacy of Stalinism. The overcentralization of planning discredited the planner and, by implication, top enterprise managers too. The rigidity of senior officials in maintaining technically unrealistic production targets to maximize the output of obsolete consumer goods left considerable cynicism at lower levels of the enterprise system. Furthermore, the privileges conferred on party activists and the widespread use of informers discouraged the open expression of dissenting views and hence disabled group-centred problem solving.

The exercise of judgement has been inhibited too, since theory and pragmatism were never brought together. Planners adopted a highly theoretical approach to decision making, based on Marxist ideas, while at the other extreme black market traders took a highly pragmatic view of opportunities for speculation and arbitrage; their insecure legal status discouraged these traders from developing long-term strategies for business growth and development. Thus the legacy of low trust and poor judgement provides a very weak basis on which to create a market economy.

In this context it is rather disturbing to note the tendency in Eastern Europe to use the United States as a model for the reformed economies. While it is natural to take institutional models whenever they are available, the present day United States economy appears to lack one of the key characteristics of a successful economy, namely a high level of trust between transactors. This deficiency is highlighted in the fourth column of the table. Although the United States has never been a very high-trust society, in earlier generations Protestant values such as shared commitment to work provided a relatively secure basis for coordination amongst the political and business elite. The relative decline of Protestant values has placed an increasing burden on the legal system as the main coordinating mechanism, a burden that the system seems increasingly unable to bear.

During the 1970s and 1980s, it has been Japan rather than the United States that has provided the best model of an advanced high-trust society. But Japan lacks a tradition of individualism, which makes it less attractive than the United States as a model for newly-liberalized economies. What Eastern Europe really requires is a model based on the best elements of the United States and Japan. It is surprising, as well as disappointing, that no such model has been advocated. Such a model can, in fact, be readily formulated, as the following discussion makes clear.

7.9   THE IDEOLOGY OF COMPETITION

Why is it that there appears to be no current working example of what theory predicts to be the most effective culture? It could be argued that the ideal culture does not exist simply because the concept of it is utopian; while any four of the five cultural characteristics can be simultaneously achieved, it could be said, all five of them cannot, because human nature simply cannot rise to such a challenge. This is a natural extension of the pessimistic view of human nature described above.

A more subtle variant of this argument would assert that all five conditions can only be satisfied in groups much smaller than the nation state. It is, perhaps, only in small face-to-face societies with stable membership that high trust can be found at the same time that other conditions are satisfied. This would suggest that family dynasties and medium-size firms are the largest units that can satisfy all the conditions.

It is possible to reject this argument, however, and to argue simply that convergence on the ideal culture is a very slow historical process. One of the recent factors hindering this convergence has been the poor quality and narrow focus of ideological debate. During the nineteenth and twentieth centuries, Western intellectual debate has centred mainly on the relative merits of two opposing ideologies: competitive individualism, on the one hand, and coercive collectivism, on the other. These ideologies obviously take opposite sides on the question of atomism versus organicism, and consequently differ in their attitude to decision making. As noted earlier, individualism tends to encourage widespread participation in essentially pragmatic decision-making, while collectivism tends to encourage theory-based decision making concentrated on an elite. But on other matters these two ideologies agree. In particular, they agree on the pessimistic view of humanity that sustains a low-trust culture. Ideology based on high-trust culture has been relegated to the sidelines as involving an improbably romantic view of the world. Yet, even if it cannot be claimed that human nature is basically good, it is possible to argue that with appropriate moral manipulation it can become much better than it would otherwise be.

In the case of collectivist societies, low-trust culture is often an unintended consequence of attempts to implement an unworkable vision of a utopian society. When the members of the society do not respond quite as the leader anticipates, his disillusionment and desire to maintain control lead to the development of a repressive political regime. In individualism, however, low trust has a more central role because it validates the emphasis on competition between individuals.

To be specific, competition is favoured by individualists because monopolists cannot be trusted. It is taken as axiomatic that a monopolist will abuse market power and dishonour any commitment to set a fair price. Unless people have a credible threat to switch to an alternative source of supply they will be taken advantage of, it is assumed. Thus, in order to negotiate a favourable price, each buyer must adopt a divide and rule strategy towards suppliers. Conversely the suppliers must adopt a divide and rule approach to the buyers. It is the interaction between these two strategies that generates the competitive equilibrium price.

Competition can, however, be viewed very differently. Taking a more optimistic view of human nature, competition can be regarded as a sporting game that allows people to achieve high social norms (Knight, 1935). Competition is significant, on this view, because no-one knows what they are capable of achieving until they have tried. Other people's efforts provide benchmarks against which each individual can assess his own performance. Direct competition in a tournament helps people to raise their game by using others as pacemakers. In this sense, the tournament becomes a cooperative exercise in achieving higher standards. Each player provides a norm for every other player to try and surpass.

This cooperative element can be strengthened by organizing competition as a contest, not between people, but between teams. People affiliate to groups and it is these groups that compete with each other. Since the most successful group is likely to be the one with the most effective internal coordination, competition of this kind actually strengthens the cooperative ethos within the team. Each team needs the other teams to help strengthen loyalty and commitment amongst its own players. The correspondence with the games ethic of the Victorian public school is quite close in this respect.

If competition is a game of this kind then it loses much of the Darwinian flavour with which it has been imbued in recent times. It is unnecessary to eliminate the weak teams from the tournament unless they directly inhibit the top teams' performance. To reduce any negative externalities, separate divisions of the tournament can be created, so that within each division teams are matched against those of comparable ability. The material risks of participation in the competitive process are also reduced, thereby providing the insurance which is missing from Darwinian competition. Although such insurance may reduce performance in the lower divisions by blunting the cutting edge of real competition, and misallocating resources by encouraging players to remain attached to a game in which their comparative advantage does not really lie, it compensates in encouraging greater risk taking elsewhere in the game, risk taking that may create positive externalities for other players in the tournament.

This view of competition promotes an alternative ideology in which cooperation rather than competition is the focus of economic organization. Price information is still generated by the competitive game, but transaction costs are lower because of the high-trust culture, and outcomes are more egalitarian because the link between competitive ability and material reward is weaker than when competition is entirely real.

7.10   THE FIRM AS A SOCIAL UNIT

This discussion of competition suggests that teams might be invented simply to reduce the intensity of competition at the individual level. In fact, of course, teamwork has an independent rationale within the economy as the basis of the production system. The basic unit of production is the plant, which combines physical inputs under conditions of technological complementarity and economies of scale. Because labour is a key input, coordination inside the production plant depends crucially on the team spirit in the workforce. Teamwork applies to groups of managers too. In a private enterprise economy wealth owners delegate the management of their resources to firms. The shareholders empower members of the management team to allocate resources on their behalf. Managers practise an intellectual division of labour in processing information and the quality of their decisions will reflect the team spirit among them. Indeed, from a managerial perspective, it is the firm rather than the plant that is the basic unit of teamwork, since one team of managers quite often coordinates several plants.

The philosophy of competitive individualism tends to overlook the fact that most production activity is organized by firms. As a result, it tends to ignore the impact of intra-firm coordination on the aggregate performance of the economy. It fails to recognize the role of national culture in promoting cooperative behaviour within the firm. It promotes a culture that is geared more to eliminating ineffi- cient firms than to improving the performance of those which remain.

From the standpoint of competitive individualism, the firm is really no more than a nexus of contracts. The contracting parties are individuals, each playing some functionally specialized role, such as shareholder, manager, worker and so on. The shareholders, as residual claimants, are specialized risk bearers, who entrust the managers with decisions in return for the power to fire them if necessary. The managers are in turn responsible for monitoring contractual compliance by other employees.

The difficulty with this view is that it ignores the social dimension of the firm. From a cultural standpoint, the firm is a sort of microcosm of the nation state. Like the nation state, the firm can function as a social group. Like the nation state, it encounters coordination problems that lead to transaction costs, and in both cases the fundamental problem is distrust. Arm's-length traders in a national economy face problems of haggling and default. Internalization reduces these problems within the firm, but agency costs are incurred instead; the manager cannot necessarily trust his subordinate to provide the informa- tion he requires.

This problem can be overcome within the firm by the same kind of moral manipulation that can be employed by the leader of a nation state. The chairman or chief executive of the firm can act as a leader, engineering a sense of obligation by articulating some legitimate objective. Enlightened entrepreneurs of the past, for example, have emphasized the inherent social value of the product they manufacture: purer foods, healthier drinks, the cleansing effect of toiletries, and so on. As a result, employees become self-monitoring: supervision costs are reduced as employees feel obliged to work hard and to share information in pursuit of the common goal (see Chapter 6).

The leader's rhetoric does not have to be directed solely at employees, however. It can be directed at the shareholders too. Shareholders who are concerned purely with profit maximization will, of course, require that any financial sacrifices made in pursuing moral objectives must generate corresponding savings from lower monitoring costs, higher productivity, and so on. But if shareholders themselves experience a sense of moral obligation then they may consent to sacrifices over and above this level. A leader who can encourage shareholders to acquiesce in the moral mission of the firm may, as a result, achieve even higher performance in terms of the mission, even though the profit performance is reduced. Provided shareholders value the emotional benefits of participation in the moral mission sufficiently, they will be unwilling to sell out to other more materialistic people who would reorient the firm to strict profit maximization instead.

Shareholders are, however, unlikely to participate emotionally in the goals of the enterprise if they only hold a small shareholding for speculative purposes, which they can liquidate at any time. Organized stock markets provide liquidity at the expense of weakening shareholders' emotional rewards and so tend to emphasize the purely material performance of the firm. In small firms, where each shareholder usually holds a significant stake on a long-term basis, emotional rewards to owners are likely to be much greater. Greatest of all are likely to be the rewards in the owner-managed firm and in those family firms whose owners regard them as an inheritance to be passed on to the next generation.

The emotional involvement of the owner with the firm is likely to strengthen the emotional rewards experienced by employees. A loyal and committed owner gives credibility by his actions to the claims he makes for the firm's moral mission, a credibility that an absentee owner simply cannot provide. This ability to enhance the emotional rewards of hard-working employees is arguably one of the major economic advantages of small-firm organization. Small size can improve material incentives too, of course, for each team member gets a larger share of any team bonus when the team is small, but morale effects are almost certainly dominant where performance is concerned.

It is often argued that small firms cannot exploit the economies of scale and economies of vertical integration that are available to large firms (Chandler, 1977). It is certainly true that the global marketing of mass-produced goods requires greater formal organization and managerial specialism than is commonly found in small firms. But advances in information technology, computer-aided design and automatic process control mean that in some industries a fairly small team of skilled workers can now operate a very large factory. Informal interaction between key workers is thus becoming more important as more of the formalities are taken care of by computer programs. Moreover, as manufacturing systems become more flexible, customization becomes more widespread and innovation becomes continuous rather than discrete. This increases the tacit content of communication and enhances the value of the informal organization typical of small firms.

So far as vertical integration is concerned, this can be seen, not so much as a strength of the large firm, but as a potential weakness, in the sense that vertical integration is essentially a response to low trust. When trust is high, different stages of production can be safely delegated to different firms, since the risk of contractual default between them is low. In principle, a network of small firms operating in a high-trust local culture can be more efficient than a single integrated firm coordinating the same activities by more formal means. The small-firm network delegates entrepreneurial decisions to owner–managers, each of whom strives to maintain the respect of his peers. By contrast, the large firm is likely to overcentralize decision making, inhibiting enterprise at the lower levels, because senior management is afraid to give too much discretion to junior salaried employees whom it does not really trust.

Identifying a preponderance of large firms with a low-trust culture is consistent with the relative importance of large firms in both the Eastern European economies and the United States. Conversely, it is consistent with the prominent role of small and medium-size firms in a high-trust economy such as Japan. While large-firm operation may have been a rational response to the early growth of mass-markets in a low-trust society like the United States, it should not, therefore, be inferred that economic performance in general is related to the presence of a powerful large firm sector. In the early 1990s it may be more appropriate to relate economic performance to the vitality of small-firm networks instead. Under contemporary conditions investment in social networks may generate higher returns than investment in more elaborate forms of large-scale organization.

7.11 VOLUNTARY ASSOCIATION

To conclude this chapter it is appropriate to set out an alternative to the low-trust ideologies of competitive individualism and coercive collectivism. This ideology may be termed 'voluntary associationism', and its principal characteristics are set out in Table 7.4. As its name suggests, it is central to this ideology that individuals naturally associate with each other, both for the purpose of production and for other activities too. The firm is one particular manifestation of association; another, for example, is the charity.

Associationist ideology is fully compatible with the economic principles outlined in section 7.2 and in Chapter 2. Individuals are assumed to be rational, in the restricted sense that they optimize within the context of oversimplified models of their environment. Individual preferences have both material and emotional components, and the latter can be manipulated by a leader's moral rhetoric.

Groups play a crucial role in associationism. Individuals are born into certain groups – the family and their local community, for example – some of which, such as the family, they can never completely leave. People can also enter groups of their own free will – the team at their place of work, clubs, charities, trade unions, churches and so on. Some teams are easier to quit than others. When choosing between teams, an individual knows that certain commitments are required by the leader when he joins, and that exit may be costly. The prospective member may anticipate that his preferences may change when he joins the team, as he comes under the leader's influence, but nevertheless he may quite reasonably decide to take this step. The commitment that the individual acquires to the mission of the group may well be a direct source of satisfaction to him. So long as he remains without commitment he may be in a stressful state.

In the ideology of associationism, individuals with common interests and beliefs are free to form their own social groups. There is freedom of entry into leadership; anyone can promote a new group, provided it is not merely a fragment or clique within an established group. Freedom of entry, coupled with voluntary membership, means that leaders effectively compete for members. Some groups may be complementary to each other, with many people being members of both, but there will also be instances of rivalry. As noted earlier, a realistic view of modern industrial economies shows that competition between organized groups is far more significant than competition between individuals, in the sense that it is firms and household units that dominate product and labour markets.

While there is freedom of entry into leadership, not everyone is equally capable of leading successfully. Leadership is a scarce quality. Leadership of a large group requires considerable judgement and also good communication skills. The engineering of trust within a group requires that the leader himself is trustworthy, and the leader's integrity in turn depends on the intensity of his own commitment to the mission of the group. While associationism endorses the democratic view that most people are reasonable and moral, it contains an elitist element too, in that the natural dispersion of abilities means that some people make much better leaders than others.

Associationism is more than just a compromise between individualism and collectivism because, as indicated above, it presumes a higher degree of trust than either of these established philosophies. It is not utopian, however, in that it does not assume that people are naturally trustworthy, only that, with suitable moral leadership, trust can be engineered. Moreover, unlike most utopian philosophies, it does not oppose institutions such as money and private property, or prefer resources to be held in common and allocated through consensus decision making. In practice, though, most utopian communities appear to rely upon strong

Table 7.4 Ideologies of economic organization

Aspect	Competitive individualism	Voluntary associationism	Coercive collectivism
Intelligence of typical individual	High	Moderate	Low
Moral autonomy of typical individual	High	Moderate	Low
Natural dispersion of intelligence and moral commitment	Low	Moderate	High
Diversity of wants and capabilities	High	Moderate	Low
Attitude to others	Toleration	Sharing	Conformity
Trust	Low	High	Low
Formality and impersonality of relations	High	Low	High
Natural form of institution	Market	Social group	Hierarchy
Primary responsibility for devising incentives	Entrepreneur	Leader	Dictator
Discretion versus subordination	Wide discretion	Mixture	Subordination
Switching allegiance between leaders	High	Low	Impossible
Leadership selection and succession	Democratic	Varied	Dynastic
Role of fantasy in leader–follower relations	Low	Moderate	High
Mobility between roles	High	Moderate	At leader's discretion
Symbiosis with family	Weak	Strong	Weak
Material incentive mechanism	Contact under law	Informal reciprocity	Unilateral threat
Emotional incentive mechanism	None	Guilt	Shame
Style of rhetoric	Appeal to self-interest	Duty to fulfil group mission	Absolute supremacy of organic group

and charismatic leadership, confirming that, despite the appearance of democracy they incline to organicism, as indicated in Table 7.5.

Table 7.5   Classification of ideologies

Trust	Atomistic	Organic
Low	Competitive individualism*	Coercive collectivism*
High – engineered by leadership	Voluntary associationism*	
High – natural		Typical utopianism

Note: * indicates economic viability.

7.12   CONSISTENCY OF ASSOCIATIONIST THEORY

The ideologies of competitive individualism and coercive collectivism each have their counterparts in economic theory. Conventional neoclassical theory takes the individualist standpoint, while neo-Ricardian and Marxist theories incline to the collectivist one. The associationist standpoint is represented mainly by institutionalist economics, but institutionalism is such a fragmented movement – encompassing writers as diverse as Commons (1934), Veblen (1890) and Coase (1937) – that it is difficult to articulate it clearly. But while no comprehensive theory exists, recent work by a number of authors, including Akerlof (1980), Frank (1985) and Jones (1984), provides a foundation on which future work can be based. Table 7.6 summarizes the associationist model developed in Casson (1991) and compares it with other strands of theory.

Because associationism represents, to some extent, a compromise position between individualism and collectivism, it might be expected that an associationist theory would lack incisiveness and rigour. In some respects, however, associationist theory exhibits greater internal consistency than does the individualistic one. The conventional neoclassical theory of the market comprises a mixture of Walrasian perfect competition theory and strategic theories of oligopoly. These coexist uneasily because in the perfect competition model everyone trusts the Walrasian auctioneer, who monopolizes intermediation, not to appropriate rents for himself, whilst in non-collusive oligopoly theory no-one trusts anyone else and even simple agreements between sellers cannot be enforced. Conventional theory also includes a mixture of profit-maximizing models of the firm, in which the managers implicitly do exactly what the owners wish, and agency models in which managers do anything but what the owners would like. Associationist theory dispenses with the Walrasian auctioneer, but substitutes a competitive mechanism that is overseen by a leader with a reputation for enforcing contracts. Associationist theory follows agency theory in going inside the firm, but unlike agency theory it recognizes the power of corporate culture in persuading agents to discipline themselves. In these respects, therefore, associationist theory clarifies and resolves issues which conventional theory has tended to fudge.

Associationist theory can be used to model the impact of many aspects of culture on economic performance. Unlike sociological theories, which typically move directly from culture to collective behaviour, associationist theory retains the methodological individualism of economic analysis. Culture alters the preferences and perceived constraints of optimizing individuals, and the principle of equilibrium predicts what the collective outcome of these individual decisions will be.

It is worth emphasizing, too, that the leader has an essentially instrumental role in associationist theory. The theory relates cultural values to economic performance and the leader is simply part of the mechanism that links the two. Many groups appear to operate without a special leader because, in a sense, the leadership function is dispersed throughout the group. The preceding discussion has personified the leadership function in terms of a single individual in each group. This has been done for analytical simplicity only, and not because all groups actually have a leader of this kind. It is the function that is important, rather than the precise mechanics of how this function is performed. Models of diffused leadership are possible in principle – they are just very difficult to construct.

This chapter has focused on the very general and sometimes rather abstract features of culture which influence national economic performance. As Chapter 6 has shown, though, it is possible to construct more detailed models, adapted to particular contexts, and to explore within these models not only the diffusion of leadership but also the effects of specific values and beliefs – the work ethic, for example – on the performance of different kinds of group. All these models share the same key feature: they demonstrate the value of morality in reducing transaction costs and the value of realistic theories in improving the quality of judgement. Just as neoclassical theory captures the ideological message of individualism by demonstrating the value of competitive markets and the dangers of interventionism, so associationist theory captures the ideological message of associationism – in particular that legitimate leadership can improve economic performance through cultural engineering.

Table 7.6 *Economic models associated with different ideologies*

Issue	Competitive individualism	Voluntary associationism	Coercive collectivism
Intelligence of typical individual	Completely rational (optimization using the true model)	Conditionally rational (optimization using a culture-specific oversimplified model)	Planner is completely rational
Moral autonomy of typical individual	Complete (preferences are given)	Partial (a preference parameter can be manipulated by other individuals or by an autonomous leader)	Dictator is autonomous
Natural dispersion of intelligence and moral commitment	None (except for the Walrasian auctioneer, who is altruistic)	Moderate (leader can encompass followers' decisions with his own model)	High (dictator has absolute moral authority and planner has unlimited calculating capability)
Diversity of wants	Extreme	Modest	Negligible
Attitude to others	Indifference	Respect for leader, who in turn sustains sense of obligation to other members of the group	Obedience to dictator, submission to the plan
Trust	Everyone trusts the Walrasian auctioneer and the integrity of the law, but they do not trust each other	Trust between firms is engineered by a national leader and within firms by corporate leaders	Coercion substitutes for trust

ACKNOWLEDGEMENTS

I am grateful to Avner Ben-Ner, John Pencavel and Andrew Van der Ven and the editors of the *Journal of Comparative Economics* for helpful comments on an earlier version of this chapter.

REFERENCES

Akerlof, G.A. (1980) A Theory of Social Custom, of Which Unemployment may be One Consequence, *Quarterly Journal of Economics*, **94**, 719–35.

Casson, M.C. (1990) *Enterprise and Competitiveness: A Systems View of International Business*, Oxford: Clarendon Press.

Casson, M.C. (1991) *Economics of Business Culture: Game Theory, Transaction Costs and Economic Performance*, Oxford: Clarendon Press.

Chandler, A.D. Jr (1977) *The Visible Hand: The Managerial Revolution in American Business*, Cambridge, Mass.: Harvard University Press.

Coase, R.H. (1937) The Nature of the Firm, *Economica* (new series), **4**, 386–405.

Commons, J. R. (1934) *Institutional Economics: Its Place in Political History*, New York: Macmillan.

Earl, P.E. (1986) *Lifestyle Economics: Consumer Behaviour in a Turbulent World*, Brighton: Wheatsheaf.

Frank, R.H. (1985) *Choosing the Right Pond*, New York: Oxford University Press.

Jones, S.R.G. (1984) *The Economics of Conformism*, Oxford: Blackwell.

Knight, F.H. (1935) *The Ethics of Competition, and other Essays*, London: Allen & Unwin.

Milgrom, P. and J. Roberts (1992) *Economics, Organisation and Management*, Englewood Cliffs, NJ: Prentice-Hall.

Putterman, L. (1990) *Division of Labour and Welfare: An Introduction to Economic Systems*, Oxford: Oxford University Press.

Veblen, T.B. (1890) The Preconceptions of Economic Science III, *Quarterly Journal of Economics*, **14**, 240–69.

Whitley, R. (1984) *The Intellectual and Social Organisation of the Sciences*, Oxford: Clarendon Press.

8.   Industrial policy in cultural perspective

8.1   INTRODUCTION

This chapter inquires why different industrial policies are pursued at different times in different countries. It offers a theoretical framework for the historical interpretation of comparative international experience in the field of industrial policy.

A broad interpretation of industrial policy is used. The objective of policy, it is assumed, is to improve coordination between different sectors of the economy. Such coordination has both static and dynamic aspects, though in practice many industrial policies address just one aspect at the expense of the other. Because of this broad definition, industrial policy is taken to include not only competition policy and regulation but also technology policy, government procurement policy, tariff policy and, indeed, any economic or financial policy which is targetted on selected industrial sectors of the economy – normally, but not exclusively, high-technology manufacturing industries and utilities.

The most obvious distinction between industrial policies is whether they are interventionist or not. Neoclassical political economy suggests that the extent and direction of intervention will reflect the economic interests of those groups that dominate the political process (Tullock, 1967; Tollison, 1982; Becker, 1983). In a traditional society agriculture may be protected to preserve the value of aristocratic landholding, while in a democratic industrial society manufacturing may be protected to maintain the wages of the urban working class. A cohesive intellectual elite may succeed in subsidizing technological research, whereas party electoral competition in a pluralistic society is more likely to eliminate subsidies in the interests of consumers and taxpayers as a whole.

Historically, though, it is difficult to explain all industrial policy regimes in these terms. For example, why are some European industrial democracies persistently more inclined to protectionism than others? Why have some European countries made a much stronger commitment to subsidize long-term R & D than others? It is difficult to see how a strictly neoclassical approach can contrive to explain all of the relevant phenomena without encountering major complications. It may be simpler to admit at the outset that cultural factors are an important influence on industrial policy, and to recognize that it is the interaction between cultural factors and economic ones that governs policy choices.

Section 8.2 reviews the various routes by which industrial policy can have an impact on national economic performance. It presents a 'systems view' of the economy and shows how different industrial policies impinge selectively on different linkages in the system. Section 8.3 indicates how the neoclassical political economy framework must be extended if cultural factors are to be introduced. It is argued that culture offers a collective vision of the economic system which can be sufficiently strong to elicit a policy consensus across potentially conflicting interest groups. Collective vision is a potentially nebulous concept, however: it needs to be sharpened up if it is to be of much use. The discussion identifies three dimensions of culture which are influential in persuading people to adopt either an interventionist or a non-interventionist stance.

Other dimensions of culture explain why intervention, when it occurs, tends to take different forms in different countries. These dimensions are discussed in section 8.4. Finally, there are two dimensions of culture which influence the success of intervention, although they work in opposite ways. A trusting attitude to other people tends to make intervention successful when it occurs, but to reduce the need for intervention in the first place. Conversely, aggression towards foreigners tends to encourage intervention in order to mobilize resources for warfare, but often generates poor results so far as coordination is concerned. These dimensions are considered in section 8.5.

Section 8.6 examines how far the switch away from interventionist industrial policies in many countries during the 1980s can be seen as a part of a more general process of cultural change. A model of cultural change based on ideological competition is set out. It is suggested that, while culture can, in principle, adapt efficiently to changing circumstances, the adaptation that occurs in practice is often inappropriate because of ideological influences.

Section 8.7 gives an example of the way in which changing perceptions of the competitive process have influenced policies towards national monopolies, and section 8.8 summarizes the conclusions.

8.2 A SYSTEMS VIEW OF THE ECONOMY

Figure 8.1 offers a simple schematic view of a modern national industrial system. The system consists of a set of related activities. The figure identifies various types of activity and illustrates the network of linkages between them. For simplicity, some of the minor linkages have been suppressed. Furthermore, because of the high level of aggregation, each 'activity' is in fact a sub-system in its own right (for further details see Casson, 1990, ch. 2). Indeed, it is possible to visualize a lengthy regress in which each activity in each sub-

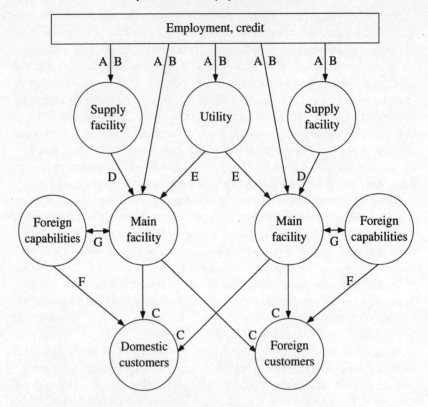

A   Employee motivation; efficiency of the labour market.
B   Creditor confidence; efficiency of the market for ownership and control.
C   Effectiveness of competition in product markets.
D   Good supplier relations.
E   Harmonious sharing of utility output.
F   Harmonious trade relations.
G   Harmonious foreign ownership relations.

Figure 8.1   A national industrial system with international linkages

system is itself a sub-system, and so on. A good industrial policy will always take account of this inherent complexity of the system to which it is applied.

Factor markets for labour and capital – particularly risk capital – appear at the top of the figure. These factors flow into both upstream and downstream production activities. The upstream activities include utility operations (energy, transport, and so on) and the supply of raw materials and components to downstream manufacturing and assembly activities. Downstream producers in turn sell to customers (both private and government) at home and abroad. At the same time foreign firms can sell into domestic markets. Furthermore, some domestic plants may be owned by foreign firms, or license technology from them, whilst domestic firms may own branch plants abroad and form partnerships with foreign licensees.

Each of the linkages shown in Figure 8.1 raises particular strategic issues which an industrial policy may seek to address. These issues are identified by the letters A–G; a key to the issues is provided at the foot of the table. The issues relate both to competition between activities – such as between domestic and foreign production – and to cooperation between activities – such as component supply and assembly, or the link between an energy utility and a manufacturing plant. One of the key points that emerges from the subsequent discussion is the importance of maintaining the correct balance in industrial policy between these competitive and cooperative requirements.

Those who favour interventionist industrial policies tend to emphasize the technological complementarities between the different activities shown in the figure. Although they recognize that each activity may itself be a system, they tend to assume that systems and sub-systems form a natural hierarchy, so that it is quite meaningful to analyse the system at the sectoral level without reference to the details which are revealed at the microeconomic level. They also believe that a 'systems view' is useful in planning major infrastructure investments. This reflects another aspect of interventionism – a concern with dynamic rather than static efficiency gains. This vision of a tightly coupled system whose performance is to be optimized over time suggests that the institutions of industrial policy should be based on centralized control.

Those who favour non-interventionist policies, on the other hand, tend to emphasize substitution possibilities. They believe that, when the systems and sub-systems are 'unpacked', no simple hierarchy of strategic dependence will emerge. Simultaneity and interdependence among a myriad of small activities is the key characteristic of the system, giving rise to intricate chains of substitution possibilities which only a market organization can detect. Non-interventionists regard dynamic efficiency simply as an intertemporal analogue of static efficiency and believe that infrastructure projects should be evaluated by exactly the same criteria as those applied to ordinary manufacturing projects. The role of industrial policy should be to 'complete the market' by refining and extending property rights and not to weaken existing property rights by extending the realm of arbitrary government *fiat*.

8.3 EMBEDDING INDUSTRIAL POLICY IN A CULTURAL CONTEXT

Debate over interventionism tends to focus on issues such as economies of scale, sunk costs, technological spillovers, environmental externalities and the like, and the possibility of dealing with these successfully through the market mechanism. The central issue addressed in this chapter is not, however, whether the logic on one side of this debate is better than that on the other, but rather why the concepts that dominate debate on industrial policy, and the assumptions that are most commonly made, vary over time and across countries.

The short answer to this question is that not everyone sees the world as an economist does. Different people see the same issue from different perspectives; indeed, in extreme cases they may not even be able to agree even on what the issue is. Differences of this kind may be not only individual but also collective. One group of people may share a view which is quite different from that of another group. Where different social groups correspond to different nation states (or, more precisely, to the governing elites of these nation states) different perceptions of the same industrial issue may lead to very different national policies being used to address it.

Differences of interpretation are not the only kind of difference that can prevail between two groups. The objectives or missions of the groups may differ too. One group, for example, may believe that its social institutions are superior to those of other groups and may seek to impose these institutions by conquest. In this context technology policy may be driven by military ambition. Another group may be more concerned with material issues such as the standard of living, and view technology instead in terms of its civilian use in consumer goods industries. Again, one country may strive for technological leadership and therefore feel obliged to develop a capability for basic as well as applied research, while another country may be content to be a follower and so may focus instead on applied research of an adaptive kind.

A conventional economist might object to these remarks about groups on the grounds that groups exist, if at all, only in the minds of their members, and certainly do not have minds or wills of their own. This is a valid criticism, but only up to a point. Groups are objective in the sense that members of the same group normally interact more frequently with fellow-members (insiders) than with non-members (outsiders). The group concept is also institutionalized in a wide variety of forms, from the family, school and club on the local level to the church, trade union and political party at the national level. It is also useful, for certain purposes, to consider firms and governing elites as social groups, rather than just as production units and legislators, respectively.

It is, however, correct to insist that the objective or mission of the group exists in the minds of its members and has no independent reality outside them. One of the features of a group, however, is that its members are likely to be standardized on their mission. This is because the mission is usually articulated by a single leader who emerges from a division of labour within the group (see Chapter 2). Pursuit of a collective mission can be a source of satisfaction (and hence of economic value) to the followers, and so the mission becomes a kind of intangible public good that is produced by the leader and is consumed by the members of the group.

It is not only the achievement of a collective goal that can be a source of satisfaction to the members, though: personal achievement can be important too. The leader can set performance norms for various roles. Citizens must be honest, employees must be loyal, managers must be competent, workers must work hard, and so on. Individuals who live up to these norms obtain an emotional reward; those who fail to do so may incur an emotional penalty instead.

This leads to an important distinction between those cultures which take an *atomistic* view of the group, and those which take an *organic* view (see Chapter 7). The atomistic view suggests that an individual's emotional satisfactions stem from his own behaviour – the morality of his own actions and his own personal achievements. The organic view, on the other hand, suggests that it is the individual's participation in the collective mission of the group that is really satisfying. It is the sense of having contributed in a small way to something very significant – so significant that only a group and not an individual could achieve it – that carries the greatest emotional weight.

The atomistic view suggests that emotional rewards are very much like material rewards, in the sense that they relate more to what the individual himself consumes than to what other people do. It encourages belief in the autonomy of each individual and offers a vision of the group in which these autonomous individuals themselves create the group through a social contract. Because the individual is morally prior to the group, the role of the social contract is to secure the initial rights of each individual to property, privacy and so on.

The organic view, on the other hand, emphasizes that members share in the emotional rewards of collective activity and so the analogy between emotional rewards and material rewards suggests that material rewards should be shared as well. From this perspective, the private appropriation of material resources seems like an attempt to deny other people the opportunity to share in their enjoyment. Thus social ownership, or ownership in common, is preferred to private ownership.

This stance is further supported by the view that the group has moral priority over the individual, since without the support of the group the individual could not survive. The emphasis of law, therefore, is on the obligation of the individual to the group, rather than on the right of the individual to isolate himself socially from the group when he desires to do so. Since the generation of emotional rewards hinges crucially on collective activity, and the efficiency of such activity often requires conformity in behaviour, the organic view offers less scope for personal freedom than does the atomistic view.

The organic view not only influences the perception of society, it affects the perception of the industrial system too. Writers who incline to an organic view emphasize the relatedness of the technologies employed in different industries.

They recognize, for example, that the introduction of a new technique in one industry may have to wait on the innovation of a different technique in another industry. Capital goods industries are often crucial constraints in this respect: a process innovation in a consumer good industry may have to wait upon a product innovation in a capital goods industry. Relatedness also involves the exploitation of economies of scope in basic technologies. An emphasis on relatedness, for example, encourages efforts to discover and exploit generic physical principles which, when applied in different fields, will generate a whole family of engineering solutions to specific problems.

Those who incline to an atomistic view, on the other hand, often perceive different aspects of technology as separable. They are concerned that each particular innovation should be assessed in terms of its calculable effects, and not in terms of ill-defined spillovers. While the organicist believes that technological appraisal must be carried out within the framework of an integrated industrial policy, the atomist favours decentralizing appraisal to individual entrepreneurs within a market system.

Another important distinction is between *elitist* cultures, which assume that the distribution of intelligence and managerial ability is very unequal, and *democratic* cultures, which assume intelligence and ability are fairly evenly spread. Modern Western culture strongly endorses the democratic view; certainly, a key assumption is that the general standard of intelligence is sufficiently high to warrant a universal franchise.

There is a tendency for atomistic attitudes to be linked with democratic ones, because the moral autonomy of an individual is normally assumed to rest on a certain minimum level of intelligence. There is also a link between organic attitudes and elitism. Thus the organic metaphor suggests that the elite should act as a 'brain' to control the 'body' of the state. This attitude is less evident today, though, than it was amongst the late nineteenth-century intellectuals, who lived before European fascist dictators came to power. Having said this, it is not unreasonable to suggest that even today those who favour interventionist industrial policies tend to exhibit organic and elitist values, whilst those who dislike intervention incline to individualist and democratic values. Thus, while many contemporary interventionists would deny any elitism, it is noticeable that they often appeal to academic authorities with strong elitist views, Schumpeter (1934) being the most noticeable example, of course. Furthermore, a comparison of those countries, such as Japan and France, which have very active industrial policies with those which do not, such as the United States and the United Kingdom, would tentatively support the association of interventionism with organic and elitist cultural values (see Table 8.1 below).

It is a mistake to suggest, though, that atomistic democratic cultures are opposed to intervention of all kinds. They are only opposed to the kind of *active* interventionism in which, for example, state control of strategic industries is seen as crucial for long run national growth. When it comes to the regulation of utility prices, say, an atomistic culture may actually favour intervention because it is required to protect individual consumers against monopoly power. An organic culture, on the other hand, might see the high profits of unregulated monopoly as providing a boost to further large-scale investment, and hence consider it better not to intervene.

This suggests a third dimension along which cultures differ, namely consumer orientation and producer orientation. Consumer orientation means that people are visualized principally as shoppers, and the role of the industrial system is seen as being to fill the shops with exciting value-for-money products. Competition is seen as important both in maintaining low prices for standardized products and in encouraging variety through the continued innovation of novel products. Natural monopoly due to economies of scale in the utilities is perceived as an awkward exception to the beneficial rule of competition. Because unregulated competition would drive down prices to marginal cost and result in persistent losses in the utilities, intervention is required, but only for this limited purpose.

Producer orientation, on the other hand, means that people are visualized principally as workers, and industry is seen as a valuable source of employment. The larger the scale of the enterprise, the more jobs are created. Intervention is required to subsidize the investment which is needed to create sufficient jobs. Conversely, the desire to preserve existing jobs may encourage the subsidization of declining industries. Indeed, once created, large enterprises may be very difficult to close down, for neoclassical political economy indicates that industrial workers concentrated in large plants are more likely to mobilize political support than are consumers and taxpayers who are dispersed throughout the economy (Olson, 1982).

The three dimensions of culture identified above are listed in Table 8.1. In each case the dimension is identified first by the characteristic that tends to promote interventionism and secondly by the characteristic that promotes non-interventionism instead. Intervention is understood to be the active form of intervention described above. To clarify the interpretation of these concepts, some popular stereotypes of national cultures are indicated (for additional stereotypes see Casson, 1990, ch. 4). The most obvious comparison of cultural extremes involves the United States and Japan, but a comparison of France and the United Kingdom is quite interesting too. These stereotypes relate to the 1970s – before the rapid cultural changes of recent years induced a degree of convergence in the cultures of the industrialized countries. (The process of cultural change, and its implications for industrial policy, are considered in section 8.6.)

For each country, the degree of interventionism, predicted from cultural considerations, is indicated on the bottom line. The numerical index indicates the number of interventionist characteristics associated with the stereotype. Casual empiricism suggests that the measures of interventionism shown in the table capture quite successfully the overall degree of intervention actually observed in each economy at the time, although the extreme subjectivity of the stereo-typing means that little weight should be placed on individual results.

Table 8.1   Three dimensions of culture that affect industrial policy

Intervention	Non-intervention	Japan	USA	France	UK
Organicism (O)	Atomism (A)	O	A	O	A
Elitist (E)	Democratic (D)	E	D	E	E/D
Producer orientation (P)	Consumer orientation (C)	P/C	C	P	P
Degree of interventionism		2.5	0	3	1.5

Japan is shown as an organic society, having a clear sense of national unity deriving, in part, from its racial homogeneity and island location. Japan is consumer-oriented so far as export-oriented industries are concerned, but producer-oriented so far as its domestically-oriented service industries are concerned. France too is shown as an organic society, built around the cultural symbol of the revolutionary Napoleonic state. It has a highly educated elite which, unlike the Japanese elite, is less concerned with consumer requirements in export markets and more concerned with producer interests in the state-owned utilities.

The United States and United Kingdom are shown as sharing an atomistic view of society. They are also democratic rather than elitist, although the United Kingdom is less democratic than the United States because it has a hereditary social elite, exemplified by the constitutional trappings of the monarchy and the House of Lords. The United States is, however, more consumer-oriented than the United Kingdom. United States citizens lack the commitment to trade union solidarity found in the United Kingdom and perceive themselves more as consumers and taxpayers who must take individual responsibility for earning their living.

8.4   THE CULTURE OF INTERVENTIONISM

Because elitism encourages intervention it is likely that the attitudes of the elite will be a major influence on the form of the intervention and on the process used to implement it. Much will depend on whether the elite is a traditional or modern one (Hoselitz, 1960). A modern elite is likely to include politically networked intellectuals who will seek a rational grounding for intervention in some theoretical scheme. A traditional elite, on the other hand, is likely to be suspicious of grand ideas. It will reject theory in favour of a more pragmatic approach.

A theoretical approach often suggests radical solutions. Theory raises intellectual possibilities that have never been put into practice before. At the same time the simplifying assumptions distract attention away from the complications that may be encountered. The mathematical elegance and logical consistency of the theory create a sense of confidence that nothing unexpected is likely to happen when implementation occurs. By contrast, a pragmatic approach favours incremental change. The pragmatist lacks the theorist's confidence that change is necessarily for the better, and so proceeds by trial and error in a sequence of small steps. The pragmatist, in other words, is much more sensitive to the risks involved.

The major intellectual product of the modern world view is natural science. A modern elite will therefore seek to present intervention as a scientific process based, for example, on the optimal control of the economic system. Intervention will involve large-scale data gathering, the formulation of computable models and the setting of explicit targets. In addition to this mimicry of scientific method in the intervention process, intervention is likely to involve subsidies for experimental work in natural science. The overt rationale may be long-term investment in new technology for economic growth, although the real motivation may simply be to subsidize the intellectual pursuits of the elite.

By contrast, a traditional elite is more likely to be interested in artistic pursuits. Support for traditional arts and crafts is likely to be favoured above radical experiments with new forms of expression. Scientific research will not necessarily be ignored, but is likely to be regarded purely instrumentally, as a means to an end (Wiener, 1981). It is unlikely to be subsidized for reasons of enjoyment or prestige.

A final aspect of modern attitudes is a belief in the importance of formal and impersonal administrative structures. Traditional attitudes tend to favour informal personal arrangements instead. Personal orientation is institutionalized in economic organizations, such as family firms, which are based on informal relationships between members of small, compact and stable social groups (Ellickson, 1991). Relationships are governed by traditional factors such as age, gender, paternity and so on. Impersonal orientation, on the other hand, is institutionalized in large formal organizations in which a clear distinction is drawn between an office and the person who holds it. Relationships are defined in terms of offices, and office holders are supposed to behave quite impartially. Showing favouritism towards family and friends is not acceptable, as it is with personal orientation, but is condemned as corruption instead. Impersonal orientation is reflected in a desire for transparency of structures and external accountability in organizations, whereas personal orientation involves an acceptance that relationships within an organization may well be opaque to outsiders and that secrecy will be maintained.

There is a paradox, however, in the attitude of a modern elite which sets up impersonal institutions to implement its interventionist policies, namely that elites of any kind often function best when they operate traditionally through frequent face-to-face contacts amongst their members. The methods of coordination that the members of a modern elite employ amongst themselves are therefore often ones whose efficiency they ostensibly deny. Their commitment to formal and impersonal structures means that they do not understand the informal and personal mechanisms on which the cohesion of their elite depends. It is perhaps for this reason that intervention by elites so often fails in practice. Instead of informally diffusing their enthusiasm for intervention to the administrators they employ, the elite reduce intervention to formal bureaucratic routine and thereby alienate the very people who are directly responsible for making it work.

The four dimensions of elitist culture reviewed above are summarized in Table 8.2, which also extends the previous national stereotypes to illustrate how the dimensions may be used. Not surprisingly, France emerges as the country with the most modern elitist attitudes and the United Kingdom with the most traditional ones. Japan's fundamentally traditional attitudes have been ameliorated by the positive attitude towards Western technology stimulated by the Meiji restoration, while the modern attitude of the United States is tempered by its Anglo-Saxon inheritance of incremental and pragmatic attitudes to innovation.

Table 8.2   Four dimensions of elite culture that influence interventionist strategies

Modern	Traditional	Japan	USA	France	UK
Theory (T)	Pragmatism (P)	P	T/P	T	P
Radical (R)	Incremental (I)	I	R/I	R	I
Scientific (S)	Artistic (A)	S	S	S	A
Impersonal (M)	Personal (P)	P	M	M	P
Degree of modernism		1	3	4	0

8.5   SUCCESSFUL INTERVENTION

Highly personalized societies are good at generating trust within small groups, such as the family firm and local community. Whether trust exists between members of different groups within the society is another matter, though. If it does then we have a high-trust society. High trust exists when other members of society are expected to be honest whatever specific allegiance they may have (Polanyi, 1944, 1977).

A high-trust society relies on moral sanctions. Its leader engineers a culture of integrity by offering emotional satisfactions to followers who pursue an honest strategy (see Chapter 7). If each follower who is influenced in this way believes that other followers are influenced in the same way, then a social equilibrium based on mutual trust can emerge. Each follower becomes sufficiently optimistic about others for him to behave in a way which validates other people's optimism about him.

High trust encourages spontaneous cooperation and hence reduces the need for intervention to prevent, or correct for, dishonesty of various kinds. Conversely, low trust undermines spontaneous cooperation. It creates a need for intervention because it encourages people to behave dishonestly.

Unfortunately, though, the need for intervention is difficult to meet in a low-trust society. The problem is that in a low-trust society people not only cannot trust each other, they cannot trust the intervenor either. Indeed, since the intervenor often has more power than anyone else, particularly if he is backed by the coercive power of the state, he is more to be feared than other people. Although there are evils that need correcting, therefore, they cannot be tackled because the solution – namely intervention – is feared more than the problem itself.

Fear of intervention means that trust becomes focused, not on people, but on processes instead. Intervention, when it occurs, is governed by rules: discretionary intervention is disliked because it is believed that discretionary powers are easier to abuse. Rules make it easier to detect when the intervenor cheats.

Formal rules do not, however, offer complete security against cheating. Dishonest judges, false witnesses and other forms of corruption are always possible in a low-trust society. As a result, a low trust society with no discretionary intervention is always potentially inferior to a high-trust society with discretionary intervention.

Engineering trust through leadership can be a mixed blessing, however. This is because the easiest way for a weak leader to engineer trust is to demand loyalty against a common enemy – to encourage people to 'close ranks' against an outsider whom they fear.

External *aggression* is therefore widely used as grounds for intervention. It justifies protectionism as a means to self-sufficiency; it also justifies export controls as a safeguard for technology, and managed markets as an aid to procurement of military supplies. Its disadvantage is that civilian consumers lose priority, and workers may even be conscripted to fill high-priority jobs. This is quite apart from the cost of damage resulting from war itself.

While both high trust and external aggression are conducive to intervention, therefore, they lead to very different forms of intervention, one of which is likely to be beneficial, and one of which is not.

Table 8.3 extends the national stereotypes to trust and external aggression. It suggests that in the 1970s all four countries were peaceful rather than aggressive, although it should be noted that Japan, France and the United Kingdom have all demonstrated a capacity for aggression at various times in their history. Although the United States has been involved in a variety of conflicts, its normal strategy (officially, at least) is one of third-party intervention to 'restore democracy' in a country where conflict has already begun.

The United States is a more notable exception in the trust dimension. It is a highly legalistic society, whose citizens are distrustful of any discretionary intervention. The constitutional validity of national regulation of industry is constantly under scrutiny and so it is not surprising that under these conditions interventionist industrial policies in the United States have enjoyed little success.

Table 8.3   Cultural factors affecting the propensity to intervene, the type of intervention and its success

Intervention	Non-intervention	Japan	USA	France	UK
High trust (H)	Low trust (L)	H	L	H	H
External aggression (A)	Peacefulness (P)	P	P	P	P

The combination of low trust and external non-aggression in the United States might at first seem paradoxical, for surely a low-trust society would be distrustful of its neighbours too? The explanation seems to be that in the United States aggression is directed towards fellow citizens, whereas in high-trust societies aggression is directed away from them towards an outside enemy. The highly individualistic and competitive culture of the United States may therefore be a significant factor in its attitude of indifference towards other societies. It is concerned about the political process employed in these societies, but has little interest in the outcomes of this process unless US economic interests are directly affected.

8.6   CULTURAL CHANGE

Culture is often portrayed as something inert, the 'dead hand' of the past, inhibiting desirable modernization. This is a very misleading view. As indicated above, culture is not just an attribute of traditional societies: modern societies have a distinctive culture too. Unfortunately, though, the image of the rational and autonomous individual created by the modernist has encouraged neoclassical economists to neglect cultural influences on behaviour (Hagen, 1964). The transition from traditionalism to modernism is not therefore, as some economists believe, the end of culture, but simply the continuing process of cultural change at work.

The appropriate response for a modernist thinker is not to reject culture but rather to model cultural change. This is not just a question of modelling the transition to modernism; it includes, for example, modelling the transition from modernism to post-modernism too. The modelling of change needs to avoid an unnecessary commitment to the progressive view that change is always for the better. Indeed, it is suggested below that recent cultural changes appear to be impairing economic performance and not improving it.

Figure 8.2 presents a simple model of cultural change in which the legitimacy of existing leadership depends on its ability to meet its own performance norms. The leader sets the culture, which is expressed in two main ways. The first is the values and beliefs of people, as determined by the leader's example and by his rhetoric. The second is the institutions – firms, markets, the state and so on – through which individual incentives are mediated. It is these institutions that determine the constraints that optimizing individuals face.

The culture disseminated by the leader is chosen by him in order to achieve his own particular goals. The culture is set in the light of the leader's perception of his environment, and in the light of the lessons which the leader draws from comparing past performance with his own performance norms. Past performance reflects the collective outcome of previous individual behaviour, as determined by the interplay of values, beliefs and institutional constraints.

A leader can normally remain in power so long as his past failures do not catch up with him, that is so long as the performance for which he is deemed responsible meets the cultural norms he has set. There is always potential competition for leadership. In democracies it is institutionalized in the electoral process, whereas in dictatorships military mutiny and revolutionary insurgency are the most common threats.

Leaders do not operate in an intellectual vacuum, however. The complexity of the economic system is so great, and the task facing the leader so overwhelming, that leaders usually refer to a simple ideology when setting culture. An ideology is a small set of related assumptions which provide clear guidance on major issues and simple justifications for the chosen policies. Ideologies are crucial to leaders in legitimating their position: the survival of a leader may well depend on his having a convenient ideology which allows him to lay the blame for failure on other people.

Throughout much of the twentieth century Western European countries have been dominated by a single ideological struggle between capitalism and socialism. Capitalism articulates an atomistic, democratic and consumer-oriented

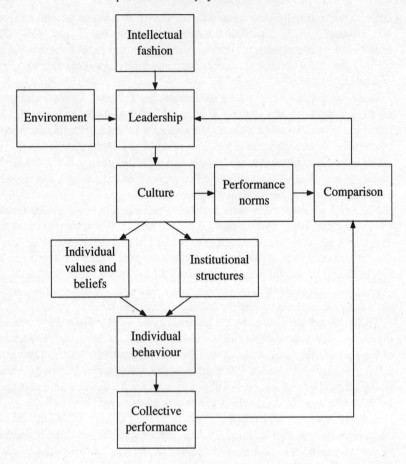

Figure 8.2   Culture, conduct and performance

view of society and is essentially non-interventionist in its approach. Socialism represents an organic elitist producer-oriented view of society and is essentially interventionist. (Some socialists would dissent from its characterization as elitist, but the fact remains that intellectual elites have played a prominent role in the formulation of socialist policies and that lack of democracy has been characteristic of many socialist countries.)

The First World War marks a turning point in this ideological struggle. Before 1914 capitalism had largely held its ground against trade union agitation and increasing socialism in urban government. After the war pro-capitalist leadership groups in several countries were discredited, and experiments in practical socialism became common. Intellectual fashion increasingly favoured the Marxian interpretation of history, which suggested that industrialization was the key to economic growth. Rapid growth in turn depended on producing capital goods rather than consumer goods, which suggested an emphasis on heavy industries. Nationalist sentiments encouraged countries to import technology in heavy industries so that they could master the technology themselves. A sense of military insecurity engendered by the war encouraged self-sufficiency in armaments-related industries. To secure a market for domestic producers, protectionism was introduced, especially in strategic industries such as steel and vehicles.

After the slump of 1929–33, these trends were reinforced by liberal democratic thinkers such as Keynes, who favoured an increased role for government in maintaining full employment. Maintaining investment levels became a government responsibility and this financial commitment, combined with nationalist and socialist ideologies, strengthened the case for nationalization of industry. Keynes regarded the Second World War as a transitory period of high employment, after which the West was liable to stagnate. Capitalism could only continue as part of a mixed economy in which the state had a major role. This fitted in well with the emerging call for a welfare state. Keynesianism supplanted Marxism as the intellectual fashion. As a result, government became an employer of last resort, with much of the employment being created by overmanning in the public services.

Unfortunately, the commitment to full employment allowed trade union leaders to pursue independently another socialist agenda, the raising of wages. But in countries where productivity growth was very limited (notably Britain) the raising of money wages merely fuelled inflation and real wages did not rise much at all. At the same time the value of 'take home' pay was being eroded by the increasing levels of taxation needed to fund the public sector.

Following the first of the oil price shocks, wages needed to fall in some industries in order to compensate for the much higher price of energy inputs, but the necessary adjustments did not occur. Unemployment rose as a result. Social security payments became an increasing burden on the budget, and fears grew that the tax increases needed to fund them had created a serious disincentive to enterprise and hard work. The Keynesian compromise between socialism and capitalism became discredited and it seemed as though it was the socialist component that was to blame.

During the 1980s the reaction against state intervention in the economy rapidly gathered momentum. Privatization replaced nationalization as the key element in industrial policy. Monetary stability and labour market flexibility engendered by curbs on trade union power replaced fiscal policy as the mechanism of macroeconomic management. The pendulum of intellectual fashion had swung back to its pre-1914 position, close to the capitalist extreme.

But something else happened as well. The ideological concept of capitalism was different in one crucial respect. The contemporary concept of capitalism has much more emphasis on interpersonal competition and on the importance of the 'rule of law' in sustaining the competitive market system.

Superficially, it could be said that this is because contemporary notions of capitalism are borrowed from the United States, which is a legalistic low-trust society, rather than from the United Kingdom, which in the late-Victorian period was very much a high-trust society. But the enthusiasm with which the new concept of capitalism has been embraced suggests that the explanation goes deeper than that. For the United Kingdom itself has now become a more low-trust society than it used to be. Intellectual fashion has driven Western culture as a whole away from the high-trust view of society which was prevalent a century ago. What is so noticeable today is the deeply pessimistic view of human nature on which the ideological case for capitalism is based.

Modern emphasis on distrust stems from a belief that people are selfish and materialistic in their attitudes. Since there is bound to be a conflict between the material interests of selfish people, any kind of collective mission must be an illusion. Furthermore, if people are intelligent their selfishness may reveal itself in very devious forms. In these extreme conditions, it is claimed, people can almost never be trusted except under a stringent rule of law.

The intellectual basis for this pessimistic view of human nature stems in part from the popular interpretation of Darwin and Freud. Darwin's theory of evolution is deemed to have undermined the Judeo-Christian view of man as superior to the animals but subordinate to God. By reducing man to the level of the animals, and eliminating God from the design of man, Darwin legitimated as perfectly natural the material desires which romantics, idealists and religious believers had traditionally condemned. By appearing to identify the satisfaction of these desires with psychological health, Freud encouraged his followers to dismantle the traditional taboos on which the customs of informal personal societies depend. As a result, society has come to be perceived simply as a growing population of human animals competing with each other for a fixed (or even declining) supply of resources from which to satisfy their desires. The roots of interpersonal conflict are only too obvious. Moreover, those traditional institutions which derived their authority from the power and mystery of God having been undermined, only the law stands between society and anarchy.

The good news, according to modern libertarians, is that the law will emerge spontaneously where the benefits of cooperation warrant it; it does not need to be invented by an elite and imposed by a monopolistic state (Hayek, 1960; Popper, 1957). Competition between the alternative legal arrangements adopted by different groups will select as efficient a liberal constitution based on private property and a market system – the only arrangement which is in harmony with human nature. Coordination occurs under these arrangements purely as the unintended consequence of selfish action, thanks to Adam Smith's 'invisible hand'.

This libertarian view is, however, just the latest in a series of intellectual fashions which have influenced industrial policy. By ignoring the moral dimension to human behaviour it wrongly implies that the low-trust form of society is inevitable. Its results depend crucially on the assumption that individuals cannot be manipulated morally, which in turn means that a high-trust equilibrium cannot be sustained. This reflects a view that individuals cannot relate to an argument (of the Kantian type) that individual morality is necessary to sustain a collective mission. This in turn stems from a failure to recognize that individuals may desire to participate in such a mission because they value the emotional rewards that they will obtain.

The current intellectual fashion for libertarian industrial policy will, in due course, be superseded, but exactly what will supersede it is not so clear. If ideological debate remains as one-dimensional as it has in the past, then the pendulum is likely to swing back again towards the Keynesian position. It may even acquire sufficient momentum to reach the organic extreme, but this seems unlikely for the time being. But if debate is to move society towards an improvement in industrial policy making, then it seems essential that the dimension of trust should be recognized explicitly, turning ideological debate into a two-dimensional affair.

The two relevant dimensions are shown by the horizontal and vertical axes in Figure 8.3. The continuum between atomistic and organic societies is represented by the horizontal axis, while different degrees of trust are measured along the vertical axis. The top part of the figure illustrates the trajectory of twentieth century change in the West, beginning with the high-trust capitalist society in 1900 and finishing with the low-trust capitalist society in 1990. The intermediate position is represented by the Keynesian consensus of 1945, which marks the reversal of the trend to socialism.

This trajectory summarizes the changing culture of an international intellectual elite. Politicians in many countries came under its influence, sometimes directly in the peripheral countries and sometimes simply by following what politicians in leading countries did. The impact of cultural change on any particular country was mediated by its own distinctive environment and history. This is indicated in the bottom part of the figure, which compares the pattern of cultural change across the four countries that were discussed above. Although the same trends can be discerned in each country, the absolute and relative magnitudes of the trends differ in each case.

Even if the ideological debate in future becomes a two-dimensional affair, many important dimensions of cultural variation will still remain suppressed. It is therefore unlikely that ideological debate can move societies to any kind of cultural optimum. Nevertheless, explicit recognition of trust would prove crucial in reversing recent decline into a low-trust situation, and thereby help to eliminate a major source of inefficiency in contemporary industrial systems.

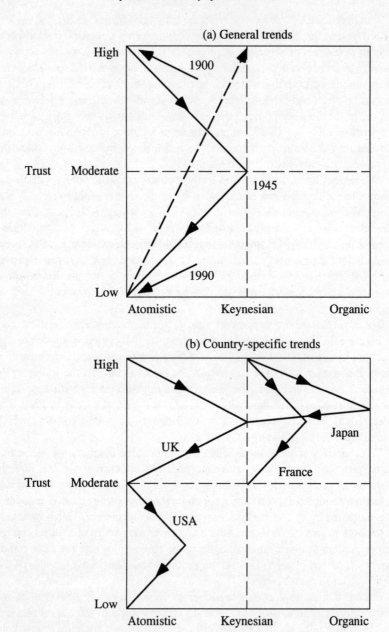

Figure 8.3   Cultural change in the twentieth century

The logic of this argument suggests that societies need to move towards a high-trust position about midway along the atomist–organic spectrum. How far and how fast they can reasonably move in this direction depends, though, upon their own traditions. The kind of trajectory required is indicated by the dashed line in the top part of the figure. If ideological debate does have the potential to respond intelligently to pressing problems, then theory suggests that this is the direction in which culture will begin to change over the next few years.

8.7   COMPETITION POLICY IN A CULTURAL CONTEXT

The preceding remarks are rather general and an illustration may help to clarify some of the points. Competition policy and natural monopoly regulation provide a useful case study. In the 1950s and early 1960s, Western economists approached competition policy with a simplified view of markets derived from Walrasian general equilibrium theory. Any distortion from the Walrasian ideal was deemed to establish a *prima facie* case for intervention. The classic distortion was monopoly power. Since scale economies in utility industries create natural monopoly, it seemed natural to treat utilities differently from the rest of the economy.

Theory identified marginal cost pricing as the rational rule for utilities, even though they would make a loss unless fixed charges (such as connection charges) could be levied as well (Berg and Tschirhart, 1988). Where fixed charges were difficult to collect (as in the railways) subsidies from the taxpayers would be required instead. No difficulty was initially anticipated in attracting managers of suitable competence and integrity to operate these utilities in the public interest. It became evident in the 1960s and early 1970s, however, that the 'soft budget constraint' under which nationalized utilities were operating resulted in surprisingly large losses, with adverse implications for taxes and the growth of the national debt. Tightening up the budget constraint resulted in higher prices rather than the lower costs which had been expected. To strengthen financial discipline, therefore, regulation was introduced.

No problem was expected in finding government officials equal to the task of regulation, but once again expectations were disappointed. As the problem of 'regulatory capture' was recognized (Peacock, 1984) concern arose that the regulators were being too friendly to the monopolists they were supposed to regulate. This applied whether the monopolists were in the public or the private sector. Gradually public attitudes hardened. The regulators were not simply being too friendly, they were not doing their jobs properly and were letting down the consumers and taxpayers. Initially idleness was suspected, but then suspicions began to include unrecorded perks, leading to allegations of corruption as well.

To explain the behaviour of regulators, it was argued, they had to be seen as selfish individuals, acting for themselves and not for the public interest. Only by promoting good regulators and penalizing bad ones could the public interest be maintained. To demonstrate that they were doing a good job, and so deserved reward, regulators felt obliged to adopt an adversarial stance towards the utilities they had previously befriended. An atmosphere of distrust led to secrecy on both sides. Accountants and lawyers had to be employed to extract the kind of information that the regulator required, and to check its accuracy. Both sides began to manipulate the media in order to win public support.

At the same time, the economist's concept of competition was changing to a more strategic one (Jacquemin, 1987). Although the physical assets employed by utilities might be naturally monopolistic, it was still possible to achieve entry and exit in a utility industry by changing the owners and operators involved (Baumol, Panzar and Willig, 1982). Moreover, some assets, though large, were more versatile than they might seem. Thus, while aircraft afford economies of scale on a given route, it is possible to switch aircraft between different routes fairly easily. It seemed, therefore, that deregulation of certain utility industries might be feasible after all. Deregulation would eliminate the problem of dishonest regulators and allow competition between owners which would keep down the costs of utility operation. Problems could still arise over monopolistic pricing, but these could possibly be dealt with by imposing competition on the distribution channels used by the utilities.

Utilities cannot, of course, be bought and sold between firms so long as they remain in the state sector. Hence the urgent need for privatization. Privatization places the assets in the hands of people who can, if necessary, sell them on to others who are better equipped to run and operate them – the important thing is simply to eliminate state involvement and create a market for the shares in the utility. The trend to privatization is therefore a natural consequence of the view that the managers of state-owned enterprises, and even professional regulators, cannot be trusted to operate in the public interest. But the question needs to be asked whether this is not in the nature of a self-fulfilling prophecy. When government officials and the heads of nationalized industries enjoy high prestige, and where moral notions of stewardship and patriotism are well developed, the problems of securing effective management of nationalized industries seem to have been less acute, as with municipal enterprise in late Victorian Britain, and in high-technology industries in post-war France and Japan. In a low-trust society deregulation has much to recommend it. But deregulation is not so well suited to utilities such as railways, gas and water where the costs sunk in the infrastructure have to be recovered through the exercise of monopoly power. Where such utilities play an important role in promoting economic development it remains an open question whether a switch to an interventionist high-trust society might not produce better results in the long run.

8.8   SUMMARY AND CONCLUSIONS

Most economic analysis of industrial policy is written from a prescriptive point of view. It attempts to identify when and where government intervention can improve welfare. Since, however, different countries have often pursued very different policies towards the same industries, it is difficult to explain actual government behaviour as a response to economists' prescriptions. Some of the differences may be due to different stages of economic development, or different technical and geographical constraints. This chapter has explored another possibility, that national industrial policy is a cultural product and reflects the different values, traditions and beliefs of each society. This cultural perspective is sufficiently broad to encompass some political aspects of industrial policy too.

The analysis has identified a total of nine dimensions of national culture which affect the degree of intervention in industrial policy, the form that intervention takes, and the way that intervention is carried out. Differences between countries in industrial policy towards similar industries can, in principle, be explained by corresponding differences in national cultures.

Culture affects conduct, and conduct in turn affects performance. In a given environment, some cultures may produce better performance than others. In this respect a key dimension of culture is the level of trust it sustains. It has been argued that high trust usually improves performance very significantly. Certainly the case of Japan – which has until recently enjoyed a very high-trust culture – would appear to support this view.

Culture is not an immutable constant, though; it changes steadily over time. In the twentieth century cultural change has tended to follow global trends. National cultures have changed in the same general direction, albeit beginning in different positions and changing at different rates. Intellectual fashions in humanities and social science have been important in determining the kind of lessons that have been drawn from the turbulent events of the twentieth century. These fashions have been reflected in the kind of policy advice that has been derived from economic analysis, notably the recent preoccupation with privatization.

It is natural to suggest that cultural change will be driven by the need to improve economic performance. The range of possible responses is, however, limited by the range of available ideologies. When ideological debate is narrowly focused, or becomes too pessimistic, culture may either fail to change at all, or change in discrete jumps, or change in the wrong direction altogether. It has been suggested that the switch from high-trust culture to low-trust culture, which has occurred in many societies, examplifies a change in the wrong direction. The repeated attempt to explain intervention failures in terms of the frustration of the public interest by private self-interest has acquired a self-fulfilling quality. Intervention stands little chance of working while society remains locked into a low-trust culture. The need for change is not difficult to discern, but where the intellectual vision and the political conviction will come from still remains obscure.

ACKNOWLEDGEMENTS

An earlier version of this chapter was presented at the December 1992 Meeting of the SPES Economic History Network at Worcester College, Oxford. I am grateful to the organizer, James Foreman-Peck, and the discussants for their comments. A revised version was presented to the German–British Colloquium on Innovation and Entrepreneurship at the University of Bonn in May 1993. I am grateful to the organizer, Professor Hans Pohl, to my colleague Professor Geoffrey Jones, and to the members of the colloquium for their comments on this version. I take, of course, full responsibility for the final version.

REFERENCES

Baumol, W.J., J.C. Panzar and R.D. Willig (1982) *Contestable Markets and the Theory of Industry Structure*, New York: Harcourt Brace Jovanovich.

Becker, G.S. (1983) A Theory of Competition amongst Pressure Groups for Political Influence, *Quarterly Journal of Economics*, **98**, 371–400.

Berg, S.V. and J. Tschirhart (1988) *Natural Monopoly Regulation: Principles and Practice*, Cambridge: Cambridge University Press.

Casson, M.C. (1990) *Enterprise and Competitiveness: A Systems View of International Business*, Oxford: Clarendon Press.

Ellickson, R.C. (1991) *Order without Law: How Neighbors Settle Disputes*, Cambridge, Mass.: Harvard University Press.

Hagen, E.E. (1964) *On the Theory of Social Change: How Economic Growth Begins*, London: Tavistock Publications.

Hayek, F.A. von (1960) *The Constitution of Liberty*, Chicago: University of Chicago Press.

Hoselitz, B.F. (1960) *Sociological Aspects of Economic Growth*, New York: Free Press of Glencoe.

Jacquemin, A. (1987) *The New Industrial Organization: Market Forces and Strategic Behaviour*, Oxford: Clarendon Press.

Olson, M. (1982) *The Rise and Decline of Nations*, New Haven, Conn.: Yale University Press.

Peacock, A. (ed.) (1984) *The Regulation Game: How British and West German Companies Bargain with Government*, Oxford: Blackwell.

Polanyi, K. (1944) *The Great Transformation*, New York: Holt, Rinehart and Winston (reprinted New York: Octagon Books, 1975).

Polanyi, K. (1977) *The Livelihood of Man* (ed. H.W. Pearson), New York: Academic Press.

Popper, K. (1957) *The Poverty of Historicism*, London: Routledge and Kegan Paul.

Schumpeter, J.A. (1934) *The Theory of Economic Development* (trans. R. Opie), Cambridge, Mass.: Harvard University Press.

Tollison, R.D. (1982) Rent Seeking: A Survey, *Kyklos*, **35** (4), 575–602.

Tullock, G. (1967) The Welfare Costs of Tariffs, Monopolies and Theft, *Western Economic Journal*, **5**, 224–32.

Wiener, M. (1981) *English Culture and the Decline of the Industrial Spirit*, Cambridge: Cambridge University Press.

9. Brands: economic ideology and consumer society

9.1 INTRODUCTION

This chapter is concerned with the implications of branding from the standpoint of society as a whole. It is not primarily concerned with the profitability of branding from the company's point of view, but whether what is profitable for the company is also beneficial for society.

Contemporary economic analysis of this issue tends to argue that branding is socially beneficial. It sees a harmony between the private interests of the firm and the goals of society. If a brand adds value to the company, it adds value to society as a whole, it is said.

This view is oversimplified – so oversimplified, in fact, that it is seriously misleading. It is a product, not so much of rigorous economic analysis, as of contemporary social values. These values reflect the dominant ideology of the market system, which is based on an atomistic and consumer-oriented culture. Contemporary culture is atomistic in the sense that it perceives society as a collection of rational and autonomous individuals rather than as an organic entity that transcends these individuals and moulds their preferences. It is consumer-oriented in the sense that individuals are assumed to derive their principal satisfactions from the private consumption of goods rather than from their work or from participation in communal activity.

This emphasis on the value of private consumption highlights the potential role of branding in ensuring that the experience of consumption matches its expectations. Rational consumers cannot be misled by branding, it is said, and will only buy branded products (particularly for a second time) if it is in their interests to do so. These individual interests are sovereign because of the atomistic nature of society. Thus the very fact that consumers choose branded products in preference to others shows that branding makes people better off, and so society, as a simple aggregate of individuals, must be better off as well.

This view of human nature is not, however, shared by those responsible for the actual marketing of products. To put it simply, an evening spent watching TV advertising does not suggest that the typical viewer is believed to be a rational and autonomous individual. Advertisers derive their professional expertise not from economic models but from psychological theories of cognition and motivation. They attempt to exploit factors, such as hidden needs, of which consumers themselves may not be fully aware.

Since TV advertising involves large sums of money spent by some of the most successful firms, it is reasonable to suppose that the advertisers know what they are doing. This chapter accepts the advertisers' point of view and reconsiders the implications of branding in this light. With a rather different view of human nature, these implications are a good deal more ambiguous than contemporary opinion suggests. To emphasize the practical relevance of the arguments, applications are given to a particular industry which is heavily involved in branding and TV advertising – food and drink.

The chapter also relates branding to a number of other issues. These include whether branding facilitates the exploitation of economies of scale, and whether brands are a separable asset in the firm's portfolio. There is also the question of whether the premium price of branded goods constitutes a regressive tax on poorer consumers, who are the major purchasers of certain types of branded good. Finally, the chapter attempts to relate the historical growth of branding to long-term economic and cultural change.

9.2   BRAND REPUTATION AS MARKET INFORMATION: A CRITIQUE

This section considers whether the economic theory of markets gives the kind of support to branding that is often claimed. It argues that the most familiar supporting arguments do not, in fact, refer to brands at all (see Balasubramanyam and Salisu, 1994). They relate instead to product differentiation, quality control and producer reputation. Most arguments for branding assume that in the absence of branding these factors would be undersupplied, so that there is a market failure which branding helps to correct. But even in the absence of branding there could be too much of some of these factors, notably product differentiation. Even if there were too little, it does not follow that branding will necessarily provide more. Branding will normally improve the situation only if it enhances the quality of consumer information. Branding can certainly do this, but it can also be used to suppress information. Most significantly, however, there are other ways of improving consumer information, and some of these tackle the issue more directly than does the use of brands. Thus brands are not necessarily the most effective way of doing the things that it is claimed that they do.

Product Differentiation

According to Lancaster (1979) each product may be regarded as a bundle of characteristics. The relevant characteristics of a motor car might be acceleration, fuel economy, passenger capacity, and so on. Consumers demand characteristics, not products. The demand for products is a derived demand, the intensity of demand for a given product reflecting the desirability of the particular mix of characteristics it offers.

A differentiated product does not have to be branded because it is always possible to order it by its specification. This is exactly what happens when customized products are made up to individual order. When just a small number of standard varieties are offered, then each variety can be ordered either by specification or by a reference number of some kind. When only one variety is available, then the generic name can, of course, be used. Thus a brand name is not necessary to signify the product under any circumstances. In this context the advantage of a brand name lies only in the economy of communication. The longer the string of distinguishing characteristics that must be enumerated, and the more subjective and qualitative these characteristics are, the greater is the advantage of using a brand name instead.

The learning of a brand name, and its mental association with particular characteristics, involves a set-up cost for the consumer, however. This is in addition to the cost to the producer of devising and publicizing the name. It follows immediately that a brand name is most useful in two circumstances. The first is repeat trading. The customer learns the name the first time he buys the product. This investment is paid back in subsequent transactions when only the name needs to be specified. The simpler and shorter the name, the easier it is to specify.

The second case is where the product is advertised away from the point of sale. The customer then needs to remember what he wants from the time he reads the advertisement until the time he makes his purchase. He also needs to remember it from one purchase to the next, of course, so that memory is relevant to repeat trading too. But since it is easier to remember a product that has already been purchased than one that has not, memory may not be quite so significant in the repeat-trading case.

Learning costs can be reduced if the brand name resonates with the characteristics claimed for the product. The consumer's demand is a demand for the characteristics, as noted above, and the translation of this into product demand is facilitated by association of ideas. A brand name should not only be succinct and memorable, therefore, but be imbued with relevant associations too.

The link between branding and repeat purchase indicated above works well in the food industry. Because of their bulk and perishability most food items are purchased repeatedly and this may explain why many foods, although their characteristics are relatively simple, are heavily branded. The subjectivity of the key characteristic, taste, is also likely to be important. Within the food sector branded goods purchased in single small transactions – confectionery and snack bars distributed through newsagents and drug stores, for example – are particularly prominent. Perhaps this is because the typical consumer of these products is in great haste and so places economy of communication at a premium.

Quality Control

The essence of product differentiation is that products are different by design and not by accident. Each variety is unique, but each unit of a given variety is the same. Customers dislike variability between units because this creates uncertainty about the characteristics of any particular purchase. Their concern is typically asymmetric, however – they dislike too little of a good characteristic, but are not averse to too much of it. Quality control is therefore normally concerned with assuring minimum standards. The probability that a unit is below the minimum standard defines the defect rate.

To a certain extent the defect rate is just another characteristic of the product. It does not require a brand name to indicate that the defect rate is low. Producers are, however, remarkably coy about publishing their defect rates. Even the top producers prefer to cultivate a general quality image rather than publicize low defect rates. For example, a top-quality car rental firm does not advertise that 'Only 3 per cent of our customers say they are dissatisfied,' even though internally managers may be quite proud of the fact. This indicates one of the ways in which branding can suppress information. Inter-brand competition focused on defect rates would impair valuable subjective characteristics with which the generic product is imbued (see below) and thereby damage producer interests in the industry as a whole. The suppression of defect information is therefore a rational collusive response by producers to the fact that consumers really do not want to know about the risks of a product. Although on average consumers' welfare may be improved by withholding unwanted information, such collusion may damage their welfare when, in an emergency, serious hazards remain concealed. Since the hazards may impinge on other people besides the consumers themselves, there is a potential externality problem here.

Another special feature of the defect rate is that it provides a particularly strong incentive for the producer to cheat by claiming that the defect rate is lower than it really is. With natural variability in production inputs, a lower defect rate normally implies a higher rejection rate, and hence more waste of output (Duncan, 1974). To lower the defect rate without raising the rejection rate it is necessary either to purchase higher-quality materials or to improve the sorting or filtering process so that fewer good items are wrongly rejected along with the bad ones. Both of these strategies involve extra costs.

Advocates of branding argue that it overcomes this incentive problem by allowing producers with low defect rates to gain a reputation for good quality. This is true, but only up to a point. Branding is neither a necessary nor a sufficient condition for this to occur.

The key issue is the nature of the sanctions against a cheat. The most obvious sanctions are fines and imprisonment effected by the state. The state can either respond to complaints made by consumers or make its own investigations. The state brings to bear on the issue its monopoly of force and its reputation for impartiality, as reflected in its legal procedures. It also has access to expert opinion.

The main limitation of the state is its requirements for evidence. Evidence is difficult to obtain when key characteristics are subjective or qualitative or where the evidence is liable to be destroyed in the act of consumption – both of which apply to food and drink. The collection and weighing of evidence constitutes a fixed cost, so that legal procedures are prohibitively expensive where small-value transactions are concerned – which again applies to food and drink.

In some cases the role of the state can be delegated to a producers' association. Like the state, a producers' association has access to expert opinion but, unlike the state, it is not weighed down with onerous rules of evidence. Fellow-producers have an incentive to punish cheats provided that they feel that the industry as a whole is in danger of being brought into disrepute. They may even be able to share the revenue generated by a fine levied on the cheat. If the producers' association has a statutory monopoly then it has a powerful sanction to extract a fine, since it can force the cheat who does not pay up to leave the industry. In the absence of statutory monopoly, however, some other exclusion mechanism may be required. The existence of an industry-wide public good, such as a cooperative distribution system, may be required for this purpose. The main disadvantage is that a producers' association can maintain prices at monopoly levels, discourage innovations that would disturb market sharing agreements, and so on. The prices maintained by a producers' association are therefore likely to reflect not merely a quality premium, but a monopolistic mark-up too.

Producer Reputation

Both of these approaches are, in essence, collective ones. Advocates of branding argue that punishment should be delegated to the consumer. The consumer's sanction is to withhold his repeat purchase, normally by switching his future patronage to a different brand. The more quickly information on defects diffuses through the market the more the producer's reputation is 'on the line'. Branding is valuable because by reducing communication costs (see above) it strengthens reputation effects.

The advantage of this approach is that it relies upon competition between firms rather than on the monopolistic powers of a producers' association or the state. It has a number of weaknesses however, related to this reliance on reputation effects.

To begin with, it is driven by the consumer's own evaluation of defects, rather than on expert opinion. The 'defects' may arise because the consumer is misusing the product without realizing it. If there is no feedback of information to an expert – for example, because no warranty claim is made – then the consumer as well as the producer may lose out.

More significantly, the reputation effect relies on consumers collecting sufficient information on defective items for them to be able to appraise the relative defect rates of different varieties. They need to combine this information with data on other characteristics in order to make an informed choice. Because it is relative defect rates that matter, the consumer needs information about defects in the products he does not buy as well as in those he does. Since it is the defect rate, and not just the incidence of a single defect, that is relevant, the consumer also needs information from a number of different units taken from different batches of each product. These information requirements constitute a very 'tall order' indeed.

It is not sufficient to say that a satisfied consumer should repeat-buy the product, because this does not provide information on the other products as well. Consumers need to learn from each other wherever possible. This does not mean, though, that every instance of a defect should attract maximum publicity, as some sections of the contemporary media seem to believe. The objective is not to expel from the industry every producer that supplies defective items, because the optimal defect rate is not normally zero. The requirement is rather that consumers should share their experiences, both good and bad, and learn as much as possible from each other before deciding on future purchases.

Finally, the sanction of loss of future custom is far more serious for some firms than others. A firm that is optimistic about market growth, or which has a low cost of capital (and hence discounts future profits relatively little) will attach more weight than others to a loss of future revenue. More significantly, a firm that has sunk a large amount of non-recoverable capital into the product is far more vulnerable to loss of custom than a 'hit and run' entrant with versatile equipment and negligible sunk costs. This is one reason for long-lived firms enjoying a reputation for quality and integrity that start-up firms do not.

The problem of the 'hit and run' entrant does not arise with state regulation because the penalty in that case is a fine, although a 'hit and run' entrant might attempt to evade the fine by strategically filing for bankruptcy. The problem could arise with a producers' association if the entrant preferred to leave the industry instead of paying the fine, but then the association may well have the power to keep the entrant out unless he is willing to commit sunk costs at the outset.

It has been argued that the problem of insufficient sunk cost is not a problem where brands are concerned because the building of a brand reputation is precisely a sunk cost of this kind (Klein and Leffler, 1981). The difficulty with this argument is that it does not explain why the firm wants a brand name in the first place. It explains why, given that the brand is valuable, the irreversible nature of the investment in the brand will discourage cheating. But investing in a brand name that has no independent value does not increase the penalty of cheating, since a loss is incurred as soon as the expenditure is made, and no further loss is involved if and when cheating occurs.

Thus it is a mistake to suggest that, say, celebrity endorsements build up brand reputation just because the payment of well-publicized celebrity fees assure consumers that the firm has much to lose from poor quality. For if the consumers really believed that no one is influenced by these endorsements then they would consider that the endorsements were a waste of money anyway, and they would suppose that the firm had already written off its investment whatever its product quality turned out to be. Only if the consumers believed that the managers believed (wrongly) that they (the consumers) were influenced in this way would the consumers expect product quality to be signalled by endorsement fees.

Further Observations

In practice collective and competitive incentive systems can be used together. Where defects are potentially hazardous and difficult to detect by inspecting the product, statutory regulation of production is the norm. A uniform standard is set by professional experts reporting to the state. Hygiene regulation in the food industry is an obvious case in point. Consumers do not rely on brands to avoid food poisoning. Because food poisoning is so hazardous to health, and bacteria are so difficult to detect, inspectors are given statutory powers of entry at the point of production. State intervention can also take account of the externalities associated with the spread of contagious or infectious diseases through the handling of food by affected people. It is the quality of taste, and not the purity of the product, that is assured by the brand.

In some less developed countries, however, state regulation is weak or unreliable, and here brands have a significant role in assuring basic levels of quality. Reduced incidence of salmonella could be a real selling point in this case. More generally, the higher are cultural standards of quality relative to regulatory standards, the greater is the scope for brands in assuring quality.

Historically, self-regulating producer associations have been an important alternative to the state. Like the state, they have concentrated on setting a uniform industry-wide standard of quality. Allowing producers to set their own standards, and to be judged on their own individual claims, is a more recent innovation associated with the growth of brands. Thus the trade marks favoured by medieval guilds were not intended to build brand reputations but were an aid to detecting those suppliers of substandard items who were putting the reputation of the group at risk.

Fears that associations introduced to raise quality may eventually turn to rent-seeking activities are supported by the experience of medieval guilds (and of many craft trade unions too). The guilds' concern with quality gradually gave way to price fixing and to lobbying for protection of the local market. This probably explains why the state rather than the producers' association seems to have gradually become the dominant authority in collective quality control. It is the combination of state control of basic quality and brand incentives governing premium quality that is characteristic of the modern market economy.

Policy Implications

The common thread that runs through the preceding analysis is that brands promote efficiency if and when they improve the quality of consumer information. But there are many other ways of improving consumer information.

One of the problems with brand loyalty is that customers are far better informed of the characteristics of the product they do consume than of the products they do not. This problem can be overcome if firms offer free samples to loyal consumers of rival products. Consumers can then check whether or not their loyalty is misplaced. Producers can also offer ordinary customers tours of their factory, thereby disseminating information which might otherwise remain locked into the official factory inspectorate. (It is rather ironic that recent European hygiene legislation designed to protect consumer interests makes such 'see for yourself' factory tours more difficult to arrange.) Producers can also submit to independent quality audit by reputable organizations who apply standards above the statutory minimum. Specialized media, such as magazines for enthusiasts and connoisseurs, play an important role in this, although there is a potential conflict of interest because of the dependence of the media on advertising revenue from the producers.

Producers can also reassure customers by offering generous warranties and readily enforceable money-back guarantees which avoid the need to make small claims in the courts. They can also sink costs in relevant activities, such as automated quality control. Such investments are doubly useful: they are not only directly relevant to quality but they demonstrably penalize poor quality because the firm is so dependent on future sales to pay the investment back. Producers can also take action to strengthen reputation effects by encouraging consumers to socialize with each other. By organizing their own enthusiasts' clubs they not only promote interest in the product but also provide a mechanism for disseminating information about the defect rate.

None of these mechanisms is directly linked to branding, in the sense that they can be employed for unbranded products too. One of the general insights of economic theory is that most incentive problems should be tackled at source wherever possible. Indirect solutions are only second-best. In the present context this means that incentive problems caused by imperfect information should be tackled by measures that directly improve information flow. Branding sometimes complements these measures but is not a direct measure of itself.

9.3   BRANDING AND CULTURAL CHARACTERISTICS

The most important motivation for branding, it is suggested here, is that it imbues products with cultural characteristics. Giving the product a name makes it possible to think of a 'personality' that goes with that name. The characteristics can then be linked to the personality of the product.

Unlike the physical characteristics of a product, cultural characteristics are not objectively measurable. They are economically relevant, however, because they are characteristics for which consumers are willing to pay. It is not irrational for consumers to value cultural characteristics. In economics rationality is an instrumental concept by which consumers determine their purchasing behaviour from given preferences (see Chapter 2). Preferences establish a priority ordering and rationality translates this ordering into appropriate behaviour under scarcity constraints. Economists do not say that one set of preferences is more rational than another, however peculiar some people's preferences may appear to be. Preferences are only said to be irrational if no consistent ordering prevails.

Consumer preferences for cultural characteristics are taken as given. This means that, when the cultural characteristics of a product are modified by branding, preferences with respect to products will change. Thus, by imbuing products with new cultural characteristics, branding manipulates consumer demand.

Four main types of cultural characteristic may be identified. The first simply makes the consumer feel good in a purely private sense. It is the emotional analogue to the material satisfaction gained from private consumption. The emotion may be related to a private fantasy: when sipping Australian wine I may be mentally transported to the Australian bush (see Merrett and Whitwell, 1994). The fantasy may activate pleasant memories or simply compensate for the fact that I will not be able to go there (or go back there) again.

A variant on the fantasy is the dream. The economic significance of dreaming is slightly different. Dreams may well come true, and the realization of a dream is often a focus for ambition, and hence a motivator for work (Schumpeter, 1934). Indeed, a product imbued with dream-like qualities may offer more emotional rewards before it is consumed than when it is consumed because the reality lacks the dream-like quality of the image on which expectations were focused. A camping holiday in the Australian bush might come into this category.

Another kind of private satisfaction is the sense of virtue in consuming a product which is morally good. Moral and religious systems are widely used (often for good reasons) to promote certain kinds of fantasy and dream and to censor others. A morally acceptable fantasy therefore provides more emotional benefit than an unacceptable one, which will be impaired by feelings of guilt. A consumer's morality is therefore an important determinant of his preferences for cultural characteristics. Thus a Protestant fundamentalist might condemn the consumption of an organic wine for its intoxicating effect, whilst an ardent environmentalist might approve on the grounds that it is ecologically sound. This moral dimension is considered further below.

The second main type of cultural characteristic is the badge of allegiance. It has social rather than private significance. Blue jeans, VW Beetles and Renault 2CVs can all be used to make a personal statement of values to other people. The economic significance of a badge of allegiance is that it facilitates the operation of social groups. People with shared values can recognize each other through their conspicuous consumption of symbolic products. Since social groups can reduce transaction costs between their members (Casson, 1991), badges of allegiance may serve to promote efficiency.

There is, however, an important difference between badges that unify hitherto disparate individuals and those that segment hitherto homogeneous groups into rival factions. While the former reduces transaction costs, the latter raises them. Thus, while blue jeans may promote economic interactions amongst the young, they may reinforce a generation gap which inhibits economic interactions between young and old. The net contribution to efficiency depends upon which of these interactions is the more important. In the case of blue jeans it could be argued that, because so many young people are employed by older people, the cost of widening the generation gap is greater than the benefit of promoting social solidarity amongst young people.

The third type of characteristic is related to status. Status is a social phenomenon, like allegiance, but is concerned with the differences and not the similarities between people. Reinforcing status-related characteristics through branding is economically wasteful. To appreciate this, consider a group divided into two factions: the 'haves' and the 'have nots'. The haves possess the status good and the have nots do not (Hirsch, 1977). When two haves, or two have nots, meet each other, the encounter is emotionally neutral (any positive effect would fall under allegiance, as described above). But when a have meets a have not the have feels good and the have not feels bad. This creates a strong incentive to acquire the good: if you meet a have, you avoid feeling inferior, while if you meet a have not you feel superior, so that whoever you meet you feel better off. If the good is reasonably priced, and the emotional benefits are strong, then everyone may buy the good. Since no-one is then inferior, no emotional benefits are obtained. But everyone needs the good because they would feel inferior to everyone else if they were the only person without it. Actually, no-one is better off emotionally than if no one had the good at all. Yet everyone buys the good, and so is actually worse off by an amount equal to the purchase price. Individually it is rational to buy the good because of the fear of feeling inferior, but collectively it is stupid because when everyone buys the good there is no-one to feel superior to.

If status is so inefficient, it may be asked, why are status systems so important and why have they lasted so long? Historically status has been an important form of occupational reward and, indeed, a good deal of status is still related to occupation today. Status rewards can compensate for missing pecuniary rewards in activities where the social benefits are difficult for the producer to appropriate. Thus a doctor may enjoy high status to compensate for the fact that he cannot charge his poorest and sickest patients much for his skills. This is not the only way of rationalizing status, of course. But, even in this context, allowing people to buy status tends to diminish efficiency. For if people who can appropriate rewards can acquire through consumption the same status as those who cannot, then status will eventually be devalued and recruitment to important occupations will be impaired. Other mechanisms, such as higher pay for directors, will have to substitute for the weakened status mechanism.

The final type of characteristic is one that makes the product suitable as a gift. It is important to remember that trade itself appears to have originated in gift giving, and that many gifts are still given in the expectation of receiving some unspecified future benefit in return. This reflects the fact that gift giving continues to support a wide range of non-market economic activity, for example the production of household services within the family. The difference between early and modern societies is simply that in modern societies the market sector has expanded and been formalized, and that most gifts used in the non-market sector are now procured through this market sector instead of being produced by the donors themselves.

A product does not make a suitable gift simply because it is useful to the recipient. There are many utilitarian items which are quite inappropriate as gifts. Indeed, if mutual convenience were the dominant criterion then most gifts would consist of money. A gift is rather an expression of the esteem in which the recipient is held. A gift contains information to the recipient because he is unsure of exactly how his reputation stands. A gift is therefore a symbolic statement of the reputation of the recipient, as interpreted by the donor.

Because gifts are such an important coordination mechanism in the non-market economy, the inculcation of relevant attributes through branding is potentially very valuable. By allowing the donor to pick off the shelf a highly distinctive and apparently exclusive product, the costs of finding suitable gifts are dramatically reduced.

Comparing the four types of characteristic discussed above suggests that the branding of products as status symbols is very inefficient (from the social point of view) compared with branding them as badges of allegiance. In terms of emotional rewards, status is typically a zero-sum game, because in every encounter the superior feeling of one party is offset by the inferior feeling of the other. When played out with branded products, however, it becomes a negative sum game because of the waste associated with the production of the product.

Badges of allegiance have an ambiguous effect because they can either unify people into a group or fragment an existing group into factions. Because badges of allegiance are mainly of significance to adolescents, few of whom are engaged in significant economic activity, the impact of badges on economic performance is probably fairly slight in any case.

Branding designed to imbue products with fantastic and dream-like qualities can be regarded favourably from a hedonistic perspective, provided that the fantasies do not have adverse externality effects (such as the incitement of aggressive behaviour). Gift-related characteristics can be particularly commended because of the continuing importance of gift giving in organizing economic activity within the household, and in clubs, societies and other small not-for-profit organizations.

9.4 FURTHER IMPLICATIONS

Because of its wide-ranging nature the preceding analysis has implications for a number of other issues that are commonly raised in connection with brands.

Barriers to Entry

It confirms the view that brands can be an important form of barrier to entry. It has already been noted that a long-lived incumbent firm demonstrates by its continued presence in the market that it is not a 'hit and run' entrant seeking to profit from poor quality. Consumers are also likely to believe that long-lived firms have accumulated more production experience than others, and that they are therefore more competent in assuring quality than their newer rivals.

Incumbent firms also have an opportunity to imbue their products with cultural attributes which are difficult to imitate. Foods and drinks containing mysterious ingredients or made to secret family recipes appear to consumers as inherently difficult to copy, so that any entrant must be under suspicion if it claims to offer an identical product. Of course, if the ingredients or the recipes are not particularly tasty then new firms can enter with their own secrets and mysteries. Marginal customers will be attracted away from incumbent firms until profits in the industry are reduced to normal levels.

The analysis also confirms the view that advertising persuades as well as informs. Advertising does not persuade by argument so much as by stimulus of the imagination. This explains why so many advertisements are important cultural artefacts, even if they fall slightly short of being major works of art. It is advertising that typically imbues the branded product with its cultural characteristics, although celebrity endorsements, sponsorship of sport events and other marketing ploys also have a role in this.

The fact that advertising is not really intended to inform is emphasized by the fact that so much relevant information is left out of advertisements – most notably the product price. Even where products are advertised as being good value for money, price information is often withheld. Many advertisements also fail to mention at which stores the product can be found, which is another vital piece of practical information.

Accounting for Brands

An important debate in accountancy concerns whether the capitalised value of a brand should appear on the firm's balance sheet, and this is reduced to the question of whether brands are separable from the firm's other assets (Barwise, 1990; Napier, 1994). In so far as brands are linked to quality control, a reasonable case can be made that the brand is inseparable from the firm because quality assurance depends on the training of the personnel and the management procedures used, which customers would believe to be different if ownership were to change. If, on the other hand, a brand is no more than a distinctive combination of cultural characteristics, it is much more independent of the firm. Note, however, that, while these characteristics may be independent of the ownership of production, they often depend on the location of production: an obvious point in the case of, say, whisky brands. Firms that acquire brands therefore need to be careful about the subsequent rationalization of production locations.

Mass Marketing

It is sometimes suggested that brands are socially beneficial because they facilitate the exploitation of economies of scale. This may be true historically in the case of the transition from customized production to mass production, or the integration of regional into national markets. In these cases branding provides the boost in sales that is needed to get a new large plant fully utilized. In other cases, however, such as petroleum refining, an integrated market for a generic product may be segmented by branding into smaller markets with a consequent loss of some economies of scale. In general there is no particular reason to associate branding with either economies or diseconomies of scale.

Distribution of Income

Mass-produced branded products are often aimed at consumers in the lower socioeconomic groups (Ward, 1994). One reason for this is simply that they are the most numerous. On the other hand, they are certainly not the wealthiest. Nor are they likely to be the groups most concerned with intrinsic product quality. The most probable explanation is that these consumers are the ones most likely to value the cultural characteristics with which advertisers associate their branded products. This sensitivity to cultural characteristics may in turn reflect the consumers' underlying concerns about their social status which they believe that branded products can help alleviate. It may also reflect the poorer urban environment in which these consumers live, which places a large premium on the fantasy element in the consumption of branded goods.

Two things follow if this interpretation is correct. The first is that the premium prices charged for branded products are borne by mainly poorer people, so that the pricing structure is regressive: wealthy shareholders extract rents from poor consumers, in other words. This is not to deny that the consumers benefit: they would not buy the products if they did not appreciate the fantasy and feel that their status had been enhanced. It does mean, however, that there may be better ways of improving welfare than selling branded products as compensation for low social status and a depressing environment. Given that status seeking is at best a zero-sum game, tackling status problems head-on might be a better approach. The same goes for the quality of the environment: creating new fantasies may be second-best to improving reality, at least up to a point. The second consequence is therefore that intensive demand for branded products is not necessarily a tribute to the success of the market system: it may actually be a compensating reaction to some of the failures of the system.

9.5   IDEOLOGY AND BRANDS

The emphasis in this chapter on the cultural significance of brands suggests a reappraisal of the standard historical interpretation of the growth of brands (see Wilkins, 1994). Conventional wisdom relates the growth of branding to a combination of rising incomes, improved transport and mass-production technology which has widened the market area over which consumer goods are distributed. Particular emphasis is placed on the role of packaging in maintaining the quality of the product between factory and consumer and in permitting colour and design to enhance point-of-sale display. Packaging also enhances the subjective degree of product differentiation, so that consumers perceive a greater variety of choice as well.

The arguments elaborated above are broadly consistent with this story, but they add a further dimension, namely the link between the growth of brands and cultural change. Cultural historians (for example, Williams, 1982) have shown that one of the consequences of commercial growth and industrialization has been the erosion of the monopoly power of traditional religion and the emergence of a moral pluralism sustained by mutual toleration. The promotion of brands through advertising taps into this moral pluralism by linking products to appropriate consumer lifestyles (Earl, 1986). Morality, particularly in its puritan manifestations, no longer provides such a tight constraint on consumerism. Morality becomes more permissive, and the choice between different moralities may even degenerate into just another aspect of consumerism itself.

The moral system which has achieved the greatest advance in its influence during the past two decades is the one centred on the ideology of the market. It is this system of thought which justifies making individual autonomy supreme and subordinating traditional moralities to the status of taboos which people may respect as they wish. As noted at the outset, it is from this point of view that most of the conventional analysis of brands is written. This analysis purports to show that brands are beneficial because branding is a product of the market system. Brands are good because this system is essentially good. It is admitted that the system is not perfect, but it is claimed to be better than any feasible alternative. Indeed, the recent downfall of socialist economies is cited in support of this.

The evidence on the growth of brands suggests a rather different interpretation, however. The major role claimed for branding, namely quality control, is in fact performed by statutory authorities in most developed countries. It is, ironically, only in developing countries that branding demonstrably performs a quality assurance role. The evidence suggests that the major role of branding is to imbue products with cultural characteristics – characteristics increasingly linked to the major lifestyle options of a pluralistic society.

The view of human nature indicated by this evidence is rather different from that of the calculating materialistic consumer promoted by market ideology. It suggests a rather imaginative and even romantically-inclined individual searching for objects with the kind of meaning and significance that the symbols of the great religions once had. It is an individual preoccupied with his acceptance by society and his status within it, who uses products as part of a strategy for social advancement. This individual prefers not to be informed about some of the risks he runs, thus information about defect rates is usually not desired, as explained above. To indulge his fantasies he needs to sustain a degree of self-esteem which objective self-appraisal might undermine. He therefore prefers to be rewarded by flattering gifts rather than by money payments which would indicate objectively his market value.

Brands 'add value' for this individual mainly because they support his fantasies, rather than because they reduce his anxieties about defect rates. But just as there are alternatives to brands in assuring product quality, so there are also alternatives to brands in generating emotional satisfactions too.

In her study of French intellectual attitudes to consumerism, Williams (1982, p. 152) notes that religious dogmatism is one answer to the needs of the individual who is 'determined to rise above the banality of mass merchandising'. In pre-industrial society religious observance certainly seems to have afforded many of the emotional satisfactions which in a secular society are generated by lifestyle experiments supported by branded goods. Market ideology encourages individuals to satisfy their emotional needs through consumption, but it seems possible that, for some individuals at least, these needs might be better met in a more traditional way. This suggests, therefore, that branding is neither an essential quality assurance mechanism nor an indispensable source of emotional satisfaction, as market ideology seems to suggest.

REFERENCES

Balasubramanyam, V.N. and M.A. Salisu (1994) Brands and the Alcoholic Drinks Industry, in G. Jones and N.J. Morgan (eds) *Adding Value: Brands and Marketing in Food and Drink*, London: Routledge, 59–75.

Barwise, P., with C. Higson, A. Likerman and P. Marsh (1990) Brands as 'Separable Assets', *Business Strategy Review*, Summer, 43–59.

Casson, M.C. (1991) *Economics of Business Culture: Game Theory, Transaction Costs and Economic Performance*, Oxford: Clarendon Press.

Duncan, A.J. (1974) *Quality Control and Industrial Statistics*, Homewood, Ill.: Richard D. Irwin.

Earl, P.E. (1986) *Lifestyle Economics: Consumer Behaviour in a Turbulent World*, Brighton: Wheatsheaf.

Hirsch, F. (1977) *Social Limits to Growth*, London: Routledge and Kegan Paul.

Klein, B. and K. Leffler (1981) The Role of Market Forces in Assuring Contractual Performance, *Journal of Political Economy*, **89**, 615–41.

Lancaster, K. (1979) *Variety, Equity and Efficiency*, Oxford: Basil Blackwell.

Merrett, D. and G. Whitwell (1994) The Empire Strikes Back: Marketing Australian Beer and Wine in the United Kingdom, in G. Jones and N.J. Morgan (eds) *Adding Value: Brands and Marketing in Food and Drink*, London: Routledge, 162–90.

Napier, C.J. (1994) Brand Accounting in the United Kingdom, in G. Jones and N.J. Morgan (eds) *Adding Value: Brands and Marketing in Food and Drink*, London: Routledge, 76–102.

Schumpeter, J.A. (1934) *The Theory of Economic Development* (trans. R. Opie), Cambridge, Mass.: Harvard University Press.

Ward, V. (1994) Marketing Convenience Foods between the Wars, in G. Jones and N.J. Morgan (eds) *Adding Value: Brands and Marketing in Food and Drink*, London: Routledge, 259–90.

Wilkins, M. (1994) When and Why Brand Names in Food and Drink? in G. Jones and N.J. Morgan (eds) *Adding Value: Brands and Marketing in Food and Drink*, London: Routledge, 15–40.

Williams, R.H. (1982) *Dream Worlds: Mass Consumption in Late Nineteenth-Century France*, Berkeley, Cal.: University of California Press.

10. Entrepreneurship, regional development and minority language

10.1 INTRODUCTION

This chapter examines the role of entrepreneurship in regional development, with special reference to the question of minority language. Does minority language influence entrepreneurial attitudes and thereby have an impact on regional economic performance? If so, what is the magnitude and direction of this effect? This leads on to the policy question of whether it is advantageous to promote an entrepreneurial culture within a minority language community through the medium of the minority language itself.

The conceptual issues which these questions raise are very large ones, while the communities to which they apply in practice are often very small. This perhaps explains why so little research has been done on the subject from an analytical perspective. Indeed, works of literary fiction probably outnumber analytical social scientific works where the relation between entrepreneurship and minority language is concerned.

The use of a minority language is tied up with a sense of history and feeling for the 'spirit of place'. In the light of this, the specificity of the history and geography of each community make it difficult to generalize about the impact of minority language. This does not mean, however, that there are no general principles which work themselves out in different ways in different communities at different times and places. Indeed, this chapter attempts to discover principles of this very kind. These principles are sufficiently general, it is claimed, to apply to Gaelic communities in the west of Ireland and the Highlands and Islands of Scotland as well as Friesian-speakers in the Netherlands, the Québecois in Canada, the Basques in Spain, and so on.

To address the specificity issue, the chapter examines in some detail the application of the principles to the Welsh-speaking community in Wales. This application shows how the general principles, when applied to specific circumstances, generate predictions which have an important bearing on local policy debate. These principles are expressed below using the language of economics. Although they encompass social issues as well as narrowly economic ones, they have been embedded in the rational action approach set out in Chapter 2. In this approach optimizing individuals interact through institutions to attain (or at least to approach) an equilibrium where their plans are harmonized.

The chapter is organized into three parts. The first part (sections 10.2–10.6) deals with the impact of entrepreneurial culture on regional development, independently of any minority language effects. The focus is on the role of an enterprise culture in attracting able individuals into the local private sector. The rival attractions of private sector employment, public sector employment and emigration is the key theme.

Local career opportunities in the private sector are strongly influenced by the region's ability to attract inward investment. This partly depends on profit opportunities stimulated by the region's resource base and infrastructure. Interregional competition for investment flows means that subsidies are important, too, and these often require regional aid to finance them. If the region's political bureaucracy is skilful in winning such aid then it can prevent emigration by boosting private-sector employment opportunities and thereby retain its most promising entrepreneurs.

The second part (sections 10.7–10.9) introduces minority language effects. Minority language is an important carrier of culture because it provides unique access to the history of the group. But conversely, the culture of the group affects the attitude to the language itself. A minority language that promotes an entrepreneurial culture may well promote its own extinction (at least so far as business use is concerned).

The use of language is ultimately a matter of personal choice, and is therefore governed by economic incentives just as other decisions are. Like other decisions, it is also framed by culture – a culture in whose formation it has often played a significant part. But another important influence on culture is simply the history of the group, in which migration plays a very important role. Recent immigrants, for example, are often entrepreneurial and their children are keen to assimilate. On the other hand, indigenous groups whose numbers have been eroded by emigration tend to have very different attitudes. This is because migration is a selective process, in which the entrepreneurial move and the less entrepreneurial stay behind. Even forced migration caused by political persecution is often focused on entrepreneurial groups who have prospered at the expense of the natural population; alternatively they have been too independent to conform to political or religious constraints, a behavioural trait which also reveals entrepreneurial qualities, albeit of a slightly different kind. The converse is that those who remain are the least successful, or the most willing to conform.

The final part (sections 10.10–10.12) considers the policy implications, with special reference to Wales. Three cultural groups are distinguished: the monoglot English-speaking workers of industrial South Wales (the largest group); the political elite, with their academic and radical political leanings; and the rural population of mainly Welsh-speakers. The culture of the rural areas, with its 'organic' view of society, dislike of personal ambition and parochial interests, is what might be expected amongst a group of people whose ancestors rejected emigration and so passed up the opportunities provided by the Industrial Revolution and the Empire trading system.

There are positive points in the culture of all three groups, however: in particular, a Protestant-type work ethic (often regarded as a legacy of the chapels), a desire for education and a facility for social networking, all of which are vital ingredients of an entrepreneurial culture. Unfortunately, though, the limited resource base of the area, reinforced by the decline of Cardiff as a commercial metropolis following the closure of the coal mines, has denied young people role models of successful businessmen and reduced their opportunities to gain relevant management experience too. Most major employers are now branch plants of firms headquartered elsewhere. The facility for networking suggests, however, that more could be done to build up large independent sub-contractors to these branch plants. If such efforts were successful then the training opportunities, coupled with a demonstration effect that boosted local confidence, might generate a more entrepreneurial regional culture, creating a new equilibrium in which 'success breeds success'.

10.2   THE CONCEPT OF ENTREPRENEURIAL CULTURE

During the 1980s the concept of an entrepreneurial culture became closely associated with competitive individualism. It became embedded in a simple ideological view of society, in which competition between individuals has a crucial role. This ideology was promoted by radical liberals who gained political control in a number of industrial countries, including Britain. Economic analysis of entrepreneurship, however, suggests a rather different interpretation of entrepreneurial culture (see Chapter 4).

Entrepreneurship of a 'high-level' kind is associated with heroic innovations which involve a major irreversible commitment of resources to a risky project. Much more common, though, is 'low-level' entrepreneurship, some of which still involves significant risks – speculation and arbitrage, for example – and some of which does not – small retail operations, for example, where the risks are largely confined to the value of the stock. What high-level and low-level activities have in common is that they involve an element of judgement (Casson, 1982). An unprecedented situation arises and a decision must be made by synthesizing whatever information is available. No handy rule or formula is available. Unprecedented situations often call for unorthodox solutions. It requires imagination to think of an appropriate solution, and a willingness to reject conformity in order to carry it out. This is the individualistic aspect of being an entrepreneur.

It requires a good deal of confidence to be an individualist of this kind. Not only can serious losses arise from a mistaken decision, with the prospect of sleepless nights while awaiting the outcome, but there is also the difficulty of justifying the decision to others once it has been taken (quite independently of how it turns out). Overconfidence is, of course, to be avoided. True confidence will normally be based on breadth of experience, for experience not only provides useful information but also develops skills in weighing up the different factors involved in complex situations. Clear thinking and oral fluency are also useful in legitimating decisions to other people.

Entrepreneurship is competitive: entrepreneurs compete to discover potential innovations, and also face competition from imitators once a successful innovation has been made. But entrepreneurs need to cooperate as well. Innovations in related activities are often complementary: in manufacturing, for example, processing firms need to collaborate with capital equipment suppliers, assemblers need to collaborate with component manufacturers, and so on. Such collaboration is often best effected through informal long-term contracts based on mutual trust.

Sometimes more formal arrangements are required. Economies of scale in upstream or downstream activities are best exploited by the corporate users clubbing together, for example to provide general training, basic R & D, representation at export trade fairs, and so on. Members of the club need to trust one another if the arrangement is to work well.

Individualists can certainly be trusted – but not if they are ruthlessly aggressive too. There are certain moral standards to which the individualist must conform if they are to be taken seriously. An agreement that is dishonoured is usually worse than no agreement at all, hence honesty is a top priority. Loyalty is important too; people who switch allegiance at short notice can often cause considerable harm by disrupting a relationship on which their partners have come to depend.

From this point of view, voluntary association is probably a better principle than competitive individualism so far as entrepreneurship is concerned (see Chapter 7). Association implies a degree of commitment to relationships with other entrepreneurs which individualism ignores. But the voluntary principle is preserved, leaving the individual free to innovate, and to associate with whom he likes in order to make the innovation succeed. An entrepreneurial culture built around voluntary association is likely to be more successful in the long run than one built on competitive individualism, as that concept has been articulated in recent years.

10.3   COMPETITION IN LOCAL POLITICS

Even the principle of voluntarism has its limitations, though. While voluntary association is a useful principle in promoting entrepreneurial clubs, there are important instances where it is difficult for club members to exclude 'free-riders' (Olson, 1982). For example, a new firm entering a district might attempt to poach newly trained staff from members of a club which had invested heavily in them.

In such cases it can be advantageous for the state to intervene in order to compel all those who benefit to contribute to the cost. From an economic perspective, this inability to exclude people from the benefits of a facility is the main rationale for coercing them to join the organization that operates the facility. The classic application of this principle is, of course, to the provision of defence, where everyone who benefits from defence is obliged to become a citizen so that they can be taxed (and if necessary be conscripted into military service). In the present context, however, the provision of infrastructure such as roads is the more obvious application, even though the administrative problems of exclusion are generally not quite so great in this case.

Unfortunately, though, the element of compulsion can also be used to distort the relationship between benefit and cost in order to cross-subsidize favoured interests. Investment in infrastructure and the redistribution of income can become mixed up together. Where private businessmen are concerned, the maximization of income and the provision of charity are conceptually quite distinct: one is effected through the firm and the other through philanthropic institutions. Where public sector projects are concerned, however, who will benefit in terms of job creation and who will lose in terms of additional tax payments often receives more attention than whether the overall benefits outweigh the costs.

An institution that can coerce wealthy people into membership offers considerable scope for extracting rents. A leader who is in a very secure position can extract these rents for himself, as with medieval monarchs and republican dictators. In modern democracies the opportunities are more limited because leaders face periodic re-election. This does not apply to all areas of state activity, though. Some public bodies which administer very large funds on behalf of the government are managed by unelected political appointees whose jobs are quite secure so long as the same political party remains in power. Some bureaucrats may also enjoy considerable power; while they may find it difficult to extract rents in the form of income, they can extract them in other ways through various privileges afforded by their status.

When leadership is subject to electoral competition, rival leaders may have to dissipate prospective rents in order to purchase support. Leaders of factions may emerge, offering greater rewards to those individuals who agree to participate in selling their votes as a block. Thus some of the rewards of leadership may be dissipated by the winner in payments to his supporting factions, with the leaders of these factions creaming off some of these payments for themselves. This is reflected in the way that electoral victors usually display considerable favouritism to those who have organized support from the constituencies.

Competition for leadership positions can itself be regarded as an aspect of entrepreneurship. The market for political power is different from an ordinary market, however. In any ordinary market the skills that achieve victory over rivals are the same skills that deliver quality of service to supporters: that is, the firm's customers, employees and financial backers. In a political market, however, the skills that win leadership are not necessarily the skills that produce successful decisions once the leader is in power. The leader who gets elected may be the one who makes the most cynically unrealistic promises, and who is intent on extracting the greatest rents for himself. Even an ideologically committed leader who is honest to begin with can finish up in this position. He overestimates the material benefits that he can deliver and finishes up promoting prestigious but useless projects from which he derives emotional satisfaction and from which he believes his supporters will derive emotional satisfaction too.

The public sector and the private sector therefore offer two distinct channels of advancement for the entrepreneur. The rewards to entrepreneurship in the public sector come more in the form of status than of income, of course. They include the satisfaction of contributing directly to social welfare too. Public-sector entrepreneurship will therefore appeal to some people more than to others. Cultural influences may well play their part in this, leading to entrepreneurs from different cultural backgrounds coming to dominate the different sectors.

It is not necessarily the case that the private sector requires the best entre-preneurs. Countries such as Japan, France, Germany and Singapore have achieved good economic results using active industrial policies formulated and implemented by entrepreneurial people attracted to high-status jobs in the public sector. Conversely, the United Kingdom and the United States have achieved very mixed results by promoting free market policies and reducing the status of public-sector employment in order to channel entrepreneurs into the private sector.

Nevertheless, it could be a problem for a region if too many people of entre-preneurial ability were diverted into the public sector. It could also become a problem if the public and private sectors developed very distinctive cultures, so that entrepreneurs in the two sectors could not easily communicate with each other. If both the public sector and the private sector were dominated by local people this would not be too much of a danger, but if locals dominated in one sector and 'immigrants' in another then it could be a different story altogether. Local networking could be impaired and local industrial policies might fail as a result.

10.4 ENTREPRENEURSHIP AND MIGRATION

According to the ideology of popular capitalism, everyone 'has what it takes' to become an entrepreneur. In practice, however, successful entrepreneurship requires distinctive qualities, in particular confidence generated by wide experience. In the private sector, for example, the standards required by 'high-level' entrepreneurship such as major technical innovation are much higher than those required for 'low-level' entrepreneurship such as market trading or local shopkeeping. It is therefore realistic to think of entrepreneurship, particularly the high-level kind, as a relatively scarce attribute.

If this somewhat elitist view of entrepreneurship is accepted, then it becomes important to consider whether those who have the necessary qualities will use them or not. It is also important to determine whether they will be used inside or outside the region where the entrepreneur was brought up (Sowell, 1983).

It is generally easier for recent immigrants to an area to achieve advancement in the private sector than in the public sector, because advancement in the public sector often requires local contacts and an empathy with local attitudes. This suggests that those who prefer to make a career in the private sector are the most likely to emigrate from a region. Emigrants are therefore more likely to be a potential loss to the local private sector rather than to the local public sector. Conversely, people who prefer to advance themselves in the public sector will be easier to retain.

In any region, therefore, a higher proportion of local people will tend to be found amongst the political elite than amongst the business elite. Conversely, a higher proportion of immigrants will be found amongst the business elite than amongst the political elite. It is also likely that a higher proportion of those who emigrate make their career in the private sector than do those who remain behind.

Emigration is a selective process not only so far as the public versus private orientation of careers is concerned. Emigration also selects between entrepreneurs and non-entrepreneurs. Entrepreneurs are more likely to emigrate from a declining region than are non-entrepreneurs because they are more aware of outside opportunities and are more confident of their own ability to exploit them. This form of selectivity is crucial for the dynamics of regional growth. If a region experiences a disturbance (for example, the exhaustion of its natural resources) and profit opportunities decline relative to those elsewhere, then a selective exodus of entrepreneurs will occur, reducing the proportion of entrepreneurs amongst those who remain behind. Furthermore, by establishing themselves elsewhere, these emigrants provide a base to which subsequent entrepreneurs can emigrate. This social network encourages a 'chain' of migrants which can lead to a major agglomeration of regional exiles elsewhere.

In extreme cases a distinctive 'overseas' group may evolve who are more entrepreneurial than the indigenous group. While the region may benefit from the subsequent repatriation of profits to family members, the maintenance of second homes and 'back to my roots' tourism, the spillover effects of such activity are generally lower than if the entrepreneurs had been able to establish similar operations at home. It is unlikely, however, that they could have succeeded just as well at home because of the diminished opportunities, and so this comparison may not be a very useful one.

The selective exodus of entrepreneurs may also alter the balance of informed opinion within the local community by removing those who would tend to oppose populist redistributive policies. Thus the decline of a traditional industry in a region may begin a vicious cycle of policy changes in which the remaining industry is increasingly hampered by heavy taxes levied to provide for those made redundant – first in the declining industry and then, as the spillovers increase, in other industries too. The local economy sinks into an equilibrium in which the only way for anyone to become rich is to use political power to extract resources from other people who are already poor themselves.

10.5   MANUFACTURING: THE POLITICAL ECONOMY OF RESTRUCTURING

In the post-war period the economic environment of several minority-speaking regions has been significantly altered by the global restructuring of manufacturing industries. This restructuring has been stimulated by trade liberalization and improvements in freight transport logistics (Williams, 1994). It has encouraged multinationals to abandon the multidomestic structure in which each national subsidiary produces for its own (protected) national market in favour of a globally rationalized structure in which each plant specializes in a particular set of components, or product varieties, and supplies a large proportion of the firm's global market through export. This has freed plants in the regions of low-growth economies from the constraints imposed by the domestic market. Although many foreign multinationals in the United Kingdom have always produced with the European market in mind, there is little doubt that liberalisation in the European Community has stimulated export demand relative to home demand so far as foreign investors in UK regions are concerned.

A related point is that manufacturing industries have become relatively footloose. Because of their modest sunk costs, low-skill assembly-type activities have always been relatively footloose. The same is now true, to some degree at least, of sophisticated operations involving the use of robots. Because of this footloose nature, competition between regions is now intense, not merely to attract investment but to retain it as well. It is not just new investment that is the subject of competition, but the entire stock of footloose investment.

At the same time, foreign aid and domestic financial assistance of various kinds have been provided to help peripheral regions attract foreign investment. In Latin America and Africa the funds have come from the World Bank and a fairly select group of donor governments who are seeking political influence in the areas concerned. In the European Union the regional fund has been the major source. All the funding programmes aim to create jobs. In Europe the emphasis has been on replacing jobs in 'sunset' industries, such as coal and steel, with jobs in 'sunrise' industries such as electronics, office equipment and household electrical equipment, while in Africa and Latin America the emphasis, until recently, was on basic industrialization instead.

The funds have been put into infrastructure improvements and into tax-breaks of various kinds for the investing companies. Entrusting state officials with the disbursement of large sums in this way creates obvious opportunities for corruption, so much so that the World Bank has 'grasped the nettle' and made good government an explicit criterion that recipient countries must satisfy. The problems of corruption in public procurement of construction work afflict not only developing countries but many developed countries too. Less is known about corruption in negotiating tax-breaks, because for allegedly commercial reasons these deals are usually shrouded in official secrecy.

Quite apart from corruption, however, there are obviously many perks to be enjoyed by officials charged with marketing their region to foreign investors using external donors' funds. The presence of these external donors may indeed help to explain why many regional governments have been so keen to offer financial incentives to foreign investors rather than to tax them heavily for redistributive purposes, as the traditional form of local populism would suggest. Basically, by focusing donor funds on the business support function, funds generated from local taxation and so on have been released to buy political support. External funding has therefore bought off local political elites who might otherwise have stifled local entrepreneurship through populist redistributive policies.

10.6   JAPANESE INVESTMENT

The rise of Japanese manufacturing investment, based on a distinctive philosophy of 'just in time' material flow, 'right first time' quality and continuous incremental innovation through factory-based R & D, has provided yet another opportunity for new regions to enter into competition for foreign investment. The Japanese appear to favour regions where they can influence local labour market institutions. They seem to avoid areas already dominated by United States investors, and to favour local communities which were traditionally based around a single plant, as in the coalfield towns of the north-east of England and South Wales.

They also favour 'relational' subcontracting based on informal long-term contracts to the backward integration typically undertaken by their United States rivals (Price, Morgan and Cooke, 1993). Potentially, this offers greater scope for local entrepreneurs to gain spin-offs from the foreign investment. It is, however, often difficult to find local entrepreneurs who are fully aware of the customer's requirements, so far as precision, product reliability and speed of response are concerned.

This is particularly true of regions which have no major indigenous firms of their own. Many of the most successful subcontracting operations seem to be set up by former employees of the customer firm, who already know what the relevant quality standards are. Where an indigenous firm is concerned, it is relatively easy for a locally recruited manager to rise to a position of seniority where he can acquire knowledge of this kind. But where a foreign firm is concerned, this may be more difficult. It is particularly difficult for employees of multinationals whose overseas operations are run by a cadre of parent-country managers on short-term postings from head office.

This kind of 'hands on' control of local operations by managers with a strong allegiance to headquarters seems to be characteristic of the early stages of a firm's foreign investment. Experienced foreign investors are often much more relaxed about delegating authority to host-country managers. This point is particularly relevant to recent Japanese investment in the European regions. It is not uncommon for the Japanese managers of new subsidiaries to refer even quite minor decisions to headquarters. If Japanese firms follow the same kind of evolutionary path as their United States predecessors, however, then the opportunities for indigenous entrepreneurs to gain managerial experience with potential customer firms should increase over time, and backward linkages with the local economy should be strengthened as a result.

10.7   THE BASIC ECONOMICS OF LANGUAGE

Since language is so fundamental to human society it is strange that little has been written on the economic theory of language *per se*. But then, again, perhaps it is not so strange after all, for economics has tended to shy away from fundamental issues of this kind. Although there is a literature on the economics of particular language groups (see, for example, Pellenbarg, 1993; Van Langevelde, 1994) the nearest that conventional economics comes to a theory of language is an analogy between a language group and a telecommunications network (for an attempt to develop an economics of language, see Buckley, Casson and Chapman, 1994).

The telecommunications network metaphor highlights the obvious point that there are major economies of standardization where language is concerned. In addition to the basic *compatibility* requirement – the listener must speak the same language as the speaker – there is the *networking* factor: when n people speak the same language, $(1/2)n(n-1)$ pairs of people can communicate with each other. Because they can communicate, they can set up trades, arrange productive teamwork, avert negative externalities, and so on. Thus for each person the value of the language is directly proportional to the number of other people (or potential partners, at least) who speak it. Indeed, further economies may arise because trading opportunities are often multilateral rather than bilateral and cannot be realized until a very sophisticated division of labour has been achieved. Thus the $(n+1)$th person speaking the language may provide even more benefit to the other members of the language group than the nth person did. This implies that everyone should belong to the same language group.

The benefit of a large group can, of course, be obtained by combining a number of smaller groups, but the disadvantage of combining different language groups in this way is the cost to each person of learning several languages instead of just one. It is, of course, possible that each distinct language group might have a natural frontier across which little trade could ever take place. It would then matter relatively little that the groups could not communicate with each other because the value of the forgone opportunities for inter-group trade would be relatively small. There are, however, no such frontiers left in the modern world. Transport costs have fallen, and at the same time advances in mass-production technology now afford significant economies from a division of labour effected on a global scale.

Moreover, improvements in communications mean that economies of standardizing language in academic research and popular entertainment are greater as well. Historically, different international elites have sometimes standardized on different languages – medieval scholars on Latin, eighteenth century aristocrats on French, some nineteenth century scientists on German, and so on. But the business community's growing use of English, reinforced by United States influence in the media, has now established English as the international standard in most fields. Now, more than ever before, failure to standardize on the dominant language is costly in narrow economic terms.

If the preservation of a minority language is to be justified in economic terms, therefore, it must be justified purely in terms of the pleasure it affords to those who speak it – and perhaps also to those who like to know that it is spoken, even if they cannot understand what is being said.

In political debates over minority language, much is made of the costs of a language 'dying out'. This is essentially an argument for treating the spoken language as an investment, on the grounds that the most effective way of keeping it available for future generations of 'consumers' is to transmit it orally rather than to create an archive of books to which they can refer. Whether experience with languages such as Latin and Classical Greek, or even Anglo-Saxon, bears this view out is a moot point, for, though dead, they seem to have been resurrected quite effectively from time to time.

It would probably be safer to ground the argument for preservation on the simple premise that it would give considerable pleasure to many of the present generation of minority language-speakers to know that their language will outlive them. Since the spoken language is a social artefact, this is not something that any one of them individually can achieve. There is certainly a case, therefore, on this line of argument, for the establishment of clubs to promote the use of the language amongst the younger generation. But whether everyone should be obliged to finance this club through taxes, whether they wish to preserve the language or not, is very dubious.

The idea that everyone in a region should subsidize the speaking of the minority language could only be justified on strictly economic grounds if those who did not speak the language actually benefited from having it spoken around them. They would then be 'free-riding' on the clubs' activities if they did not pay an appropriate sum in taxes. There may indeed be some people who fall into this category, as suggested earlier – for example, romantics who appreciate cultural diversity but choose not to contribute to the clubs that help to support it. But equally, there will be other people who dislike the fact that those around them are speaking a language which they cannot understand. They may even believe, rightly or wrongly, that it is being done to ostracize them (see below). There is no case for making such people pay for the preservation of a minority language.

The case for a minority language that is only a second language is, however, somewhat stronger than for a minority language which is the only language spoken at all. This is because the economic losses associated with the failure of inter-group communication are much lower than in the single-language case. The case is not significantly stronger, though, because the fact that the language is only a second language also means that fewer elements of the traditional culture are likely to be preserved by those who speak it. On the whole, therefore, the economic logic of state support for the preservation of a second language is tenuous, to say the least.

10.8 LANGUAGE AND CHOICE

Because the use of a common language affords significant network externalities, most people will wish to adopt the language which is in most common use around them. The use of a second language is, however, very much a matter of choice. While children may be under the influence of parents or of school, adults definitely face a choice. Those who have not learnt the language can begin to learn it, and those who have already learnt it can allow it to lapse.

Because language is kept alive by its social use, a commitment to a second language implies a commitment to belong to social groups where this language is regularly used (local churches, organizing committees for cultural festivals, and so on). The opportunity to use a second language is increased by residence in an area where such users tend to agglomerate. Where a minority language is concerned, this generally means not only the homeland but also particularly areas of it. This in turn means that the preservation of the language generally rests with people born in particular parts of the homeland who choose to remain there.

A strong attachment to the homeland may prevent people from gaining experience elsewhere. A spell of time away may seem easy to accommodate, but once people have made the break they may, for various reasons, decide not to return. Thus the native-speaking population in the homeland is likely to contain relatively few people with outside experience. Encounters with visitors to the homeland make native speakers increasingly aware of how out of touch they have become. Young native speakers therefore face a stark choice between remaining with the group or breaking their allegiance and 'catching up' with events outside. This gap will tend to undermine the confidence of the native speakers. They hesitate to compete with outsiders because they see the outsiders as being more competent and more up-to-date than they are themselves. This discourages them from making a commitment to entrepreneurial activity because they perceive the risks as being too great.

Even the most successful entrepreneur has occasional misfortunes, and the setbacks, when they come, have to be taken in one's stride. But those who lack confidence may also lack perseverance: they may impute the setback to their own shortcomings, and so give up when their first setback appears. They may even consider that they have been 'taught a lesson' for attempting to achieve something that is beyond their reach.

In areas that are poor in natural resources, and relatively isolated too, local residents may quite reasonably take the view that the chances of entrepreneurial success are rather remote; the chances are so low that it is not worth making the effort to start a business in a non-traditional industry, and this provides a useful self-justification for remaining relatively poor. It can be a considerable blow to people's self-esteem if a local person 'makes good'. Local people can no longer tell each other that poverty is inevitable and therefore not their own fault. The successful entrepreneur may well be ostracized as a result. The occasional person who does become successful may therefore have to leave the area anyway, if they wish to be on good terms with their neighbours. This is another reason why it does not pay to strive for success. Success is something that comes to those who leave, and is to be avoided by those who prefer to stay.

Use of a minority language can also function as an exclusion mechanism (Steiner, 1975). It is a means of talking secretly about people even in their presence. More generally, it is a powerful way for native speakers to distinguish between 'us' and 'them'. Such attitudes can backfire, however. It becomes easy for the group to reject ideas that come from 'them'. Even if 'they' live on our doorstep, they are 'foreigners' whose attitudes have no place within our own group. Anyone who deals too frequently with the foreigners, or adopts their ways, also runs the risk of ostracism, just as the high achiever does. If acceptance by the foreigners is by no means certain, then the 'deviant' may be left with no social support at all. The risk of exclusion therefore encourages a high degree of conformity in the language group.

Another aspect of minority language use is that it provides access to a cultural heritage which can otherwise only be tapped through translation. This cultural heritage is likely to be much stronger on the artistic side than on the scientific side, and is therefore likely to develop the artistic capabilities of the student more than it does the scientific ones. It may also provide a taste for 'high' culture of the kind to which access is gained through university education, and induce a corresponding rejection of the 'low' culture associated with commercialism. This may bias minority language speakers towards careers in education and the arts, and against careers in commerce, industry and sciences, though how strong such effects are in practice is difficult to say.

It is also relevant to note that the poems and historical narratives which occupy a key place in many minority language cultures are very often connected with the early stages of nation building through great battles fought by warrior-kings. The sense of history suggests that 'we' have always been different from 'them'. It also suggests that the loss of self-esteem caused by 'our' economic inferiority can be compensated for by the use of force against 'them'. The very people who induce the feelings of inferiority are themselves shown to be inferior because of the fear that the use of force creates in them. This indicates that the link between minority language use, nationalism and terrorism found in some countries – notably Ireland and Spain – is not a coincidental one.

All societies have their exclusion mechanisms, of course, and their myths and legends too. The point is not that these cultural factors are peculiar to minority language groups, but rather that they express a fear of outsiders which comes from having become marginalized as a 'minority group' in the first place. The message of the myths is likely to be that the group has survived only by being cunning and devious, by members of the group recognizing one another through their use of the language and by organizing collusion against outsiders amongst members of the language group.

This sense of being different may also be reflected in a distinctive set of laws and customs enforced by the group's own punishment system. In some cases this system may contravene the formal law established by the majority language group. The use of informal legal systems is not confined to minority language groups, of course. The case of the Mafia in Sicily indicates that relative poverty and remoteness, coupled with weak central government, are probably more important factors in creating an independent system of law and order. Nevertheless, the Mafia in the United States definitely constitutes a minority language group, and the linguistic affinity of its members may well have helped in building the sense of solidarity needed to transplant its code of secrecy there. The evolution of distinctive customs may prove a much greater obstacle to business relations with the majority language group than does the language difference itself.

It should also be noted that the differences which define the cultural identity of the language group may appear as romantic and exotic to the outsiders. Members of a competitive and individualistic commercial society may imbue the organic solidarity of the minority language group with a sense of mystery. They positively desire to see the members of the group as emotional and irrational even when the kind of collusive activity that the group is engaging in is perfectly explicable in materialistic economic terms (Chapman, 1992). Just as it is unfair to allege that collusion is the principal aim of minority language users it is also unfair to suggest that minority language speakers are not sufficiently rational to use it in this way when circumstances warrant it.

10.9 AGRICULTURE AND RURAL POLITICS

Minority language use is likely to have the greatest appeal in areas of traditional activity, notably agriculture. The small farm is typically both the 'firm' and the 'household' rolled into one. It is an undifferentiated economic institution in which family and workforce coincide, where managerial seniority and paternity are closely linked, and where training and parenting go hand in hand (Gasson and Errington, 1994).

There are, of course, good reasons why such a family-centred institution should continue to thrive in agriculture. Family loyalties can overcome incentive problems which, given the difficulty of continuous supervision on a farm, are difficult to tackle through a conventional wage system. Similarly, the long-term nature of investments in farming can be tackled using the concept of stewardship, in which the farm is viewed as being held in trust for future generations of the family.

So long as agriculture remains in a steady state, such values contribute to productivity. But when labour-saving technologies appear, and new sources of competition emerge, such values can impede structural change (Jenkins, 1971). Furthermore, institutions which support family farming, such as farmers' clubs and agricultural cooperatives, can become vehicles for political lobbying to delay adjustment. While some delay may well be warranted – to permit retraining of redundant labour, for example – lobbyists may well succeed in delaying it for much longer than this by threatening political leaders who will not promise protection or subsidies with a loss of votes.

An unambiguously positive aspect of farming values is the work ethic. Farmers are used to long 'anti-social' hours, to strenuous effort in unpleasant conditions, and to assuming great responsibility, as in caring for livestock. If they leave the land to work in manufacturing then they usually take these values with them and so make excellent employees. Unfortunately, when they relocate to an urban environment they often fail to pass on these values to the next generation. This is one reason why newly industrializing countries and regions often experience a short-lived productivity bonus in manufacturing industry as the first generation of industrial workers leaves the land.

The connection between agriculture, rural life and minority language is very important in mobilizing support for linguistic nationalism. The idea of a rural 'heartland' or 'homeland', undefiled by industry and commerce, holds romantic fascination for successful emigrants who plan to return to their roots one day. Activists can tap their money and their political influence to promote the language – and buy off the farmers with subsidies at the same time. This external support can also help the linguistic nationalists to outmanoeuvre their political opponents in the region, and so appropriate more of the already limited economic rents for themselves.

10.10 WELSH CULTURE

A naive approach to entrepreneurship and regional development would suggest that to improve economic performance in a lagging region the local culture needs to be made more entrepreneurial, and that local leaders therefore need to be persuaded to promote appropriate values. A checklist of appropriate values could be derived, these values compared with the actual values, and major discrepancies identified. Propaganda would then be aimed at the values that had been isolated.

It is interesting to see how this approach would work in the case of Wales. Chapter 7 identified the five key characteristics of an entrepreneurial culture which are reproduced in Table 10.1. The first characteristic, scientific differentiation, refers to the separation of religious and secular issues in a manner that facilitates scientific inquiry. High tension refers to the desire for achievement, and for recognition as being successful. Atomism is a view of society as a collection of autonomous individuals linked by a social contract; it contrasts with organicism, in which society is believed to transcend the individual and require him to conform. High trust implies that in the atomistic society individuals accept an obligation to treat others with consideration and to respect their property, even in the absence of law. Judgement represents a realistic view of the environment which is typically the product of sophisticated education and wide practical experience.

Table 10.1   Strength of five key aspects of entrepreneurial culture

Aspect	Wales	England	USA
Scientific differentiation	3	4	5
High tension	2	4	5
Atomism	2	4	5
High trust	4	3	2
Judgement	2	4	4

These are not the only factors that are important in entrepreneurial success, of course, but many of the other factors, such as hard work, high savings and bargaining skills, can be subsumed under one or more of these headings.

The table rates Welsh culture on a five-point scale ranging from one (weak) to five (strong). It suggests that Welsh culture inclines to an organic view of society. There is a fairly optimistic view of people's moral potential (as reflected in high trust) but a rather pessimistic view of their economic potential (as reflected in low tension). It is also characterized by rather parochial concerns (Williams, 1985), which means that, in spite of good education, narrow experience makes the quality of judgement rather weak.

Inevitably, ratings of this kind reflect a stereotype, but they should not be rejected out of hand just because of this. Stereotypes often contain useful information about the typical attitudes of members of a group, even though there may be considerable diversity within the group. Stereotypes do, however, tend to be rather out of date. A stereotype is a form of collective reputation and, like all reputations, it tends to be based on recollections of the past rather than on the reality of the present. Subject to this qualification, however, it is often reasonably accurate. (Indeed, stereotypes may to some extent be self-fulfilling, in that people searching for an identity deliberately live up to their stereotype.) It is suggested that the ratings given in Table 10.1 apply to attitudes in the late 1960s and early 1970s, a period in which the Welsh seem to have lived up to their reputation for social conscience rather more than they do today (see below).

Minority language cultures often use the majority language culture as a foil, to define their identity in terms of what they are not. The virtues of the minority language culture are expressed in terms of the vices of the majority language culture that it avoids. This is certainly true in the case of Wales, where a stereotype of English culture is widely employed to define what Welshness means.

Groups are often far more disdainful of neighbouring cultures, however, than they are of cultures further away. There is always tension with neighbours, which amplifies perceived cultural differences, so that quite minor differences are seen as extreme. More remote cultures, on the other hand, are less threatening and seem more romantic, so that differences that are genuinely extreme may hardly be recognized at all.

Differences between English culture and Welsh culture are, in fact, quite modest compared with those between Welsh culture and, say, United States culture. This is certainly what the numbers entered in the table are meant to suggest. This is an important point, because Welsh culture seems to have become much more competitively individualistic since the 1970s, and some of this may be due to US media influence.

In the 1960s and 1970s, the cultural differences between Wales and England were broadly the same as those that prevailed, in turn, between England and the United States. Thus Wales was at one extreme, the United States at the other, with England in the middle. This was consistent with the view that the more enterprising people are continually migrating to the most promising areas. The entrepreneurial Welsh have historically migrated to England and many of the entrepreneurial English have historically migrated to the United States. From this perspective, cultural differences between England and Wales are just a modest local manifestation of a larger international phenomenon driven by the cumulative influence of selective migration on local cultures.

What has happened since the 1970s is that Welsh culture, and to a lesser extent English culture, has shifted significantly towards United States culture. This is most apparent amongst the monoglot English-speakers of South Wales, whose voting patterns in recent British general elections have become almost indistinguishable from the rest of southern England. These English-speakers are the people whose forebears moved into the valleys at the end of the nineteenth century to develop the coalfields. They acquired Welsh accents but did not assimilate the language. They developed a distinctive culture whose hero was the skilled self-educated and politically active working man. This culture of the valleys, symbolized by chapel, temperance movement, trade union and Labour Party, now verges on collapse. Once a local hegemony, the power of Labour Party radicalism is now largely confined to local government. The reaction against those organic values for which the Labour Party stood has been strongest in the very area in which they seemed to have been most deeply entrenched.

One clue to the explanation is that the area has also witnessed changes in its economic structure. The dramatic decline of mining, and the rise of light manufacturing and distribution services, have stimulated a significant increase in female employment and a consequent shift in the balance of economic power within the family. A declining respect for traditional family values and increasing concern over material consumption standards may be an important factor in the political shift to more atomistic values.

Amongst the intellectual elite cultural change has taken a slightly different turn. The traditional Welshness of the Labour Party activist has been rejected by many intellectuals in favour of linguistic nationalism. An attempt is being made to fashion a new culture which, while resonating with the past, is sufficiently modern to generate cultural products, such as television drama, which can compete for media exposure with popular United States output. This is a sophisticated nationalist culture that is tailored to the needs of the 'Postmodern' world.

The Welsh elite, perhaps because of its outstanding oral tradition, seems always to have been effective in politics. From the time of the Tudors through to David Lloyd George and Aneurin Bevan, they were influential in Westminster politics. This influence has recently been used not only to attract subsidies for regional development but to establish a special bureaucracy, the Welsh Office, based in Cardiff, which holds administrative responsibility for many functions which in England are carried out by specialized Whitehall ministries. Increasing use of Welsh within this bureaucracy has attracted many Welsh-speakers to Cardiff. It has created a new demand for Welsh language education but has also stimulated protests about discrimination in public employment against non-Welsh-speakers. Some English-speaking Welsh allege that the Welsh language is now being used not only to win subsidies for Wales, as in the past, but also to concentrate the benefits on the Welsh-speaking population to the detriment of themselves.

The people apparently least affected by the cultural change are in the rural communities of North and West Wales. Here hill farming and quarrying are the traditional industries, although quarrying has mainly died out and farming is becoming economically marginal in the light of recent changes in the Common Agricultural Policy. Current concerns amongst Welsh policy makers about lack of entrepreneurship in Wales are focused on these areas. It is in these areas that the proportion of Welsh-speakers is highest. Although under 20 per cent of all Welsh residents speak any kind of Welsh at all, over 80 per cent of the population in some of these rural areas speak Welsh. Because their population densities are so low, however, the impact on the statistics for Wales as a whole is relatively small.

It is also in these areas that surveys have found a lack of confidence about the chances of success in small business start-up (Menter a Busnes, 1993). A tendency to blame oneself for failures, rather than to rationalize them in terms of a 'learning experience', has also been noted. At the same time, there is no reliable evidence that these self-assessments are misplaced. It may well be that because of their inexperience, and a lack of desire for achievement, new businesses founded by Welsh-speakers would indeed be likely to fail.

As already noted, the probable reason why these negative attitudes developed is that these areas have suffered a steady exodus of their most enterprising people, either to other parts of Wales or further afield. This in turn reflects their historically poor resources endowments. The quality of the agricultural land is low, the mineral resources have been fairly quickly exhausted in intermittent mining booms, and the areas have been too remote to attract major manufacturing investment. Moreover, the climate is not sufficiently warm and dry to encourage mass tourism, particularly in an age of holiday jet travel.

Some factors, such as climate, cannot be changed, of course, but other factors can. Motorways, expressways and ordinary road improvements have begun to open up some of these areas both to manufacturing and to cultural tourism. Cultural tourism is a form of tourism favoured by the increasing numbers of educated people who retire early, and which is less dependent than ordinary tourism on favourable weather conditions. This means that there may be greater opportunities than before for enterprising young people who wish to remain in rural Wales to achieve prosperity close to their 'roots'. Not all areas are equally affected, however, and the 'trickle down' effect to the more remote areas may still be slow.

Tourist development in the past has largely been undertaken by English immigrants, however. The same is true of the early industrialization of the Vale of Neath, the Cardiff area and the Wrexham connurbation (John, 1950). Access to capital and a knowledge of export markets appear to have been crucial factors giving advantage to the English entrepreneurs, but a general lack of enterprise amongst Welsh-speakers cannot be ruled out. Although some Welsh-speakers have proved very enterprising, the enterprise has generally manifested itself outside Wales – in the steel industry of Pennsylvania, for example, or the retail milk trade in London (Davies, 1992).

If enterprising people are to remain in Wales, therefore, they need to find a way of acquiring skills that their parents and grandparents have generally lacked. They also need to be liberated from the anti-entrepreneurial culture of their families. It is important that they acquire their skills locally, however, for once enterprising people leave Wales they are unlikely to return. Local acquisition of skills, in this context, must signify access to a business centre of some substance, and this naturally points to Cardiff. Although once a major metropolis – a hub of international business empires in coal and shipping – Cardiff has since lost much of its financial sector. It no longer, unfortunately, hosts the headquarters of major multinationals, as London does, but only the subsidiary offices associated with branch plants. Local opportunities for incubating entrepreneurial talent are therefore limited.

Perhaps the best prospect for developing an indigenous group of entrepreneurs lies in large-scale subcontracting for foreign investors in the area. If stronger links could be developed between local firms and foreign multinationals then greater opportunities would exist for giving young managers practical experience in these local firms before they founded their own businesses in the more rural areas.

10.11   IMPLICATIONS FOR REGIONAL DEVELOPMENT

On the face of it, the implications of this analysis for regional development are not particularly encouraging. Regional development agencies, and other departments of local government mandated to attract industry, could be considered as just another of those public-sector institutions which recruit entrepreneurial minority language-speakers who might otherwise have gone into the private sector and have done the very kind of job that the regional development agency ostensibly wants them to do. The social cost of this depends upon whether the entrepreneurs would really have gone into local industries, or simply emigrated elsewhere.

Elaborating this cynical view, it could be said that the value of a regional development agency to the local political elite is that it symbolizes a commitment to the advancement of local people which a populist political agenda requires. Because it is concerned with the promotion of enterprise it is also acceptable to the major providers of financial assistance to the region, and so does not need to be funded at local expense. It can also claim support from nationalists in the elite, provided that its enterprise culture is not perceived as a corrupting influence. Theory therefore predicts that regional development agencies and analogous institutions are likely to appear, whether they actually advance the interests of the region or not.

An obvious criticism of concentrating regional development initiatives on minority language speakers is that this promotes the interests of a language group rather than the interests of the region as a whole. This criticism is dubious, however, in so far as greater prosperity for the language group will create local externalities that benefit other businesses in the region too. A more convincing argument is that the money directed at changing attitudes in the language group may be better employed in giving assistance to those outside the group who already have the right attitudes, but because they come from poor backgrounds, lack start-up finance.

A potential problem in directing policy at a language group is that the positive discrimination involved reinforces the view that they are different from other people. By strengthening their own sense of identity their tendency to collude against outsiders may be reinforced. The resources of the development agency may be used not to develop outward-oriented activities that will strengthen interaction with other groups (industrial subcontracting, cultural tourism and so on) but 'import-substituting' activities designed to reduce 'dependence' on other groups (a wholesale cooperative for local retailers, for example). Where outward-oriented activities are concerned, there may be a tendency to try to restrict the benefits to the language group itself (encouraging cultural tourists to patronize only businesses owned by members of the group, for example).

Another important point concerns the distinction that needs to be made between promoting the economic interests of the speakers of the language and promoting the business use of the language itself. While promoting the business use of the language may be part of the local political agenda, it is doubtful whether it can be justified in narrowly economic terms. For a start it will tend to impair communication between the minority group and the monoglot majority, if for no other reason than that the individual members of the majority feel ostracized as a result. This will reduce beneficial externalities between the sectors by impairing trade between them in intermediate products. If the monoglot sector is the more dynamic then this will harm the minority sector more than it harms the monoglot sector, which may have little difficulty in obtaining its intermediate inputs elsewhere.

It is also unclear why entrepreneurial values need to be disseminated to the minority language group through the medium of the minority language itself when the majority language is already perfectly adequate for this purpose. This is particularly true in the case of Wales, for English is already the recognized medium of international business communication in most parts of the world. Although English (interestingly enough) does not have its own word for entrepreneurship, it has at least adopted the French one. If the Welsh language needs to adopt a large number of such business-oriented words then this is a further reason why entrepreneurial ideas should be communicated in English rather than Welsh. Moreover, it could be claimed that the cultural heritage embodied in Welsh language form reinforces the anti-entrepreneurial attitudes that naturally develop amongst people in rural areas who reject the opportunities afforded by emigration. Although the language is not a cause of anti-entrepreneurial attitudes, it may help to reinforce them once they have developed.

In spite of this, however, the Welsh language may still be of economic value if it provides access to a cultural heritage which is of some commercial value. It has already been noted that the modern media, and the leisure and tourist industries, provide ample opportunities for extracting rents from cultural artefacts. Even if the Welsh language has little future *in* business, it may prove a valuable resource *for* business. This economic value may well prove important in maintaining the Welsh language in use for artistic and cultural purposes.

It could, indeed, be argued that local culture has been exploited less effectively as a commercial asset in Wales than it has been in, say, Scotland, and perhaps even Ireland too. One of the great advantages of businesses based on cultural tourism is that the economies of scale in operating attractions are relatively small, so that it is easy for them to begin on a small scale and then grow through reinvested profits. The development of the cultural concept and its transformation into a marketing strategy require a mixture of imagination and careful calculation, but this does not involve complicated logistics or sophisticated accounting systems. It is true that it is often difficult for local people to recognize exactly what it is about their locality that appeals to visitors and that advertising can be impaired by limited access to the social networks in the places that the visitors come from. Nevertheless, there is no reason why Welsh-speakers should not play a more active role in the development of cultural tourism and its supporting industries in Wales.

10.12   SUMMARY AND CONCLUSIONS

This chapter began by asking whether a minority language makes an impact on culture sufficiently strong to affect regional economic development. The analysis suggests that minority language is not an autonomous influence of any great significance. It can serve to amplify some of the anti-entrepreneurial attitudes that develop in indigenous rural populations that have survived several generations of emigration, by encouraging attachment to a romanticized view of the past. But on the whole it is more appropriate to regard the use of minority language as an effect rather than a cause. It is the result of choices made by people who value attachment to their roots over material success. As such, it is a correlate of the history of immobility which is the key factor in the culture of the group.

The more fundamental issue that emerges from the discussion, however, is whether the dominant culture of the private sector is really compatible with a culture of commitment to a minority language. There is a definite conflict between the logic of global markets, on the one hand, and the use of minority language for business purposes, on the other. Furthermore, the concept of a minority language group as a nascent nation state, which seems to be part of the cultural heritage, fits uneasily with the dominance of multinational organization in the private sector.

Linguistic nationalists naturally dissent from this view. They point instead to the way that many Western societies are fragmenting into different factions, centred on different languages, religious sects or extreme political beliefs. Regional identity and linguistic identity can, they claim, be seen as products generated to satisfy individuals' desire for meaning in this 'Post-modern' world. In economic terms, there is certainly nothing objectionable in presenting minority language as a consumer good in this way. The economic problems only arise when those who wish to 'consume' attempt to gain political power in order to make others pay for their consumption. The cost of the exercise is further increased when the language ceases to be centred on 'hearth and home' and is transplanted to the office, where it makes little economic sense. Legislation which requires the use of the minority language in local government and in local business normally increases costs because the minority language does not replace the majority language but merely duplicates it. It may well be true that in certain regions the minority language is increasingly seen as an economic asset by those who speak it, and that the number of speakers is even beginning to rise as a result, but there is little comfort to be gained from this if the driving force is simply legislation that is raising administrative costs in the region and making it less competitive than before.

Another key point in the chapter, however, is that it is not only the culture of linguistic nationalism which has its faults: the culture of the modern private sector has problems too. The aggressive enterprise culture of the 1980s was too strong on competition and individualism, and dangerously weak on cooperation and association. If the culture of capitalism changes towards cooperation and association – and there is evidence that, at least in the more intellectual circles, this is happening – then the gap between enterprise culture and the typical minority language culture will be much reduced. With more realism and less romanticism on the nationalist side, and more emphasis on social networking on the capitalist side, the cultural fit with private industry would be much improved.

In the context of Wales, better cultural fit should lead to more rapid advancement for Welsh-speaking entrepreneurs, so that more successful role models will be available for future generations. Positive role models should engender greater confidence and encourage future generations of Welsh-speakers to embark on a more varied set of careers. This would in turn broaden the range of experiences which could be shared within the Welsh-speaking community and so help the community to play a more constructive role in preparing its younger members for careers in the private sector.

This suggests that regional development agencies in Wales could play an active part in promoting cooperative values within Welsh business generally, as well as in promoting entrepreneurial attitudes amongst the Welsh-speaking community. To some extent, of course, these cooperative values are already present in Wales to a higher degree than in other parts of the United Kingdom. Many

Japanese investors already have this ethos, and so too do many of the small Welsh-owned firms. The same is not true, though, of United States and European firms. Neither is the cooperative ethos likely to be strong in branch plants of English firms, or in firms that have relocated entirely from England to Wales. Certainly small and medium-sized firms with English owners often suffer from a highly autocratic management style which, it has been alleged, tends to stifle their further growth. Thus disseminating a cooperative ethos to investors in Wales might well improve these firms' performance anyway, in addition to providing a better cultural fit with Welsh-speaking employees.

The way to do this, however, is not to disseminate entrepreneurial values in Welsh, or to promote the use of the Welsh language at work. The most appropriate way is to establish greater dialogue between opinion leaders in the two cultures, in the hope that each can influence the other. The natural way to broker between the two groups is not to interpose a translation service involving one-way intellectual traffic into the Welsh-speaking group but to make introductions and then step aside to allow two-way intellectual traffic between them.

The key to entrepreneurial success, it is now increasingly recognized, is effective social networking. In the private sector non-Welsh-speakers are already networked to the business community outside Wales, but by and large the Welsh-speakers are not. The Welsh-speakers need to be encouraged to network more effectively with local non-Welsh-speakers. While a local Welsh-speaking business network is better than no network at all, such a network is still inadequate in the context of the modern globally integrated economic system. Welsh-speakers should appreciate that their values of cooperation and community solidarity are valuable in making non-Welsh-speaking business networks more effective. They might acquire the confidence to socialize more freely with the non-Welsh-speaking community. If they were convinced that they had something useful to teach other people then this would open up new business opportunities. It would facilitate the supply of intermediate inputs to the non-Welsh-speaking sector and so allow them to learn more of modern business practices at first hand. Regional development agencies can perform a useful function in getting this kind of dialogue under way.

ACKNOWLEDGEMENTS

Research for this chapter was supported financially by Menter a Busnes. I am grateful to Adam Price for his support and encouragement. Valuable comments were received from Anuradha Basu, Eamonn D'Arcy, Christie Davies, Andrew Godley, Adam Price and Mike Stabler, and from participants in a seminar held in Cardiff in June 1994. The views expressed are not those of Menter a Busnes, but are purely my own.

REFERENCES

Buckley, P.J. and M.C. Casson (1993) Economics as an Imperialist Social Science, *Human Relations*, **46**, 1035–52.

Buckley, P.J., M.C. Casson and M. Chapman (1994) Economics and Social Anthropology: Reconciling Differences, *University of Reading Discussion Papers in Economics*, October.

Casson, M.C. (1982) *The Entrepreneur: An Economic Theory*, Oxford: Martin Robertson.

Chapman, M. (1992) *The Celts*, London: Macmillan.

Davies, C. (1992) The Protestant Ethic and the Comic Spirit of Capitalism, *British Journal of Sociology*, **43**, 422–41.

Gasson, R. and A. Errington (1994) *The Farm Family Business*, Wallingford, Oxon: CAB International.

Jenkins, D. (1971) *The Agricultural Community in South-west Wales at the Turn of the Century*, Cardiff: University of Wales Press.

John, A.H. (1950) *The Industrial Development of South Wales 1750–1850: An Essay*, Cardiff: University of Wales Press.

Menter a Busnes (1993) *Characteristics of Welsh Speakers in Business*, Aberystwyth: Menter a Busnes.

Olson, M. (1982) *The Rise and Decline of Nations*, New Haven, Conn.: Yale University Press.

Pellenbarg, P.H. (1993) Language, Economy and the Regional Image: A Case Study of Friesland, mimeo.

Price, A., K. Morgan and P. Cooke (1993) *The Welsh Renaissance: Inward Investment and Industrial Innovation*, Regional Industrial Research Report 14, Cardiff: Centre for Advanced Studies, University of Wales, College of Cardiff.

Sowell, T. (1983) *The Economics and Politics of Race: An International Perspective*, New York: Morrow.

Steiner, G. (1975) *After Babel: Aspects of Language and Translation*, London: Oxford University Press.

Van Langevelde, A.B. (1994) Language and Economy in Friesland: A First Step Towards Development of a Theory, *Tijdschrift voor Economische en Sociale Geografie*, **85**(1), 67–77.

Williams, G. (1994) Political and Economic Restructuring in Europe, Bangor: UCNW, mimeo.

Williams, G.A. (1985) *When was Wales? A History of the Welsh*, London: Black Raven Press.

11. Enterprise culture and institutional change in Eastern Europe

11.1 INTRODUCTION

Western experts advising East European countries on the transition to a market economy face an embarrassing problem, namely that there is no comprehensive economic theory of institutions on which to base their policy recommendations. As a result, the advice given by Western economic experts stresses those aspects of the economic system which can be understood using the limited range of concepts employed by conventional economic theory. One manifestation of this is the extraordinary emphasis given to adjusting real wages down to the low level of productivity in industry (Kolodko and Rutkowski, 1991). The idea is sound, but its significance has been exaggerated to distract attention from the fact that so little can be said about other equally important issues.

The real challenge is not to get real wages down, but to get productivity up. This sounds like a production problem, to be solved by installing new capital equipment, increasing the intensity of labour and incentivizing managers by privatizing the largest firms. But the relevant concept of productivity is value productivity rather than just physical productivity. Value productivity is maximized by producing the right sorts of goods, of the right quality, at the right time. The allocation of resources to producing the right goods is the key task which the reformed economies have transferred from the planning system to the market system.

It is often assumed in East European economies that Western economists know all about how markets work. This seems plausible, but is regrettably untrue. Most Western economists operate with a highly simplified and potentially misleading view of the market system. This view is rightly criticized by economic sociologists for failing to recognize how far markets are embedded in the social fabric of society (see Chapter 2). But even within the strictly economic domain, the economists' account is misleading because it fails to recognize the role of entrepreneurial intermediation in the market process.

Entrepreneurs establish market-making firms to identify and exploit opportunities for reallocating resources to a better use (see Chapter 4). The role of market making in reducing transaction costs, and its dependence on entrepreneurial initiative, are not properly recognized in conventional economic theory. This chapter attempts to redress the balance by analysing the key factors in the formation and growth of market-making firms.

In line with the arguments of previous chapters, entrepreneurial success is ascribed not merely to single-mindedly selfish and materialistic ambition, but to the building up of networks of trust between enterprising individuals with complementary sets of skills. The crucial constraints on the success of market reform in Eastern Europe include not only the lack of an entrepreneurial tradition, and the lack of understanding amongst Western advisors about the nature of entrepreneurial skills but, most fundamentally, the lack of trust in the countries concerned, caused by the social disintegration that began under the discredited socialist regimes and has been accelerated by the traumas of the reform process itself. Entrepreneurial success in creating interlocking networks of market-making firms will only be achieved in Eastern Europe when the interaction between entrepreneurship and culture is appreciated more fully at both an intellectual and a practical level.

11.2 LIMITATIONS OF THE MACROECONOMIC APPROACH TO REFORM

Many East European enterprises have suffered from the collapse of the Soviet market. Since their products are ill-adapted to Western requirements, the value productivity of East European enterprises is very low (Wyplosz, 1992). Thus, measured in terms of imported consumer goods, the equilibrium real wage is so low that many families would sink even further below the poverty line if short-run adjustments were made in full.

Because most major enterprises are state-owned, wages can be subsidized using the 'soft budget constraints' under which these enterprises work (Sachs, 1991). But this means that a large amount of government expenditure has to be allocated to subsidizing loss-making industries. Although defence expenditure has been cut back, resource savings have been limited because many workers are still employed in the state-owned defence supply industries even though there is little for them to do. Expenditure on subsidies to state-owned enterprises diverts resources from schools, hospitals, social services and so on, so that the 'social wage', which includes unpriced services, falls even if the real wage does not.

Tightening up these budget constraints has now become an objective in its own right. But if the real wage is maintained while enterprise budgets are cut, the number of people employed must fall. This should, in theory, eliminate over-manning and help to improve productivity, thereby restoring some of the balance between productivity and the real wage. In practice, however, it has proved difficult to raise productivity without new investment. Thus unemployment has risen and, in the absence of adequate social services, widespread prostitution, theft and even violent crime have materialized.

Budgetary imbalance leads East European governments into either printing more money or borrowing from abroad. These are the obvious ways for them to try and finance new investment. They could, in principle, borrow from or tax their own citizens but the margin of taxable surplus, and the willingness to lend, are both too low. Inflation caused by increases in the money supply is the obvious result (Hansson, 1991). This is, of course, yet another way in which the real wage is reduced to its equilibrium level. For, with nominal wage stickiness, inflation simply erodes real purchasing power.

Faced with these difficulties, East European governments have been obliged to turn to the International Monetary Fund (IMF) and the European Bank for Reconstruction and Development. The IMF perceives East European issues in the context of its experience in lending to less developed countries. It believes that correct domestic pricing is necessary to guide the structural adjustment process and that this is possible only if tradeable goods are priced at international levels. In extreme cases domestic price distortion can sustain industries which have negative value added at international prices. The IMF therefore favours the dismantling of protection, the abolition of exchange controls and the maintenance of monetary discipline through currency boards. The correct pricing of capital requires financial markets, and these in turn require a modern banking system. Efficient pricing of labour means not only short-run 'cold turkey' while real wages are reduced but the elimination of long-run distortions caused by high marginal rates of taxation on wage and salary income.

Bitter experience of lending to irresponsible governments has created considerable cynicism within the IMF towards public-sector investment projects. This has led to a series of related targets: to encourage privatization; to promote transparency of government finances, in order to discourage corruption and reveal the true opportunity costs of prestigious projects; and to achieve 'coherence' between the policies of debtor governments and the IMF – for example, to reduce high-pressure selling of arms and conspicuous high-technology equipment by Western firms.

There is general consensus that in the long run the key prerequisite for raising living standards is to raise productivity. It is here that the limitations of Western advice became apparent. While Western advisers are quite convincing on the question of how to reduce the real wage to match a given level of productivity, they are much less convincing on the subject of how to raise productivity to sustain a given real wage.

Raising productivity is not just a matter of increasing the aggregate capital stock, as a simplistic application of neoclassical economics might suggest. If it were, previous investments would have yielded a much higher rate of return.

The problem is not so much the aggregate capital stock but its composition. It is also the effectiveness with which labour utilizes the capital, the quality of the raw materials used, and the suitability of the product. In other words, it is a micro-level problem.

Micro-level analysis of new investment can be carried out using project appraisal techniques: private net present value calculation, or social cost–benefit analysis, to capture external effects. But for separate micro-level decisions to be properly coordinated accurate prices are needed. When markets are not in place such prices are difficult to obtain. Since, moreover, the absence of some markets distorts prices in other markets, it is a complete system of markets that is required. An incomplete system of markets could, in principle, generate such distorted prices that it was worse than no system of markets at all.

A market system is thus, to some extent, an indivisible asset. The creation of a market system requires an institutional revolution to put as many markets in place as quickly as possible. Once the system is in place, micro problems can be solved using a bottom-up approach, because the market incentive system will support an efficient delegation of decisions.

But the creation of a market system requires a top-down approach. Markets require property rights and property rights normally benefit from being centrally enforced. The framework within which rights are created and modified is usually centralized as well. The key problem is how to design this system to meet the needs of the East European economies. At the moment there is no generally accepted set of principles for the institutional design of a market system.

A market system is not a purely technical artefact. It is also a social organism. The information flows of the market system are embedded in language and culture, and in networks of trust which assure the reliability and intelligibility of the information. As such, a system needs to be adapted to local customs and traditions if it is to be used effectively. The implementation of general principles must therefore take account of local factors of this kind, but, without an understanding of these principles, appropriate forms of institutional adaptation may not occur.

11.3 ENTERPRISE AND ORGANIZATIONAL DESIGN

Western economic advice to East European enterprises tends to be practical rather than conceptual, and specific rather than general. Western experts can advise on how to set up an accounting system for cost control, how to carry out technological appraisal and market research, and so on. But the methods are usually based just on standard industry practice rather than on any explicit comparison with alternative systems.

At the conceptual level there is a general recognition amongst economists that markets and organizations are alternative coordinating mechanisms. Unfortunately, though, this insight is treated rather superficially, and its implications have not been developed in the detail that is required for practical application. Internalization theory (Coase, 1937) indicates in general terms where the boundaries of the firm and market should lie, but it does not fully analyse the choice between alternative market structures, on the one hand, and alternative organizational structures, on the other. Industrial organization theory explains the importance of avoiding monopoly. This point is usually made in the context of markets but it applies equally well within the firm, where selfish individuals or groups can use monopoly power to block necessary change. But the problem of reconciling the gains from scale economies with the costs of monopoly is still not fully resolved, as current Western controversy about natural monopoly regulation makes clear.

It is in issues that require a fully dynamic analysis that the limitations of conventional theory are most acute (see, for example, Husain and Sahay, 1992). Even down-to-earth issues, such as how to grow small enterprises to a significant level, remain opaque because they involve questions of evolution, uncertainty and change. Similar problems make it difficult to advise on the reorganization of large state-owned enterprises too (Bös, 1992). While there is general agreement that East European economies need more medium-size enterprises, there is no consensus on how this apparently desirable state of affairs is to be brought about (UNIDO 1991, 1992).

The fundamental problem, it is suggested here, is that the nature of entrepreneurship is not fully understood. A better understanding of entrepreneurship would provide several of the missing principles which the appraisal of alternative economic institutions requires. While it may be obvious at a practical level that entrepreneurship is the key to economic development within a market system, entrepreneurship has never been accorded the central place in Western social science that it deserves. Thus, while specific techniques can be taught by Western experts, these experts have little advice to offer on the general principles governing the growth of enterprise.

Part of the problem is the naive Western view that everyone is potentially entrepreneurial and that failures of entrepreneurship are simply the consequence of rigidity and repression. The repression of entrepreneurship is typically blamed on the state. Deregulate and privatize, it is argued, and you can rely on people to do the rest.

The alternative view is that entrepreneurship is a very scarce attribute. Most people wish to conform rather than to stand out, and are accustomed to following other people's opinions rather than thinking for themselves. On this view a society needs to make the most of its limited supply of entrepreneurial talent, by selectively recruiting able individuals to an entrepreneurial elite which takes strategic decisions on behalf of other people. If entrepreneurship is extremely scarce then it may be more important, in fact, to concentrate entrepreneurs in the government service and political life, where there are many big decisions to be made, rather than, say, to disperse them across medium-sized enterprises in the private sector.

These alternative views have important practical implications. The scarcity view tends to support an 'industrial policy' approach to the restructuring of state-owned enterprises. It suggests that entrepreneurial public officials, acting with Western advice, could usefully develop an integrated restructuring programme for the mature heavy industries and negotiate a comprehensive financial package underwritten by Western governments. The populist view of entrepreneurship, on the other hand, suggests that such policy formulation is premature. Only when the diverse views of individual owners of newly privatized enterprises have been sought can sound policies be devised. It is not the intellectual sophistication of the judgement that matters, on this view, but rather that the judgement is informed by the calculated self-interest of the private owners of the firm. Current privatization practice based on the distribution of vouchers to the electorate clearly reflects this second view.

In practice both views have something to commend them. Where small-scale entrepreneurial activity, such as petty trading, is concerned, the assumption that many (though certainly not all) people possess entrepreneurial potential may have some validity. But when it comes to large-scale activities, where some familiarity with scientific and managerial techniques is called for, scarcity seems to be the rule. This is, of course, the kind of entrepreneurial activity that Schumpeter (1934) had in mind when he articulated his distinctively elitist view of economic development. If this assessment is correct then more weight clearly needs to be given to the industrial policy approach outlined above.

Another implication of the naive Western view is that the emergence of appropriate institutions is a sufficient condition for entrepreneurship to flourish. Such institutions will emerge from a competitive process which selects the best adapted institution for each niche of the economy. The alleged justification for this view is that Western capitalism evolved over centuries as a result of numerous small and localized experiments in organization. The most successful of these experiments have led to the emergence of certain common organizational forms, as diverse as parliamentary democracy, the limited liability company, the stock market, and so on. In almost every country, it is stressed, these forms have emerged with local variation which is crucial to their effective performance. Thus in Britain government is centralized, companies have a single board to represent the interests of the owner as dominant stakeholder, and the stock market involves extensive participation by small investors. In Germany, on the other hand, government is decentralized on federal lines, large companies have two-tier boards to represent a diversity of stakeholder interests, and the stock market is less important than the banks in financing new investment by industry.

This theory suggests that the reasons underlying the success of these firms and the rationale of their local adaptation is too complex to be understood. There can be no grand design for an economic system (Hayek, 1960). The demise of the socialist central planning system is held to be the obvious demonstration of this. But there is no design for the market system either. The bad news is, therefore, that Eastern Europe must just wait for its own institutional structures to evolve. The main precondition for this is simply freedom – freedom for anyone to experiment pragmatically with a new organizational form, and the freedom of others to imitate a successful experiment if they wish.

Since this theory offers no 'quick fix' however, it leaves a gap in the market. Surely there must be Western models which can be taken down off the shelf and used as a basis from which local adaptations can emerge? It surely cannot be reasonable to expect Eastern Europe to replay Western European history simply to ensure that institutions are well adapted to their needs.

Sixty years ago most East European countries shared much of the Western culture of the time, and this suggests that it might be possible to reinvent the institutions of the pre-socialist era. Such reinvented institutions would presumably resonate with cultural traditions, and so stand a good chance of working effectively. Apart from the serious problem that 60 years implies a gap of two generations, during which the West and the East have grown apart, there is also the difficulty that, with one or two exceptions, such as Hungary and the Czech republic, the early twentieth century was not a particularly successful period for East European economies, partly because of the unresolved political tensions stemming from the partitioning of territory after the First World War. Thus it might be necessary to turn the clock much further back in order to reinvent a country's golden age.

This chapter argues for an intermediate position, which neither uncritically imposes contemporary Western European institutions on Eastern European economies nor simply liberalizes as much as possible as quickly as possible and waits for order to emerge slowly from the ensuing anarchy. The key to the proposed policy is that entrepreneurship and the institutions that support it are, in fact, susceptible to analysis, and that it is possible to use this analysis to design institutions that will be well adapted to local conditions. It is a medium-run strategy to be pursued over a 5–10 year period. The important thing is to be able to identify the principles governing the efficiency of entrepreneurial institutions. These principles can then be applied using the local knowledge of businessmen and politicians who are familiar with local conditions. The Western experts' contribution will comprise, firstly, the elucidation of these principles and, secondly, the development of a partnership with East European practitioners in framing the constitutions and formulating the precise organizational structures involved.

These principles are outlined in the following section and the main argument is resumed in section 11.5.

11.4 THE INFLUENCE OF INSTITUTIONS ON ECONOMIC PERFORMANCE

Entrepreneurship is popularly understood as involving the founding of small firms and their subsequent growth, first to medium-size enterprises and, ultimately, to large-scale ones. The founding of a firm is usually visualized in terms of the discovery of an opportunity that the founder decides to exploit.

Discovery

Discoveries can be imbued with very different degrees of significance. Most discoveries by small-firm entrepreneurs relate to localized changes in the economic environment. Economies are in a continual state of flux, and those who are the first to discover the latest change acquire a temporary monopoly of this information which they can exploit for profit (Kirzner, 1973). Such entrepreneurship is essentially responsive. When circumstances change again the opportunity disappears and a new one appears elsewhere.

A trivial instance is where a craftsman who has been made redundant by a large firm 'discovers' that he can still make a modest living by practising his craft out of his garden shed, doing 'odd jobs' for neighbours and bartering payment through the local 'black' economy. Businesses of this kind typically have no potential for growth. This does not mean that small informal businesses cannot grow. It is not unknown for door-to-door commission salesmen, reflecting on their successes and failures, to evolve a marketing concept with considerable potential. The difference between the craftsman and the salesman in this respect is that the former is typically oriented to the emotional satisfactions derived from indulging the 'instinct of workmanship' rather than to the income derived from providing satisfaction to other people. The marketer is geared to helping other people solve their problems whilst the craftsman's effort goes into solving his own problem of how to derive interest and enjoyment from his work (Smith, 1967).

Sometimes major discoveries can be made, however. The chance of making a major discovery enhances entrepreneurial prestige: it implies that the entrepreneur can 'make his mark' by leaving the world in a very different state from that in which he found it. These chances seemed high for the merchant adventurers of fifteenth- and sixteenth-century Europe, and for the mineral prospectors in nineteenth century Africa, Australasia and Western America. There were uncharted territories to be explored and an open geographical frontier. Most of these frontiers are now closed in the physical sense. It is nowadays in the world of ideas that the most important frontiers remain open, and in the application of these ideas to solve practical problems and improve the material standards of everyday life.

Yet in intellectual terms the frontier is far more open in some societies than in others. There are prominent systems of thought which claim that all the really important ideas have already been discovered. Marxism is, to some extent, in this category: it is amazing to realize, for example, that in the Soviet Union historical materialism was considered so definitive that two of the major break-throughs of twentieth-century physics – relativity and the uncertainty principle – were considered unsound because of their conflict with Marxist views of causality and determinism.

Religious revelations that are taken as definitive can sometimes exert a similar constraining influence. Interestingly, though, Western Christianity has embraced a Cartesian dualism in which scientific inquiry into material creation can coexist alongside moral and metaphysical speculation about the mind and soul (see Chapter 7). Occasional conflicts, as between Darwinism and Biblical fundamentalism, should not obscure the fact that religion has done little in the West to curb scientific optimism. It has, indeed, actively promoted certain lines of inquiry, for example by providing a moral impetus to fund expensive medical research.

Appropriation

Optimism about scientific discoveries and the possibility of their social appli-cation is only one of several entrepreneurial stimuli. Another concerns the possibility of appropriating ideas for private profit. Western societies take an ambiguous view on this. On the one hand, there is the attitude that what is uncharted is not yet appropriated, and so is 'up for grabs'. When allied to the view that discovery is normally a consequence, not of luck, but of dedicated effort, this view suggests that the private appropriation of a discovery is a natural reward for the expenditure involved.

On the other hand, there is the Christian view that everything is ultimately God's creation and that man is not the owner but only the steward of it. This suggests that everything is, in some sense, already appropriated, and so can only be held under licence. A similar conclusion follows from the socialist view that everything is owned by society, whether or not some individual has yet discovered it.

There is an important difference between them, however, in that society usually expresses its rights through the representatives who govern it, and these repre-sentatives therefore acquire considerable power over the disposal of these rights. In practice, this means that the discoverer must negotiate with central government in order to obtain a licence to exploit his discovery, a licence which in many cases may well be denied. The religious concept of stewardship does not have to be expressed through a powerful earthly representative, though medieval popes were not slow to exploit some possibilities of this kind. The exercise of stewardship can be decentralized through the conscience of the discoverer and the voluntary self-restraint he shows in the exercise of his rights. Central regulation is then invoked only if negative externalities emerge which call for the rights acquired as a result of the discovery to be more precisely defined.

It is evident that in the Western system the right to appropriate discoveries is much stronger than in a socialist or theocratic state, and that the pecuniary incentive to innovate is much greater as a result. The existence of a wide range of undiscovered and unappropriated ideas is taken for granted. An optimistic view of the consequences of discovery is generally taken, and this is reflected in the desire to encourage the discoverer by giving him the 'natural' reward for his effort. It is recognized that the exploitation of a new discovery may have unintended consequences. Political institutions are designed to be responsive to popular concerns about their indirect effects, and if necessary legislation can be passed to protect existing rights.

Private Ownership

Ideas themselves are notoriously difficult to appropriate. Patent infringements are difficult to detect, the litigation is costly, and the scope of the patent system is limited in any case. Often the most effective way to appropriate rewards from an idea is to focus on its application. The typical entrepreneurial idea is exploited by putting existing resources to a novel use. The entrepreneur integrates forward by buying up the resources required by the application. If these resources are in fixed supply, and he can keep his idea secret until negotiations are complete, then a pure rent can be obtained which reflects the value of the idea.

This mechanism requires that ownership of these resources can be traded freely between individuals. It also requires that ownership is a quite general right which allows the owner to deploy his resources in any way he likes, provided that it does not infringe the rights of other parties. This highlights the basic point that in an entrepreneurial economy individuals as well as corporate entities can hold rights and that, with certain minor limitations, they can acquire or dispose of them as they wish (Putterman, 1990). What is more, because the rights are quite general, the redeployment of an asset to a novel use does not require the creation of a novel right to authorize this specific use. All potential as well as actual uses are included in the ownership right (Casson, 1982).

A strength can easily become a weakness, however, and the very generality of the ownership right means that unanticipated conflicts can readily emerge. Two parties may coexist happily without coordination so long as they do not make choices that directly impinge on each other. When by chance one decides to make a different choice, the other party is disturbed and an inconsistency in the initial distribution of rights is revealed. This inconsistency has hitherto been hidden by a fortuitous combination of choices. The rights of one of the parties must now be modified, and the question of whether the party whose rights are restricted should be compensated must also be addressed. The private ownership system generates many instances of this kind, and its success depends crucially on the efficiency with which such conflicts can be resolved.

It is unfortunate that the political and legal systems of East European countries are currently ill-equipped to deal with a regular stream of cases of this kind. It is even more unfortunate that they are preoccupied with even more funda-mental problems relating not so much to inconsistencies between rights relating to different resources as to inconsistencies relating to the *same* resources – conflicts between rival claimants to the same resources stemming from controversy over whether previous transfers of ownership were legitimate or not. Until such issues are resolved, markets in these resources are effectively blighted, because no one can afford to acquire a resource if they are unsure who holds the legal title to it. Since the acquisition of resources is one of the basic ways in which entre-preneurial ideas are exploited, this is a fundamental problem which must be urgently resolved.

Screening

While small discoveries can often be exploited using the personal wealth of the entrepreneur and his immediate circle – taking a second mortgage on the house, borrowing from family and friends, and so on – it is difficult to exploit a really major discovery in this way. If an employer will not back the idea then the discoverer must become self-employed and seek support from financial insti-tutions. Such backers are likely to take a very different view of the opportunity the entrepreneur believes he has discovered than does the entrepreneur himself. The entrepreneur's very limited experience makes him unaware of the many practical difficulties that face a small business, difficulties that are only too familiar to the financial institutions he approaches.

While the entrepreneur has made an initial judgement that an opportunity exists, the financial institution must independently validate that assessment by making a judgement of its own. It is only natural that those who make 'discoveries' tend to be more confident about them than are those to whom the discovery is reported. The success of an economic system depends crucially on the quality of judgement exercised by financial institutions of this kind. Since financial insti-tutions are normally in competition with each other it is not the quality of any one institution that is crucial but the quality of the institutions as a whole. It is possible that all the financial institutions in a given country may share a particular cultural bias which influences the kind of project to which they prefer to lend. In one country there may be a bias to large high-technology projects, for example, and in another to small-scale retail projects, or to property development. There may also be cultural differences between the institutions and their borrowers, caused by differences in education, social background, urban versus rural residence, and so on. Such differences may impair communication, leading the institutions to overestimate certain risks involved and so deny funds to viable projects. A relatively homogeneous society sharing a culture that embraces a diversity of perspectives is likely to be most successful in screening entrepreneurs' ideas.

Liquidity

Financial intermediaries such as banks are not just in the business of lending to entrepreneurs, they are also in the business of supplying liquidity to their depositors. If pressed, banks may wish to liquidate their investments, and so they are interested in how much of their investment can be recovered at short notice should circumstances require it. They therefore tend to require collateral of a highly liquid form, such as land, or inventory ready for sale. In some cases these very specific collateral requirements, coupled with the short-term nature of bank lending, may be a serious constraint on the entrepreneur's ability to take a long-term view of his business.

The obvious way for a firm to mitigate this liquidity problem is to borrow funds through a stock market instead. A stock market provides the individual investor with an opportunity to liquidate his investment by selling his shares to another individual. It does not require him physically to withdraw funds from the firm, since what he withdraws is immediately replaced. The entrepreneur is still under some external pressure, however, because if the equity shares carry votes then a significant sell-out by existing shareholders could place control of the firm in hostile hands.

The efficiency implications of this are not so adverse as they may seem, however. Entrepreneurs can always make mistakes – for no one's judgement is perfect – and so it is advantageous for a firm to make as few irreversible commitments as possible until its plans have clearly survived the 'market test'. A firm which requires a large injection of outside capital to make an irreversible lumpy investment, in a large customized piece of durable equipment with no second-hand value, for example, is a less attractive economic proposition, other things being equal, than a firm which plans to make only a small trial investment in standard equipment which can be scaled up through replication if experience shows that it is successful.

It is interesting to note, in this connection, that many of the most successful individual entrepreneurs of the twentieth century have been the founders of retail chains, who have developed and refined their marketing concept by experimenting in one location before standardizing it and repeating the formula many times over elsewhere. Although their businesses rapidly grew to be very large, they were financed to a significant extent by reinvested profits, a strategy made possible by replicating small reversible investments rather than committing to a single large irreversible one. The industrial mega-projects of the East European socialist regimes illustrate the converse case, in which large irreversible commitments are made on the basis of a largely hypothetical analysis of needs and resources because the owner – the state – attaches no weight to the liquidity aspects of the investment.

Confidence

When the assets of a business are illiquid, the owners of equity are underwriting its commitments by providing insurance. The owners accept a large payment under good conditions as a compensation for low payments under poor conditions. Their 'premium' is reflected in the average rate of return.

If everyone has confidence in the firm then insurance will be forthcoming cheaply: the share price will be high and it will be easy for the firm to raise funds through new issues. But when confidence is low it may be difficult to get anyone to subscribe to new issues at all. If the degree of confidence in an enterprise reflects well-informed opinion then there is no problem of this sort, but if confidence is volatile and led by rumour and fashion then a considerable degree of distortion may be introduced into the growth of industry: fashionable industries expand at the expense of unfashionable ones, and investment proceeds in intermittent spurts as general confidence fluctuates over time. One of the dangers of 'popular capitalism' is that ill-informed investors may be attracted into the market as a boom is reaching its peak, encouraging even greater excesses of investment which defer recovery from the ensuing slump.

Conflict Resolution

When equity markets are poorly developed, as they are in many countries, confidence becomes important in a different way. Large-scale projects normally require several shareholders to finance them, and these shareholders become locked into the firm by the difficulty of disposing of their stock. While they may have perceived a common interest in backing the firm at the outset, unanticipated managerial issues may emerge which create conflict between them. While all the shareholders were initially optimistic, for example, one or two may become pessimistic and try to urge caution when others still want to expand.

Disagreements between shareholders are not the only cause of problems. There may be other stakeholders, such as employees and even major customers and suppliers, who feel (particularly if they are creditors) that their opinion should be considered. Western capitalism generally regards the interests of share-holders as dominant, but this is not universally accepted in capitalist countries and there is still a popular view, advocated by trade union leaders and socialist politicians, that natural justice requires that workers, whose effort is embodied in the product of the enterprise, should be considered to have equivalent rights. Although the capitalist employer would typically argue that these rights were voluntarily surrendered when the wage bargain was struck, the advocate of workers' rights will reply that this concession was only extracted through nego-tiation under duress, or that it is so fundamental that it is inalienable anyway.

These are not the sort of disagreements that any of the parties can easily walk away from. On the other hand, it is difficult to achieve consensus. Some political process is required which will allow each party to compromise without appearing to undermine their ideological position. If the process is perceived as fair then the outcome will be regarded as legitimate by the loser. But it is difficult for a process to appear fair if the outcome is a foregone conclusion. There needs to be an element of chance in the process, a chance mechanism which is equally likely to favour any of the parties. Voting is the preferred mechanism in democratic nations, but at the enterprise level independent arbitration is popular too. The absence of a recent democratic tradition in East Europe is a potential source of weakness in this respect. Resort to coercion is obviously an imperfect method of conflict resolution; democratic methods are required not only at the national level, but at the enterprise level too.

There is a sense, of course, in which resort to a political mechanism is itself a symptom of failure. It indicates that conflicts of economic interest are being magnified, if anything, rather than reduced, by ideological factors. If there were a single unified ideology then everyone would agree on who the stake-holders were, and on the nature of their responsibilities to other parties. From an efficiency point of view this would be preferable to the ideological conflict which is perpetuated from generation to generation even in advanced Western countries. It is true that ideological differences are a manifestation of the same intellectual vitality that sustains innovation. Serious danger arises only when the ideological positions grow so far apart that there is little common ground. Toleration of diversity is desirable, but only within the limits of a reasonably homogeneous culture. Societies with a strong cultural tradition (such as Japan) tend to have quick and peaceful mechanisms of internal conflict resolution and perform efficiently as a result.

Networks of Trust

Conflict resolution is important not only within the firm, but between firms as well. Competition is the classic conflict-resolution mechanism in inter-firm relations. Each firm plays off its trading partners against their rivals. The scope for bilateral bargaining is dramatically reduced by the threat to switch to another partner.

This threat is only credible, however, if the firm is not heavily dependent on a particular customer or supplier. If the firm has invested heavily in adapting its plant to a particular source of supply or demand, its bargaining power is undermined (Klein, Crawford and Alchian, 1978). It needs to trust in the integrity of its partner instead. Trust is also important in constraining the incentive to default on transactions. However satisfactory the outcome of a bargain may be, it is quite useless if the other party has no intention of honouring the contract. While blatant default – such as short supplies or non-payment – can be punished in law, covert default on quality is more difficult to detect. It is also more difficult to prove in court, given the way that the law of evidence normally works.

Networks of trust have proved very important in the textile and garment industry. This industry is historically important as an engine of economic development. It is labour-intensive, uses a standardized technology and has relatively small and inexpensive equipment for which a good second-hand market exists. It is therefore well suited to small owner-managed firms which can grow under constant returns to scale by reinvesting profits, as described earlier.

Each small firm requires an independent source of textile inputs and an independent buyer of its output too. To reduce transport costs and inventory levels in a highly competitive industry, the supplier and customer must be close by. Hence textile firms at adjacent stages of production tend to agglomerate into industrial districts. Within a district there is an elaborate network of inter-firm linkages in which, if the district as a whole is to be internationally competitive, the costs of transactions must be very low.

Building networks of trust between independent businesses can be very time-consuming unless there has been some preliminary socialization between the owners concerned. In many countries ethnic connections based on extended families play an important role in this. In some urban areas in less-developed countries, having ancestors from the same village may prove an effective bond between recent immigrants. In established urban communities, churches, local political parties and clubs can play an important role both in facilitating introductions and in creating an atmosphere of trust. It is interesting to note that some of the most conspicuous examples of networks of trust are found outside the Western countries from which East European policy makers typically take their lead. Powerful networks are common in the Chinese communities of South-east Asia and in Islamic towns as well. Their positive influence on the competitiveness of Japanese industries is also well known. Eastern Europe needs to borrow its institutional models eclectically if it is to reform itself along best-practice institutional lines.

The institutions which engineer trust generally operate, it should be noted, on a non-profit basis. This highlights an important point not usually recognized by advocates of market liberalization, namely that the enforcement of many market contracts hinges ultimately on the efficacy of non-market institutions. An entre-preneurial society is not, therefore, necessarily a profit-centred one. Indeed, too much emphasis on the selfish pursuit of profit will tend to undermine affiliation to these non-profit institutions. In the long run this will impair efficiency, as contracts become more difficult to enforce and a sophisticated division of labour between firms becomes more difficult to sustain.

Law and Government

If a costless system of law were available to the business community then, of course, trust would not be a problem. Every conceivable contingency affecting the rewards to contracting parties would be itemized and any disagreement referred to an impartial judge. The judge's decision would reflect a perfect comprehension of all the relevant facts of the case, facts which in everyday life are sometimes quite impossible to ascertain. The absurdity of the scenario confirms that the law is not a sufficient answer to the problem of trust in the business community.

It is equally utopian to suppose, however, that even with a rich variety of non-profit organizations the web of mutual obligation would embrace every conceivable pair of contracting parties. Ultimately, therefore, there needs to be some coercive sanction against persistent offenders against the moral code of the business community. While a system of law is not, therefore, sufficient for contractual enforcement, it is necessary in dealing with persistent offenders.

The practical difficulty lies not so much in creating an institution, such as the state, with sufficient coercive power, for even very primitive communities have a military defence force which can be deployed for civilian use. The problem lies in constraining the abuse of state power. A good legal system requires the exercise of self-restraint by judges (in refusing bribes, resisting intimidation, and so on) and a good political system requires similar self-restraint by leaders (in not suspending the democratic constitution once they have been elected, for example). Even where individual members of society cannot trust each other, therefore, they need to be able to trust the judges and politicians who intermediate between them.

This highlights the point that successful economic transition in Eastern Europe requires an efficient judicial system and reputable government (Siebert, 1992). While it may be true that a democratic system offers the best guarantee of this, democracy *per se* may not be essential. The important point is that whoever rules is widely trusted to respect rights and enforce contracts. This is important not only internally but externally too. The integrity of government is an important issue for foreign lenders (see section 11.6). While foreign lenders may tolerate a non-democratic system (for if it is stable it offers the prospect of long-term consistency of policy) they will not tolerate a government which repeatedly reneges on its commitments. One of the key issues for East European transition is therefore a political rather than an economic one, namely to find the best way of maintaining a stable and honest government that will respect individual rights.

11.5   CULTURAL INFLUENCES ON PERFORMANCE

The preceding discussion has emphasized that entrepreneurial activity is very much embedded in the social and political system. This raises the question of whether certain attitudes towards social and political life are more conducive to entrepreneurship than others. It has already been suggested, for example, that a confident scientifically optimistic attitude is required for successful innovation.

It has been suggested, too, that a high-trust atmosphere promotes effective cooperation, both within and between firms. The importance of cooperation in entrepreneurship demonstrates that the typical Western view of the successful entrepreneur as a highly competitive and assertive individualist is very misleading. It is particularly unfortunate that the low-trust attitude of contemporary Western culture reinforces the low trust that is already apparent in many East European countries because of the legacy of the Stalinist era. Not only did Stalinist thinking itself involve a suspicious attitude to others, but the increasing absurdities of overcentralized planning led to a general distrust of promises made by anyone working within the economic system. This atmosphere of distrust was exacerbated by the widespread use of informers reporting to the secret police. A low-trust attitude is, in general, a source of weakness rather than strength, and it must be hoped that the recovery of 'traditional values' in some East European countries may help to build up the kind of high-trust culture that the West is currently in a poor position to supply.

An entrepreneurial culture must combine high trust with some degree of individualism. A successful entrepreneur is usually an individualist in the sense that his views do not always conform to the general opinion of those around him; indeed, if they did he would have little value since anyone else in the group could arrive at the same decisions he did. But as an individualist, he must not be motivated by entirely selfish means (Casson, 1991). It is certainly useful for him to experience the tension of striving for something that it is difficult to sustain, for such an attitude reduces the subjective cost of hard work. But, as emphasized in the earlier chapters of this book, the striving should not be for material success alone. Many successful entrepreneurs of the past have held very naive views about the intrinsic value of the goods they produced. This naivety was a considerable source of strength in giving conviction to their personal efforts to promote their product and enabling them to motivate employees to take their work very seriously. These naive views were in turn often a manifestation of religious or philosophical convictions. Many successful entrepreneurs in both the United States and the United Kingdom have belonged to sects which demanded high levels of personal commitment from their members. The tensions of business life were reflected in the tensions these religious groups experienced between their own value systems and those of the establishment of their day. Although material success often led these entrepreneurs (or their descendants) to compromise with established values in order to win respectability, this does not detract from the fact that success was in large part attributable to the high moral value that they accorded to their early business activities. East European enterprises need to rediscover a sense of mission too. This is important in convincing customers of management's commitment to product quality and motivating employees by giving them pride in their job. Cultural factors will be important in determining whether the new business leaders emerging in Eastern Europe have these qualities or not. First impressions suggest that, unfortunately, many of them do not.

Culture can contribute not only to enhanced cooperation: it can improve the quality of decision making too. Given all the imponderables in the typical business situation, and the need for a quick decision, good judgement is extremely important. As emphasised in Chapter 7, judgement typically requires a combination of theoretical perspective and practical knowledge. This combination is found in relatively few cultures. Marxism is essentially a theoretical construct and, in countries previously dominated by Marxist ideology, theory is likely to be valued much more highly than practical experience. Although this may not apply to industrial craftsmen, it certainly applies to the political and business elites.

The West has examples of businesses run on the basis of theories too, however, and the results have generally been poor. Most theories oversimplify and suggest that just one or two factors dominate where business performance is concerned. In large Western firms concepts of 'divisionalization', 'globalization' and 'diversification' are often applied uncritically without reference to the firm's industrial and institutional environment. Where day-to-day decisions, rather than long-term strategy formulation, are concerned, theory manifests itself in the belief that one set of indicators – sales, market share, mark-up, and so on – is more important than all others. Power within the organization is given to the managers who collect the relevant figures and plan the relevant responses, while managers who deal with issues which are, in reality, no less important do not get a chance to make their views known. It is their role to implement policies handed down from the more powerful managers, and not to question these decisions on the basis of their own set of data.

A theoretical orientation also encourages a preference for radical rather than incremental change. Theory not only throws up new ideas, but provides a framework within which the practical application of those ideas can be legitimated. It gives an unwarranted sense of confidence to those who overlook the very restrictive assumptions on which the theory is based. This preference for radicalism rather than incrementalism is likely to be another instance of the Marxist legacy. It is already apparent in the very doctrinaire way in which market principles have been applied in liberalizing East European countries. One theoretical system – based on an abstract notion of a market – has been substituted for another theoretical system based on surplus value. The dilution of theory with practical experience has yet to come. One reason, of course, is that practical experience of markets is singularly lacking in Eastern Europe, for historical reasons. The speed at which it can be accumulated, and the willingness to use it, will be major factors in the success of the transition to a market economy.

Overall, it seems that the cultural legacy of Marxism may prove a major handicap in the newly liberalizing economies (Etzioni, 1991). The need for interpersonal trust in the development of business partnerships and business networks is underestimated as a result of the cynical low-trust culture promoted by the Stalinist style of management (Attali, 1992). Even in countries such as Hungary and Poland, where intermittent attempts at decentralization have been made, this legacy still seems to remain. While there is little problem in most of the countries with people being ambitious to improve their quality of life, the extent to which moral as well as material objectives are important remains unclear. In several countries the churches are still a powerful influence, but traditionally the Catholic church, which is dominant, has tended, unlike the Protestant church, to promote organic solidarity rather than individualistic values.

11.6   FOREIGN DIRECT INVESTMENT AND THE TRANSFER OF CULTURAL VALUES

The macroeconomic perspective of section 11.2 makes it clear that much of the new investment required for industrial restructuring must come from foreign sources. Pure capital, in the form of fixed-interest loans, is relatively homogeneous and can be obtained from private, governmental or intergovernmental sources. Where indigenous technology and management are weak, however, and access to foreign markets is poor, foreign expertise is required as well. Much of the expertise at the enterprise level resides in foreign firms.

It is quite possible, in principle, to obtain these different inputs from different sources using arms'-length contracts: to issue bonds to obtain capital and then invest the capital in the purchase of licences, brands and consultants' expertise

(Casson, 1979). It is often advantageous to link such procurements, however. To encourage the supply of good quality expertise it is useful to introduce an element of payment by results, and one way of doing this is to persuade the supplier to take an equity stake. This may also be advantageous from the supplier's point of view. For example, it allows a licensor to monitor the resale of technology to third parties, to control exports to markets already serviced by other licensees, and so on.

Similarly, capital investors may wish to acquire an equity stake so that they can influence the way their funds are used. This is particularly important when collateral is illiquid and intangible, and where the limited liability of equity holders makes it difficult to recover funds from an insolvent firm. It is for reasons of this kind that policies for industrial reconstruction tend to focus on the selective encouragement of foreign direct investment.

Every foreign investor is going to be concerned about the security of their property rights, and so the stability and integrity of the government is crucial to them (Samuelsson, 1992). Since foreign investment is needed urgently, governments have an imperative to acquire reputation as quickly as possible. One way of doing this is to bind themselves through treaties with other governments, giving these other governments a legitimate excuse for intervention should the rights of their private foreign investors be infringed. The current policy of making treaties with the European Community is a successful example of this political strategy.

Historically, of course, many countries have achieved political credibility with foreign investors by submitting to colonization or occupation. The post-war recovery of both West Germany and Japan involved periods of foreign occupation during which a good deal of United States technology and management practice was transferred to those countries. It might not be too fanciful to suggest that, under the veneer of reunification, something similar is happening in former East German territories now. One reason that West German technology and management practice is rapidly advancing in eastern Germany is that the political risks of private investment are so low.

From a strictly economic point of view, other East European countries might benefit from political subordination of this kind. There is no reason, in principle, why there should not be a market in government, in which one government could contract with another government to assume some of its powers for a limited period of time. The moral hazard is, of course, potentially acute, because the foreign government might be reluctant to relinquish its powers at the end of its term, particularly if it had in the meantime managed to acquire a monopoly of force.

Another objection is that government is a culture-specific activity, so that political structures do not transfer readily between countries. This is certainly supported by the nineteenth-century British experience, where an optimistic belief in the universal superiority of a very specific package of democratic institutions was belied by the very mixed results which were obtained in different parts of the world.

It is not only government that is culture-specific, though: enterprise management is culture-specific as well. Foreign direct investment transfers not only technology and management skills, but cultural values too. What is more, the cultural values are very much bound up with attitudes to technology and preferences for particular management forms, so that the cultural content cannot easily be separated out to leave a culture-free residue.

The transfer of culture may, to some extent, be a bonus so far as economic efficiency is concerned. In a social context, however, it is understandably perceived as a negative factor by those committed to the traditional values of the host country. From the perspective of this chapter the crucial issue is whether the foreign culture that is transferred is more conducive to entrepreneurship than the indigenous one.

Taking the culture as a whole, the answer must be an affirmative one. Foreign investors are typically firms that have already proved successful in their home countries, and are therefore presumably imbued with a culture that supports competitive advantage. Even if their home country culture is not particularly entrepreneurial, therefore, the corporate culture of the foreign investor will be so.

This is not to say that each individual aspect of the foreign culture is to be recommended, though. It was noted in section 11.5 that contemporary Western culture has a number of negative aspects so far as entrepreneurship is concerned. The decline of traditional religions and moral systems and the weakening sense of community caused by rising geographical mobility mean that Western values are becoming low-trust, with increasing emphasis being placed on the law as a coordinating mechanism. The law does not seem to be meeting this challenge very well in Western countries. At the social level, crime statistics show an upward trend, while at the corporate level costly investments have to be made in auditing systems to detect employee fraud, and in legal services to recover debts, prevent patent infringement and the like.

However, to compensate for this deteriorating environment many of the most successful Western firms have invested heavily in training schemes designed to inculcate values of loyalty and stewardship. These reduce the costs of supervising employees, although, because they focus loyalty exclusively on the firm, they do not afford the same social externalities that traditional moral education did. It was emphasized in section 11.5 that the Stalinist legacy of cynicism is a major threat to effective management in East European enterprise, and so corporate cultures which can address this problem should prove particularly valuable. There is a reasonable chance that major foreign investors will be free of some of the worst excesses of contemporary Western culture, so that the values transmitted through foreign investment will, on the whole, be beneficial ones. There is, however, a case for vigilant monitoring of major foreign investments to ensure that this is indeed the case.

It is often claimed that cooperative enterprises in Eastern Europe already enjoy a high-trust culture and that this culture may in fact be undermined by the import of Western values. This claim seems a rather dubious one, however. Worker participation through owner-management may well be an outward symbol of an internal state of harmony, but it is not necessarily so. In so far as harmony exists, internal efficiency gains should allow the cooperative enterprises to compete with foreign investors, at least in those sectors where access to foreign markets or technology is not essential to success. On balance, therefore, it seems reasonable to require that claims about the efficiency of cooperative enterprise should be put to the market test.

The conclusion is that foreign direct investment should be welcomed rather than censured for its role in transmitting cultural values. There is a danger that inappropriate values may be transmitted, but the danger is not so great as might be feared because foreign direct investment is a selective process in which only the more successful firms tend to participate. These firms will tend to have corporate cultures that are conducive to enterprise. The criteria that such cultures must satisfy have been set out in this chapter. It is therefore perfectly feasible to screen foreign direct investments in order to eliminate those with negative cultural externalities, although skilful judgement will be required to do this effectively.

11.7   CONCLUSIONS

The problems of economic transition in Eastern Europe have created an atmosphere of crisis. Sensing political instability, reformers in East European countries have pushed through radical measures designed to raise the costs of returning to communism to a prohibitive level. The political trade-off between changing too slowly, and allowing the communist elite to regroup, and changing too quickly, and so losing popular electoral support, has dominated economic trade-offs between different institutional arrangements. Economic liberalism has provided a simple powerful ideology for the reformers. For citizens accustomed to a simplistic Marxist ideology, an equally simplistic ideology that puts everything into reverse has a natural appeal as an explanation of what went wrong under the previous regime. So far as foreign creditors are concerned, pro-market rhetoric on the lips of local politicians sounds very reassuring. The obvious danger is that the politicians come to believe their own rhetoric and underestimate the subtlety of the problems involved.

This chapter has emphasized the importance of increasing the reputation of government in order to allow the reform process to be undertaken at a less hectic pace. More weight should be given to industrial policy in the restructuring of heavy industry as a complement to, rather than a substitute for, popular privatization. While it is true that the institutions of a market economy constitute an indivisible system, it is also true that the design of the system requires careful thought. Imitating existing Western institutions may be an adequate short-run response, but it should be regarded as a provisional solution to be used only until a more sophisticated one can be found.

The fact that East European economies have an opportunity to create institutions from scratch should not be wasted by acting as though the only way to develop an adequate set of institutions is to copy them from other countries and then adapt them to local conditions using evolutionary processes that may take hundreds of years. Sufficient is known about the conditions conducive to entrepreneurship to make it evident that many existing Western institutions perform very imperfectly. It should not be difficult for East European countries to do better than some of their Western counterparts if they simply avoid making the same mistakes. The biggest mistake is to regard the low-trust legalistic culture of the West as a source of strength rather than as a serious weakness. In this respect the institutions and value systems of Japan, or the South-east Asian 'tigers', are models that might be considered as alternatives to Western ones – at least so far as short-term imitation is concerned.

In this chapter the design of institutions has been analysed under nine headings: discovery, appropriation, private ownership, screening, liquidity, confidence building, conflict resolution, networking and legislation. A number of important principles have been identified, although there are many more which could not be covered but which are relevant too. A distinction has been drawn between the small-scale skills of the petty trader, such as a former black marketeer, and the large-scale skills of the technological innovator and system builder, and the difficulties of upgrading the skills of the former to those of the latter have been stressed. The need to create an intellectual climate which rewards large-scale private innovation as well as petty trading has been noted. The role of financial institutions in screening complex and sophisticated projects has been discussed, with special reference to reconciling the technical need for large-scale investment with the investor's need for liquidity. A variety of issues relating to conflict resolution have been considered, and the vital importance of combining a strict business morality with a legal system well adapted to resolving minor cases has been highlighted. The design of systems that embody principles of this kind provides a full agenda for economic reform in the medium run.

For the long run, it is reasonable to expect that each East European country will choose its own individual path of social and political development. The consequences of these choices can also be analysed using the general principles set out in this chapter. Some paths may emphasize a return to the values of some previous 'golden age', even if these hinder economic success in the modern environment. Such a choice may be perfectly reasonable, provided it reflects popular preferences and is based on a well-informed analysis of the consequences. Other countries may embrace Western cultural values more fully. They would be well advised to consider, however, whether such values really are as conducive to long-run economic success as current political rhetoric claims.

REFERENCES

Attali, J. (1992) The Collapse of Communism and the International Response, speech delivered at the London Business School, London, 30 March.

Bös, D. (1992) Privatization in East Germany: A Survey of Current Issues, Washington DC: International Monetary Fund, *IMF Working Paper*, 92/8.

Casson, M.C. (1979) *Alternatives to the Multinational Enterprise*, London: Macmillan.

Casson, M.C. (1982) *The Entrepreneur: An Economic Theory*, Oxford: Martin Robertson; reprinted Aldershot: Gregg Revivals, 1991.

Casson, M.C. (1991) *Economics of Business Culture: Game Theory, Transaction Costs and Economic Performance*, Oxford: Clarendon Press.

Coase, R.H. (1937) The Nature of the Firm, *Economica*, (new series), **4**, 386–405.

Etzioni, A. (1991) *Eastern Europe: the Wealth of Lessons*, Washington DC: George Washington University; The Socio-Economic Project.

Hansson, A.H. (1991) The Emergence and Stabilisation of Extreme Inflationary Pressures in the Soviet Union, Helsinki: World Institute for Development Economics Research, United Nations University, *WIDER Working Paper*, 93.

Hayek, F.A. von (1960) *The Constitution of Liberty*, Chicago: University of Chicago Press.

Husain, A.M. and R. Sahay (1992) Does Sequencing of Privatization Matter in Reforming Planned Economies? Washington DC: International Monetary Fund, *IMF Working Paper*, 92/13.

Kirzner, I.M. (1973) *Competition and Entrepreneurship*, Chicago: University of Chicago Press.

Klein, B., R.G. Crawford and A.A. Alchian (1978) Vertical Integration, Appropriable Rents and the Competitive Contracting Process, *Journal of Law and Economics*, **21**, 297–320.

Kolodko, G.W. and M. Rutkowski (1991) The Problem of Transition from a Socialist to a Free-market Economy: The Case of Poland, *Journal of Social, Political and Economic Studies*, **16**(2), 159–79.

Putterman, L. (1990) *Division of Labour and Welfare: An Introduction to Economic Systems*, Oxford: Oxford University Press.

Sachs, J.D. (1991) Accelerating Privatization in Eastern Europe: The Case of Poland, World Institute for Development Economics Research, United Nations University, *WIDER Working Paper*, 92.

Samuelsson, H-F. (1992) Foreign Direct Investments in Eastern Europe: Current Situation and Potential, Geneva: United Nations Economic Commission for Europe and United Nations Centre on Transnational Corporations, GE. 92-20047.

Schumpeter, J.A. (1934) *The Theory of Economic Development* (trans. R. Opie), Cambridge, Mass.: Harvard University Press.

Siebert, H. (1992) Transforming a Socialist Economy: the Case of Eastern Germany, Kiel: Kiel Institute of World Economics, mimeo.

Smith, N.R. (1967) *The Entrepreneur and His Firm: The Relationship between Type of Man and Type of Company*, East Lansing: Bureau of Business and Economic Research, Graduate School of Business Administration, Michigan State University.

UNIDO (1991) Industrial Restructuring in Central and Eastern Europe: Critical Areas of International Cooperation, Vienna: United Nations Industrial Development Organisation, PPD/IPP/REG.

UNIDO (1992) Foreign Direct Investment in Central and Eastern European Countries: Recent Developments and Determinants, Vienna: United Nations Industrial Development Organisation V.92-55129.

Wyplosz, C. (1992) After the Honeymoon: On the Economics and the Politics of Economic Transformation, Fontainebleau, *INSEAD Working Paper*, 92/52/EP.

Index